The thirst for annihila

An important literary and philosophical figure, Georges Bataille has had a significant influence on other French writers, such as Foucault, Derrida and Baudrillard. *The Thirst for Annihilation* is the first book in English to respond to his writings. In no way, though, is Nick Land's book an attempt to appropriate Bataille's writings to a secular intelligibility or to compromise with the aridity of academic discourse – rather, it is written as a *communion*.

Theoretical issues in philosophy, sociology, psychodynamics, politics and poetry are discussed but only as stepping stones into the deep water of textual sacrifice where words pass over into the broken voice of death. Cultural modernity is diagnosed down to its Kantian bedrock with its transcendental philosophy of the object but Bataille's writings cut violently across this tightly disciplined reading to reveal the strong underlying currents that bear us towards chaos and dissolution – the violent impulse to escape, the thirst for annihilation.

Nick Land, whose aim is to spread what he calls 'the virulent horror' of Bataille's writings, himself writes with a vividness and commitment more usually associated with works of literature than intellectual investigations. This book is of relevance to everyone interested in the philosophy of desire, the psychopathology of deviance, political and legal theory, the history of religion or poetry. It is also urgent for all those intrigued by their sexual torments or the death they mistakenly conceive of as their own.

Nick Land is a lecturer in Continental Philosophy at Warwick University.

The thirst for annihilation

Georges Bataille and virulent nihilism (an essay in atheistic religion)

Nick Land

London and New York

First published in 1992
by Routledge
11 New Fetter Lane, London EC4P 4EE

Simultaneously published in the USA and Canada
by Routledge
a division of Routledge, Chapman and Hall Inc.
29 West 35th Street, New York, NY 10001

© 1992 Nick Land

Typeset in 10/12 pt Baskerville by Columns Design and
Production Services Ltd, Reading
Printed and bound in Great Britain by
Biddles Ltd, Guildford and King's Lynn

All rights reserved. No part of this book may be reprinted or
reproduced or utilized in any form or by any electronic,
mechanical, or other means, now known or hereafter
invented, including photocopying and recording, or in any
information storage or retrieval system, without permission in
writing from the publishers.

British Library Cataloguing in Publication Data
A catalogue record for this book is available from the British
Library

Library of Congress Cataloging in Publication Data
Land, Nick, 1962–
    The thirst for annihilation: Georges Bataille and virulent
nihilism: an essay in atheistic religion/Nick Land.
    p.   cm.
    1. Bataille, Georges, 1897–1962 – Philosophy. 2. Nietzsche,
Friedrich Wilhelm, 1844–1900 – Influence. 3. Nihilism
(Philosophy) in literature. 4. Atheism in literature. I. Title.
PQ2603.A695Z74 1992
848'.91209–dc20   91–36365
                                                          CIP

ISBN 0–415–05607–1
       0–415–05608–X (pbk)

The profundity of the tragic artist lies in this, that his aesthetic instinct surveys the more remote consequences, that he does not halt shortsightedly at what is closest to hand, that he affirms the *large-scale economy* which justifies the *terrifying*, the *evil*, the *questionable* – and more than merely justifies them [N III 575].

there is nothing
except
the impossible
and not God [III 47].

Zero is immense.

Contents

Reference codes	ix
Preface	xi
1 'The death of sound philosophy'	1
2 The curse of the sun	27
3 Transgression	58
4 Easter	75
5 Dead God	80
6 The rage of jealous time	92
7 Fanged noumenon (passion of the cyclone)	105
8 Fluent bodies (a digression on Miller)	121
9 Aborting the human race	133
10 The labyrinth	160
11 Inconclusive communication	184
Notes	211
Bibliography	215
Name index	218
Subject index	220

Reference codes

Wherever a reference consists of a Roman numeral followed by an Arabic one it indicates a volume and page number in Bataille's *Oeuvres Complètes*.

Other collected works are indicated by an initial letter or letters, followed by the same key. These are:

A	Aquinas
B	Boltzmann
H	Hegel
K	Kant
L	Lukács
N	Nietzsche
S	Sade
Sch	Schopenhauer

Other codes refer to specific texts rather than collected works:

Cap	Marx, *Capital Volume One*
CG	Augustine, *The City of God*
Ch	Gleick, *Chaos*
DH	Walker, *The Decline of Hell*
Gr	Marx, *Grundrisse*
Hay	Hayman, *De Sade*
PCD	Plato, *Collected Dialogues*
PES	Weber, *The Protestant Ethic and the Spirit of Capitalism*
Pol	Aristotle, *Politics*
R	Rimbaud, *Collected Poems*
SD	Ragon, *The Space of Death*
Spu	Derrida, *Spurs*
TC	Miller, *The Tropic of Cancer*
TE	Cioran, *La Tentation d'Exister*

Preface

As though to give yourself a certain 'positive' assurance, which harbored as well a suspicion of superiority, you have often reproached me for what you call my 'appetite for destruction' [TE 113].

The reasons for writing a book can be led back to the desire to modify the relations which exist between a human being and its kind. Those relations are judged unacceptable and are perceived as an atrocious wretchedness.

However, to the extent that I have written this book I have been conscious that it is impotent to regulate the account of that wretchedness. Up to a certain limit, the desire for perfectly clear *human* exchanges which escape general conventions becomes a desire for annihilation [II 143].

*

I have always unconsciously sought out that which will beat me down to the ground, but the floor is also a wall.

*

What best befits an author is to preface a work with its *apology*, ornamenting it with the gilt of necessity. After all, one should not beg attention without excuse. That a writer provide some rudimentary justification for a book seems a modest enough expectation, but such a demand obliterates me, since this is a text which has been reared in perfect superfluity, clutching feebly at zero. There is not a single sentence which is other than a gratuitousness and a confusion; a cry at least half lamed and smothered in irony. Each appeal that is made to the name 'Bataille' shudders between a pretension and a joke. *Bataille.* I know nothing about him. His obsessions disturb me, his ignorances numb me, I find his thought incomprehensible, the abrasion of his writing shears uselessly across my inarticulacy. In response I mumble, as a resistance to anxiety, maddening myself with words. Locked in a cell with my own hollow ravings . . . but at least it is not *that* . . . (and even now I lie) . . .

In truth, Bataille seems to me far less an intellectual predicament than a sexual and religious one, transecting the lethargic suicide upon which we are all embarked. To accept his writings is an impossibility, to resist them an irrelevance. One is excited abnormally, appalled, but without refuge. Nausea perhaps? Such melodrama comes rapidly to amuse (although we still vomit, just as we die).

So I try to persuade myself that it *would have been* relatively straightforward to write a sound book on the work of Georges Bataille; a book that would have discussed the contribution he has made to the philosophical and literary culture of twentieth-century France, expositing his doctrines of 'general economy', 'base materialism', and 'atheology', appraising the excellences of his various prose styles and his poetry, recommending that his works be invested by serious reading, scholarship, and eventually a judicious estimation – by my reckoning, a *schlecht* book. Such books are always depressing enough, but in the case of Georges Bataille the situation is even more acute, touching on something akin to the pure pornography characterizing our contemporary *Nietzsche scholarship*. To succeed in writing a book of any kind about Bataille is already something wretched, because it is only in the twisted interstitial spaces of failure that contact, infection, and – at the limit – the anegoic intimacy that he calls 'communication' can take place. A recovery of the sense of Bataille's writing is the surest path to its radical impoverishment. It is as pathetic to seek education from Bataille as it is to seek comfort from Nietzsche. (Bataille is, of course, somewhat more honest than this about his own hypocrisies.)

There is no doubt that to season Bataille in preparation for his comfortable digestion by capital's cultural machine is a piece of twisted prostitution of the kind he would fully have appreciated. The delicious obscenity! A writer who tried to help us to expend, stored away with all the others in our reserve of informatico-financial assets, in order to be pimped out into the career flows of the Western academies. There are North Americans who have already learnt to gurgle 'Bataille contra Marx' for instance, although the issue is rarely this inanely ideological. More insidious is the 'he was a librarian you know' Bataille, increasingly snarled-up in the deconstructivist pulp industry of endless commentary on Logocentrism, Western Metaphysics, and other various *Seinsvergessenheiten*, the Bataille who read a lot, and had something very clever to say. Bataille may be praised or condemned in terms of his erudition, but this scarcely matters when compared with his sanctity as a voyager in sickness . . . but books make good burrows in which to hide, and few places are as redolent of the *little escape* as a library; the shelves of fiction, history, geography, each book a pretext for derealization, patiently awaiting the moment when it will be coupled to some vague reverie.

Not that this book makes any special pleading for itself, it has scratched about for needles in the most destitute gutters of the Earth, cold-turkey crawling on its knees, and begging the academy to pimp it ever deeper into abuse. Ever since it became theoretically evident that our precious personal identities were just brand-tags for trading crumbs of labour-power on the libidino-economic junk circuit, the vestiges of authorial theatricality have been wearing thinner. Who cares what 'anyone' thinks, knows, or theorizes about Bataille? The only thing to try and touch is the intense shock-wave that still reaches us along with the textual embers . . . for as long, that is, as anything can still 'reach us'. Where Descartes needed God to mediate his relations with his fellows, secular man is happy with his television set, and with all the other commodified channels of pseudo-communication with which his civilization has so thoughtfully endowed him. Such things are for his own protection of course; to filter out the terrifying threat of infection. If openness to alterity, base communication, and experimental curiosity are marks of an exuberant society, its only true gauge lies in its tendency to be decimated by sexually transmitted diseases and nihilist religion. On this basis it seems that our society, despite its own most strenuous efforts, has not yet consummated its long idealized sclerosis into impermeable atoms. The grit still exists, and it is only amongst the grit that we connect.

*

It is 03.30 in the morning. Let us say one is 'drunk' – an impoverished cipher for all those terrible things one does to one's nervous-system in the depths of the night – and philosophy is 'impossible' (although one still thinks, even to the point of terror and disgust). What does it mean for this episode in the real history of spirit to die without trace? Where has it strayed to? 'I thought of death, which I imagined to be similar to that walk without an object (but the walk, in death, takes this path without reason – "forever")' [III 286].

An extraordinary lucidity, frosty and crisp in the blackness, but paralysed; lodged in some recess of the universe that clutches it like a snare. A wave of nausea is accompanied by a peculiarly insinuating headache, as if thought itself were copulating unreservedly with suffering. A damp coldness, close to fog, creeps through the open window. I laugh, delighted at the fate that has turned me into a reptile. The metallic hardness of intellect seems like a cutting instrument in my hand; the detached fragment from a machine tool, or an abattoir, seeking out the terminal sense it was always refused.

The object of philosophy, insofar as the reflective meditation upon thought can be taken to characterize it, is arbitrarily prescribed as undisturbed reasoning (the cases of psychopathology, psychiatry, abnormal psychology, etc. do not remotely contravene this rigorous selection, because such studies of disturbed thought are constituted – in principle – without entanglement). It is thus that successfully adapted, tranquil, moderate, and productive reason monopolizes the philosophical conception of thought, in the same way that the generalized robotism of regulated labour squeezes all intense gestures out of social existence. My abnormal devotion to Bataille stems from the fact that nobody has done more than he to obstruct the passage of violent blanks into a pacified oblivion, and thus to awaken the monster in the basement of reason.

Not that the repressed is locked in a dungeon, it is stranded in a labyrinth, and connected to the daylit world by a secret continuity. A tangle of confusion comes to seem like a door, a maze like a barrier, and one says 'I', but the inside is not a cell, it is a corridor; a passage cut from the soft rock of loss. Inner experience traverses a sombre porosity, and the moans of the minotaur reverberate through its arteries, hinting at an indefinable proximity. It becomes difficult to sleep.

*

Of course, I indulge myself, in innumerable ways. 'I' tell myself the personal pronoun fails to mark the pseudo-neutral position of a commentator *this time*. That is rather a protraction of 'Bataille's' incessant *je* into a further episode of debasement. For it is remarkable how degraded a discourse can become when it is marked by the obsessive reiteration of the abstract ego, mixing arrogance with pallid humility. The chronic whine that results – something akin to a degenerate reverberation from Dostoyevsky's underground man – is the insistence of a humanity that has become an unbearable indignity. 'I' am (alone), as the tasteless exhibition of an endogenous torment, as the betrayal of communication, as a festering wound, in which the monadic knitting of the flesh loses itself in a mess of pus and scabs, etc. etc. . . . (You yawn of course, but I continue.) Yes, *I* am – *definitionally* – a filthy beggar (like God), scrabbling at the coat-tails of a reluctant and embarrassed attentiveness, driven into a guile that fuses wretchedness with an elusive element of threat. Is it mere indolence that defeats all tendency towards decorous impersonality? Scarcely. Or rather; I cannot bring myself to think so. I nag at the margins of this *discourse on the writings of Georges Bataille* as a hideous confirmation of its cowardice and moderation, simultaneous with the dreariness of its prostitution; a wheezing parody of laughter teetering upon the abject nakedness of a sob. Yet at the same time it scarcely matters whether I write of Bataille or myself. If there is a boundary between us it is only insofar as he was momentarily frustrated in his passage to the truth of his text.

Bataille's writing exhibits a marked attachment to the first person pronoun, and the confessional mode is especially predominant in his more 'literary' works, although it spreads almost everywhere. The most obvious consequence of this device is to immerse the narrative ego in the text, fusing voice and discourse in a field of immanence, and putting identity unreservedly into play (*en jeu*). Not only is most of the fiction published during Bataille's lifetime narrated in the first person – including *The Story of the Eye, Madame Edwarda, The Impossible, The Abbé C.*, and *The Blue of Noon* – but in every case more than one confessional voice is involved – even after the various egos of dialogue are excluded – whether this is the result of 'authorial' prefaces, or stratified narrative structures. *The Abbé C.*, for example, includes no less than three distinct first person narrative voices, and temporal ruptures in the order of its discourses complicate the situation still further. There is an unmanageable appeal, a plight of isolation, a voice resistant to all delimitation, an *infection*, so that reading Bataille is not a contribution to positivity, but a plea.

It does not befit beggars to garb themselves in the robes of proud neutrality, the matter is quite to the contrary; no one sinks beneath the burden of individuality as they do. If beggars are so often driven to religion it is because it can never be in the rational interest of anyone to respond to them. They must inherit the tradition of unanswered cries encrypted in monastic cells. These mendicants have certainly been destituted in an echo of the death of God, but with no space awaiting them in the secular order they are forced to live their limitless impoverishment as an impossible necessity. As for myself (Bataille also) the matter is altogether more comic.

Do not think I am unsympathetic. These thickets of abstract identity are no doubt unpleasant to stumble through. The scrawny little sign of promiscuous individuality is a perpetual aggravation; reminding you in each case of your own incarceration by self. That enunciation should be harried by an 'I' is no mere stylistic infelicity, it is a loathesomeness, and yet the only routes of evasion leading away from it are hypocritical. To try and hide the manacle-scars which wreck the complexion of the text would itself be a decisionistic celebration of autonomy, debasing the text further, branding it even more conclusively as servile matter (out of which the ego has transcended into invisibility). To write oneself out of a book can be many things; the dilettantism of one for whom writing is from the start affectation and artificiality, the professionalism of one for whom a book tends to an anonymity – if not immediately to that of the commodity, at least to that of career capital – the authoritarianism of one lost in a monological insanity close to solipsism, or the all-too-ostentatious humility of one who prefers to guide from behind the scenes. It can be genuine timidity, pomposity, inertial apathy, even experiment, but what it can never be, for as long as it is remotely deliberated, is flight.

It is still tempting to renounce the posture of the first person, even though its force of corrosive qualification reduces the risk of complacent objectivism or pseudo-collectivity. The indulgences of personality, of spurious autonomy, responsibility, and idiosyncratic affectation, are sufficiently repellent to provoke a measure of tactical carelessness. One paralyses a dimension of messy effectivity, out of distaste. But to write of Bataille in such a way is more than a little absurd, suggesting, as it does, that impersonality is a simple thing to achieve. After all: the 'I' is not to be expelled, but submitted to sacrifice. When shuffled about within a text upon Bataille it is compelled to refer not to an author, but rather, to an *ennui*, gesticulating at the void; the symptom of an absent tragic community.

*

It is a long time now since I was afflicted by Bataille's poem 'Rire' ('Laughter'):

> Laugh and laugh
> at the sun
> at the nettles
> at the stones
> at the ducks
>
> at the rain
> at the pee-pee of the pope
> at mummy
> at a coffin full of shit [IV 13].

This poem introduces three of the must crucial themes traversing Bataille's writing: laughter, excrement, and death. Such 'themes' are suspended only momentarily at the lip of philosophical intelligibility, and then released into a euphoric immolation upon the burn-core of literature, disintegrating into a senseless heterogeneous mass. His texts obsessively reiterate that the decomposed body is excremental, and that the only sufficient response to death is laughter. The corpse not only dissolves into a noxious base matter analagous to excrement, it is also *in fact* defecated as waste by the life of the species. For the corpse is the truth of the biological individual, its consummate superfluity. It is only through the passage into irredeemable waste that the individual is marked with the delible trace of its excess. It is because life is pure surplus that the child of 'Rire' − standing by the side of his quietly weeping mother and transfixed by the stinking ruins of his father − is gripped by convulsions of horror that explode into peals of mirth, as uncompromising as orgasm. 'Rire' is, in part, a contribution to the theory of mourning. Laughter is a communion with the dead, since death is not the object of laughter: it is death itself that finds a voice when we laugh. Laughter is that which is lost to discourse, the haemorrhaging of pragmatics into excitation and filth.

Bataille tells us that the universe is energetic, and the fate inherent to energy is utter waste. Energy from the sun is discharged unilaterally and without design. That fraction of solar radiation which strikes the earth resources all terrestrial endeavour, provoking the feverish obscenity we call 'life'.

Life appears as a pause on the energy path; as a precarious stabilization and complication of solar decay. It is most basically comprehensible as *the general solution to the problem of consumption*. Such a solar- or general-economic perspective exhibits production as an illusion; the hypostatization of a digression in consumption. To produce is to partially manage the release of energy into its loss, and nothing more.

Death, wastage, or expenditure is the only end, the only definitive terminus. 'Utility' cannot in reality be anything but the characterization of a function, having no sense short of an expenditure which escapes it utterly. This is 'relative utility'. The order of Western history has as its most pertinent symptom the drift of utility away from this relative sense, towards a paradoxical absolute value. A creeping slave morality colonizes value, subordinating it to the definition 'that which serves'. The 'good' becomes synonymous with utility; with means, mediation, instrumentality, and implicit dependence.

The real trajectory of loss is 'immanence', continuity, base matter, or flow. If the strictly regional resistance of everything that delays, impedes, or momentarily arrests the movement of dissolution is abstracted from the solar flow it is interpretable as transcendence. Such *abstract resistance to loss* is characterized by autonomy, homogeneity, and ideality, and is what Bataille summarizes as '(absolute) utility'.

The (inevitable) return of constricted energy to immanence is religion, whose core is sacrifice, generative of the sacred. Sacrifice is the movement of violent liberation from servility, the collapse of transcendence. Inhibiting the sacrificial relapse of isolated being is the broad utilitarianism inherent to humanity, correlated with a profane delimitation from ferocious nature that finds its formula in theology. In its profane aspect, religion is martialled under a conception of God; the final guarantor of persistent being, the submission of (ruinous) time to reason, and thus the ultimate principle of utility.

Cowering in the shadow of its gods, humanity is the project of a definitive abrogation of expenditure, and is thus an impossibility.

The humanizing project has the form of an unsustainable law. Despite the fortifications of prohibition, the impossible corrodes humanity in *eroticism*; the eruption of irreducible excess, which is the base unity of sexuality and death. Eroticism gnaws us as the inevitable triumph of evil (utter loss).

It is this passionate submission to fate (= death) that guides Bataille's own readings, in *Literature and Evil* for instance, the greatest work of atheological poetics. *Literature and Evil* is a series of responses to writing that exhibit the complicity between literary art and transgression. Bataille's insistent suggestion is that the non-utilitarian writer is not interested in serving mankind or furthering the accumulation of goods, however refined, delicate, or spiritual these may be. Instead, such writers – Emily Brontë, Baudelaire, Michelet, Blake, Sade, Proust, Kafka, and Genet are Bataille's examples in this text – are concerned with communication, which means the violation of individuality, autonomy, and isolation, the infliction of a wound through which beings open out into the community of senseless waste. Literature is a transgression against transcendence, the dark and unholy rending of a sacrificial wound, allowing a communication more basic than the pseudo-communication of instrumental discourse. The heart of literature is the death of God, the violent absence of the good, and thus of everything that protects, consolidates, or guarantees the interests of the individual personality. The death of God is the ultimate transgression, the release of humanity from itself, back into the blind infernal extravagance of the sun.

*

It is a mere consolation to the timid to imagine that philosophy has died. The fact of the matter is quite to the contrary. Philosophy will be the last of human things; perhaps the efficient impulse of the end. That humanity is fated to terminate is amongst the most basic thoughts, and no more than the most elementary qualification for philosophy, since to think on behalf of one's species is a miserable parochialism.

Man is a little thing that has learnt to stammer the word 'infinity'. In doing so it makes everything small, diminishing even itself. One need only dip into the history of monotheism to note the wretchedness of human 'infinities' in comparison to the most casual of natural immensities. It is first necessary for a thing to shrivel for it to share anything with us; to become 'humane'.

Insofar as nature can be injured or offended by us, it is mere surface, superfice, sensitive skin. Profound nature – matter – is something else; the indifferent and the inviolable. (It is deeper, therefore, than God.) This deep nature suffers nothing, resents nothing, makes no cases. It is only in the shallows that one ever finds a defence.

There is one simple criterion of taste in philosophy: that one avoid the vulgarity of anthropomorphism. It is by failing here that one comes to side with cages. The specifics follow straightforwardly:

1 Thoroughgoing dehumanization of nature, involving the uttermost impersonalism in the explanation of natural forces, and vigorously atheological cosmology. No residue of prayer. An instinctive fastidiousness in respect to all the traces of human personality, and the treatment of such as the excrement of matter; as its most ignoble part, its gutter . . .
2 Ruthless fatalism. No space for decisions, responsibilities, actions, intentions. Any appeal to notions of human freedom discredits a philosopher beyond amelioration.
3 Hence absence of all moralizing, even the crispest, most Aristotelian. The penchant for correction, let alone vengefulness, pins one in the shallows.
4 Contempt for common evaluations; one should even take care to avoid straying accidentally into the right. Even to be an enemy is too comforting; one must be an alien, a beast. Nothing is more absurd than a philosopher seeking to be liked.

Libidinal materialism is the name for such a philosophy, although it is perhaps less a philosophy than an offence. Historically it is *pessimistic*, in the rich sense that transects the writings of Nietzsche, Freud, and Bataille as well as those of Schopenhauer. Thematically it is 'psychoanalytical' (although it no longer believes in the psyche or in analysis), thermodynamic-energeticist (but no longer physicalistic or logico-mathematical), and perhaps a little *morbid*. Methodologically it is genealogical, diagnostic, and *enthusiastic* for the accentuation of intensity that will carry it through insurrection into anegoic delirium. Stylistically it is aggressive, only a little sub-hyperbolic, and – above all – massively irresponsible . . .

Such thinking is less concerned with propositions than with punctures; hacking at the flood-gates that protect civilization from a deluge of impersonal energy. It could be described as writing against reservation, but any description is inevitably domesticating. It will never find its father, or its mother; it has no ultimate ancestor of any kind. For it did not begin with Nietzsche, or with the topico-pathological furore found in Schopenhauer, or with the unconscious of the Kantian text, but ever further back ... It has been the menace that provoked even the most ancient philosophy – already Anaximander as Nietzsche suggests – to anticipate the police. Another description might run like this: libidinal materialism is the textual return of that which is most intolerable to mankind.

No one could ever 'be' a libidinal materialist. This is a 'doctrine' that can only be suffered as an abomination, a jangling of the nerves, a combustion of articulate reason, and a nauseating rage of thought. It is a hyperlepsy of the central nervous-system, ruining the body's adaptive regimes, and consuming its reserves in rhythmic convulsions that are not only futile, but devastating. Schopenhauer already knew that thought is medically disastrous, Nietzsche demonstrated it. An aged philosopher is either a monster of stamina or a charlatan. How long does it take to be wasted by a fire-storm? By an artificial sun upon the earth? It is only when the blaze in Nietzsche's brain-stem fused with the one in the sky above a piazza in Turin that libidinal materialism touched upon its realization.

Like all '-isms', libidinal materialism is at best a parody, at worst a constriction. What matters is the violent impulse to escape that gives this book its title. *The thirst for annihilation*. This name has grown on me as an ulceration in the gut. Is it desire or its negation that is marked here? The overcoming of the will, nihilism, *Todestrieb*? It seems to me that it is first of all the compulsion to abstract. Historically and anthropologically considered, this is negation torn from its logical function to become the non-objective destination of an attachment, destituted of its formality by a ferocious investment, *besetzt*, and coupled to a motor of liquidation. So that the instrument of logical dissection is at last acknowledged in its terrible materiality; negativity as an excitation. To rather 'will negation than the negation of will' [N II 839]; this is an elusive difference, twisting like a rusted nail into sensitive flesh. Is the primitive craving that seeks the abolition of reality an object of philosophical investigation, or a drive accomplishing itself *through* philosophy? What is it that makes use of subtlety here?

Subtlety grates upon the nerves, yet everything is driven by an immense crudity: death impassions us. Even before crossing over into death I had been excruciated upon my thirst for it. I accept that my case is in some respects aberrant, but what skewers me upon zero is an aberration inextricable from truth. To be parsimonious in one's love for death is not to understand.

This is not to deny that the gentleness with which Hell has treated me has been a source of considerable embarrassment. No one less worthy of sanctity has ever twitched upon the Earth. I slunk into Hell like a verminous cur, accompanied by a wanderer of an altogether more celestial aspect. According to the Sikh religion humans are the masks of angels and demons, and my own infernal lineaments bear little ambiguity (everywhere I go the shadows thicken). When I stare into the eyes of Bataille's photographic image I connect with his inexistence in a community of the kiln. I smile.

*

My wings are ragged
they have never been licked by the sun
black and hooked on iron struts
like a poison flower of death
they only open for the night

*

In the box it seems as if the choice is yours to either dismiss or accept my words when I insist: *I have been outside the box.* Like Plato, knowing is a memory for me, but unlike him I have outlived philosophy and aspiration, since I have outlived life itself. Death has no representatives, but I have at least returned from the dead (a characteristic I reluctantly share with the Nazarene). Since I have floated in death the world has desisted from all effort to seduce me into seriousness. I rest in life as a tramp rests in a hedge, mumbling these words . . .

Chapter 1

'The death of sound philosophy'[1]

Kant's great discovery – but one that he never admitted to – was that apodictic reason is incompatible with knowledge. Such reason must be 'transcendental'. This is a word that has been propagated with enthusiasm, but only because Kant simultaneously provided a method of misreading it. To be transcendental is to be 'free' of reality. This is surely the most elegant euphemism in the history of Western philosophy.

The critical philosophy exposes the 'truths of reason' as fictions, but cunning ones, for they can never be exposed. They are 'big lies' to the scale of infinity; stories about an irreal world beyond all possibility of sensation, one which is absolutely incapable of entering into material communication with the human nervous system, however indirectly, a separated realm, a divine kingdom. This is the ghost landscape of metaphysics, crowded with divinities, souls, agents, perdurant subjectivities, entities with a zero potentiality for triggering excitations, and then the whole gothic confessional of guilt, responsibility, moral judgement, punishments and rewards . . . the sprawling priestly apparatus of psychological manipulation and subterranean power. The only problem for the metaphysicians is that this web of gloomy fictions is unco-ordinated, and comes into conflict with itself. Once the fervent irrationalism of inquisition and the stake begins to crumble, and the dogmatic authority of the church weakens to the point that it can no longer wholly constrain philosophy within the mould of theology, violent disputes – antinomies – begin to flourish. Due to the 'internecine strife of the metaphysicians' polyglot forces begin to be sucked into conflict, at first mobilized against particular systems of reason, fighting under the banner of another. But eventually a more generalized antagonism begins to emerge, various elements begin to throw off the authority of metaphysics *as such*, scepticism spreads, and the nomads begin to drift back, with renewed *élan*.

Kant's critical philosophy is the most elaborate fit of panic in the history of the Earth. Its more brutish – and even more consequential – ancestor was Luther's hysterical reaction to the disintegration of Christendom. A kind of intellectual paralysis, the basic symptom of which was a demand for rigorous and consistent austerity, was common to both. Like Luther, Kant was forced into conflict with an institution steeped in tradition with which he would have been happier to conform; if only it were strong enough to keep the barbarians at bay. But whilst atheists (such as Hume) threatened to wash everything away, the pope spawned bastards and Christian Wolff pontificated absurdities. There was only one answer, revolt in the service of the establishment, and the revolt, once begun, was carried through with a steel dedication. What was also common to both of these reluctant rebels was the renewed vitality that they breathed into the antique institutions they engaged. Within a few years of Luther, the Jesuits, after Kant, Hegel. Catholicism and metaphysics both reborn. After all, fear is the passionate enthusiasm for the *same*.

*

In speaking of modernity we acknowledge that an insatiable historicization has befallen the Earth; a shock-wave of obsolescence has swept away all perpetuities. Far from escaping the frenzy of abolition, thought has been sublimed in the white heat of its outer edge, functioning as the very catalyst of history. What is new to modernity is a *rate of the obsolescence of truth*, although it is still (as I write) possible for a good idea to last longer than an automobile. It is natural enough, therefore, that critique is an instrument of dissolution; a regression to conditions – to the magmic power of presupposition – upon which all order floats. Cultures that become critical are rapidly intoxicated by lavish metamorphic forces. Reality becomes soluble in the madness of invention, such that it seems as though critique were luring nature into our dreams. Anything is allowable eventually, as long as it is extravagant enough, and nothing that is allowable may any longer be avoided. A critique only dates in the way capital does: cunningly. Both are names for metamorphosis as such, reproduced in their own substitution[2].

To describe Kant and capital as two sides of a coin is as necessary as it is ridiculous. A strange coin indeed that can synthesize a humble citizen of Königsberg with the run-away reconstruction of a planet. Yet any attempt to render such an absurdity intelligible enmeshes us in the critical machinery that will always be associated with Kant. If counter-balancing the dominant mass of the real with transcendental philosophy is deeply unjust, to which tribunal shall we appeal? To one that is more universal? – a transcendental move. Or one that is more ontologically profound? – a theological idiocy. Hegel sought to treat Kant with a sense of proportion, and his failure in this regard is also ours. This is why every variant of modern thought exhibits a complexion of retardation, critique, and aberration, since if it does not inertially resist the seduction of modernity's critical resources it is torn between the twin lures of harmonizing with them, or venturing into the expansive obscurities beyond.

Philosophy (comprehending all 'theory') has no socio-historical pertinence for us other than its relation to Kant. In the case of Bataille such a relation is superficially obscured by the prevalence of references to (a Kojévean) Hegel, but two obvious points can be made here: firstly, the Hegelian text is nothing other than a response to the predicament of transcendental philosophy, so that all of its terminology is operative from the start within a Kantian register, and secondly, Bataille's philosophical vocabulary – regardless of first appearances – is in fact, and independently of Hegelian mediation, fated to address a Kantian inheritance. A preliminary sample might include *sovereignty* (a Kantian problematic before becoming a Hegelian one), the thoughts of *limit, the unknown, possibility, objectivity*, and *end*, as well as – and above all – the crucial difference between *immanence* and *transcendence* along with its critical usage.

The importance of Hegel to Bataille is not immediate. It stems from the character of Hegelian thinking as a redemption of Kantianism; its attempt to save transcendental philosophy from the lethal spasms welling up from within. Irrespective of his own immensely confused intellectual project, Bataille's reading of Hegel is a regression into the nihilistic momentum of critique; into a thanatropism which Kant largely misconceived, and which Hegel attempted to speculatively excise. Hegel's philosophy is the life-support machine of Kantianism, the medical apparatus responding to a crisis. When Bataille explores this machine it is not primarily

4 The thirst for annihilation

in order to understand its inherent potentiality for malfunction, but to excavate the euthanasia it prohibits.

Hegel's reading of Kant is complex and multifaceted, but also of an unprecedented coherence. Its intelligibility is, in the end, coterminous with the possibility of a system of reason, or actual infinity. Hegel realized that the Kantian conception of infinity, which abstractly opposes itself to finitude rather than subsuming it, indefinitely perpetuated a dangerous tension, insofar as it ascetically suspends the moment of resolution. This *bad infinity* – the endless task of perpetual growth (capital) – is incapable of ever diminishing the prospect of utter collapse. Kantian infinity is deprived of any possibility of intervening in developmental series, leaving them vulnerable throughout their length to the catastrophic collision with a limit; loss of faith, war, the irruption of an incomprehensible death. Kantian infinity is given, whereas Hegel sets to *work*.

It is only a banal claim of Hegel's own thinking that history has no greater abjection to offer than the profound immersion in his work. Unlike the exposition such *Knechtschaft* receives within Hegelian self-understanding, however, this is not primarily because there is no depth of servility or wretchedness to which the spirit of the system refuses to descend, but is rather due to the fact that the comprehensive voyage of experience that traverses such depths has as its condition of existence the uttermost abandonment of real independence. The filthiness and ignobility of Bataille's writing follows immediately from its being steeped in Hegel. This is not to suggest that such baseness is coherent with 'Hegelianism' (in any of its variants), for however immense the powers of reflexive self-comprehension exhibited by such thinking, the supremely vicious character of intimacy with the Hegelian text cannot be grasped within it. Investment in the system is not itself a relation internal to the system, and to make it so is merely to offer a hypocritical apologia for its degradation. If Hegel's prostitution to the Prussian state can become speculatively intelligible, this is only at the cost of an etherealization which, 'in itself', is consummate abjection, deceit, and travesty, or, put succinctly, definitive humanity.

This is not to provide the 'justification' for a 'dismissal' of Hegel. Hegel remains strictly unintelligible to us, and any claims to the contrary are anaemic tokens of bourgeois apologetic. Insofar as Bataille depends upon the overcoming of Hegel he is an inanity. That 'Hegelianism' is a sad farce of the academy decides nothing as to its eventual sense, and if postmodernity depends upon a 'decision' in respect of Hegel it is a culture of accommodation analogous to Hegel's own crude response to Schelling, or to the even more devastating oblivion of Schopenhauer's thinking within the formative phase of nineteenth century German metaphysics. The internecine conflict between germinal possibilities of post-Kantian thought is appropriately 'judged' by a laughter whose measure is the preponderance of capital within modernity. It is as comic as the hatred Troskyite sects bear for each other as they squabble over the management of a future whose probability slides asymptotically towards zero.

*

A dialectical illusion is the error – exposed by transcendental critique – through which reason pretends to the transcendence of itself. It is associated, on the one hand, with an objectivistic interpretation of the intellectual forms of a representation as independently existing structures of things in themselves, and, on the other hand, with an attempt to grasp the subject as if it were an entity separable from its own operations, the latter being a mistake that Kant entitles *paralogism*. Descartes' ontology of extended and thinking substance exemplifies both of these errors. Such dialectic is the object of critique, and is always a confusion between conditions of possibility and their products. Kant describes this confusion as one between conditions of objectivity and objects, which in Marx's case are producers (labour power) and commodities, in Heidegger's being and beings, in Derrida's writing and the sign, etc. Such confusions misconceive the transcendental as the transcendent, performing a gesture that can be described as 'metaphysics' (fetishism, ontotheology, logocentrism). For Bataille it is the effaced difference between utilization (expenditure) and utility which bears the brunt of critical aggression, engaging an error to which he gives the uncompromising label 'reason'. Profane thought (reason) interprets *making use of* in terms of *usefulness*. It thus loses all sense of absolute end (the transcendental condition of value).

To repeat Kantianism (modern thought) is to perpetuate the exacerbative displacement of critique, but to exceed it is to cross the line which divides representation from the real, and thus to depart both from philosophy and from the world that has expelled it into its isolation. Critique is a matter of boundaries, or the *delimitation of domains of application for concepts*. It is inherent to critique that a terrain of unthinkability is delineated, or that limits are set to the exercise of theoretical endeavour. The Kantian name for the items within the legitimate field of theoretical cognition is *phenomena*, whilst the extra-territorial items are called *noumena* or *things-in-themselves*. Because the noumenon escapes the categories of the understanding (which include modality) 'we can neither say that it is possible nor that it is impossible' [K III 304]. Noumena are what escape the competence of theory, being those 'things' which are unknowable in principle. 'That, therefore, which we entitle "noumenon" must be understood as being such only in a *negative* sense' [K III 278].

The most influential attempt to establish a new coherence between conception and its outside is Hegel's, in particular his phenomenological solution to the delineation of experience. Hegel argues that the boundary of experience is produced by the inherently self-transcending character of reason, so that the discursive excess which is exhibited – for instance – in the word 'noumenon' expresses the negativity or freedom of spirit in relation to its content. Spirit is not confined by the difference which restricts or determines phenomenality, since it is itself its auto-differentiation. The outside of spirit at any moment of history is merely its own unreclaimed (alienated) work. This is not merely to collapse Kant's thing-in-itself back into the phenomenal world, because Hegel does not think of spirit as a timeless (transcendentally pre-given) system of cognitive faculties (in Kantian fashion), but as a historical auto-production, in which the self is really – and not merely reflectively – determined by the logically orchestrated content of thinking as and through time. Hegelian history is not formal but speculative, which means that the subject is developed – and not merely expressed – through the series of predicates by which 'it' is thought.

Hegel considered Kant's basic failing to be an inability to see that the limits of reason are self-legislated, so that when intelligibility is absolutely consummated the ethical order is recognized as commanding for nature. Spirit must abandon itself to its noumenal extinction in the confidence that it cannot be identified with its perishable pupal stages, but instead finds eternal life in the thinkability of death. Finitude is only possible through a spiritual production transcending and comprehending it as a necessary moment of itself. Humanity becomes God in the mode of a return by expiating its finitude on the cross of history, whereby alterity is neutralized into the reconciliatory phenomenology of absolute spirit = God. So much for the novelty of the Hegelian imagination.

Since Hegel the word phenomenology has fallen even further into disrepute. Compared to the majestic pomp of the Hegelian system the philosophy of Edmund Husserl – with which the word 'phenomenology' is now inextricably tangled – is a mere neo-Kantian eccentricity. There is something profoundly infantile about the egocentric obsession of Husserlian thought (one is reminded of Fichte). It is only worth mentioning at all because – primarily for socio-political reasons – it has not been without defenders. If in the Hegelian mode of philosophizing alterity is reduced into a collective auto-generative knowing, in the Husserlian mode it is reduced into a monadic 'transcendental ego' (at the limit a *petit bourgeois* parody of Hegel's absolute, God in the guise of a minor state employee), for which the Kantian noumenon is bracketed as a transcendent or naturalistic postulate. The transcendence of the object is reconstituted on the side of the subject as the intentionality or inherently outward-oriented character of experience. Experience is intrinsically transcended, i.e. to experience something as an experience *of* something beyond the experience itself is simply what experience is in itself. That thought concerns something outside itself is a transcendental structure *of thought*. Rigorous phenomenology of the Husserlian type, whereby all questions of reference are replaced by an analytic of intentionality, leads straight to idealism and solipsism and thus, as Schopenhauer persuasively suggests, to the madhouse (although it is an insipid insanity they offer us).

An altogether richer vein of thought is that initiated by Schelling, provoking Hegel's famous remark concerning a 'night in which all cows are black' [H III 22]. Like Hegel, Schelling saw the weak spot of Kantianism to lie in the impossibility of a rigorous determination of the transcendental ground of knowing, since what is transcendental has to remain immanent to its own disjunction. What differentiates these two philosophical modes is that where Hegel's *Aufhebung* or assimilatory negation passes though the other, appropriating it as a mediating pause of absolute reason, Schelling's *Indifferenz* undercuts the articulated terms, exacerbating the critical gesture, since one of the transcendentally subverted terms is in each case *the simulacrum of the transcendental*. Hegelian thought is guided by the exigency of comprehension (which at the limit grounds itself), Schelling's by that of transcendental grounding (which at the limit comprehends all difference). In their early nineteenth Century systematic forms these types of thinking can seem very similar, but as they divergently concretize themselves into contemporary philosophies of critical theory and deconstruction respectively, their difference becomes more stark. The most important rhetorical symptom of this difference is the contrast between an ever more nostalgic discourse on the failure of totality on the one hand, and an ever more complacently impotent discourse on the impossibility of radical subversion on the other. In their recent forms both discourses make frequent and preposterous claims to a Nietzschean inspiration.

It is not Hegel or Schelling who provide Nietzsche with a philosophical tap-root, but rather Schopenhauer. With Schopenhauer the approach to the 'noumenon' as an energetic unconscious begins to be assembled, and interpreting the noumenon as will generates a discourse that is not speculative, phenomenological, or meditative, but diagnostic. It is this type of thinking that resources Nietzsche's genealogy of inhuman desire, which feeds in turn into Bataille's base materialism, for which 'noumenon' is addressed as impersonal death and as unconscious drive.

Even though Bataille exhibits little interest in Schopenhauer (and even a measure of casual hostility), his location in relation to the history of philosophy cannot be pursued without attending to the meditation upon the will that Schopenhauer initiated. Kant's conception of the 'will' [*Wille*] provides a certain base-line for the thought of desire because it is the sophisticated rendering of a crudity. The folk-psychology of intentions finds a baroque justification in Kant's philosophy, but scarcely even the most fleeting interrogation. Kant rationalizes willing into transcendental agency; the more or less lucid pursuit of ends, exhaustively mediated by the structures of individualized representational subjectivity. Humanism reaches its zenith in such thinking, where the will is conceived as the condition of possibility for the efficiency of concepts; the wholly miraculous adaptation of *transcendent* reality to representation.

With Schopenhauer this notion of will inherited from Kant and early German idealism undergoes a profound transformation. Such terms as 'will to power', 'libido', and 'orgone', for instance, can be seen to negotiate with the terminology of Kantianism only after their specifically Schopenhauerean modulation has been recognized. Schopenhauer no longer understands the spontaneity of will as a predicate serving to differentiate the transcendental subject from the inertia of matter, as Kant does. Rather, the terminology of the will (desire) is guided through its first faltering steps towards a notion of increate matter. Schopenhauer reserves the word 'matter' [*Die Materie*] for the fundamental determination of objectivity within representation, which he distinguishes from the will, whereas later thinkers beginning with Nietzsche – and including Freud as well as Bataille – shift the sense of matter towards the substratum of appearances (impersonal, unconscious, and real) that Schopenhauer calls will. Increate matter is a translation of will or noumenon; a designation for the anti-ontology basic to any *positively* atheistic materialism ('[t]o say the World was not Created ... is to deny there is a God' writes Hobbes in his *Leviathan*). Such a thought is at variance with the most prevalent scientific conception of matter only insofar as science has – despite many of its pronouncements – tended to be implicitly agnostic, or even theist, rather than virulently atheistic in tendency. Due to this dominant attitude, first systematized by Kant in his determination of theological ideas as postulates of practical reason, matter has continued to be implicitly conceived as *ens creatum*, distinguished from a creative being which is determined as an extrinsic spontaneity. Matter as *ens creatum* is essentially *lawful*, whilst increate matter is anarchic, even to the extent of evading the adoption of an essence. This is why Schopenhauer considers the principle of sufficient reason or logicality of being to have a merely superficial validity.

Schopenhauer reverses the traditional relation between intellect and will, for which willing is the volitional act of a representing subject, and re-casts the will as a pre-representational ('blind') impulse. His advance is nevertheless an extremely limited one in certain respects. He considers the anarchic character of the pre-ontological cosmic bedrock to be morally objectionable, and merely replaces its traditional theistic determination with an extrinsic moral principle of absolute negation (denial of the will). This anti-materialist dimension of his thinking can be seen as stemming from the requirement that unlawful being should retain the (idealistically grounded) juridical potentiality for the condemnation of itself. Without rigorously interrogating the basic values of his moral heritage he continued to associate that which is not God with radical imperfection and sin, so that unregulated will is thought of not as irresponsibility but as malice. Perhaps it should not surprise us to learn that Schopenhauer lent his opera glasses to a Prussian officer in 1848, in order, as Lukács tells us [L IX 179], that he should have 'a better view of the rioters at whom he was shooting'.

*

Pessimism, or the philosophy of desire, has a marked allergy to academic encompassment. Schopenhauer, Nietzsche, and Freud all wrote the vast bulk of their works from a space inaccessible to the sweaty clutches of state pedagogy, as, of course, does Bataille. The most perfectly distilled attack upon institutional philosophy is probably that found in Schopenhauer's *Parerga and Paralipomena*, in its section entitled 'On University Philosophy'. By the end of this text Schopenhauer has argued that the university is inextricably compromised by the interests of the state, that this necessarily involves it in the perpetuation of the monotheistic dogmas that serve such interests, and that the consequent subservience to vulgar superstition completely devastates it; degrading it to a grotesquely hypocritical sophistry, fuelled by a petty careerism spiced by an envious hatred of intellectual independence, and articulated in a wretchedly obscure and distorted jargon that allows its proponents both to squirm away from the surveillance of the priests, and to hypnotize a gullibly adoring public. It is scarcely surprising that he comes to conclude:

> if there is to be philosophy at all, that is to say, if it is to be granted to the human mind to devote its loftiest and noblest powers to incomparably the weightiest of all problems, then this can successfully happen only when philosophy is withdrawn from all state influence [Sch VII 200].

This distaste has been fully reciprocated. One need only take note of Heidegger's remarks on Schopenhauer to get a taste of the university's revenge upon its assailants. The crass dismissal of Schopenhauer's aesthetics in the first volume of Heidegger's *Nietzsche* lectures is a quite typical example, and others can be found in *Introduction to Metaphysics*, his Leibniz lectures, *What is Called Thinking*, etc. What is at stake in both cases is not argument, however rancorous, but the relation of mutual revulsion between the academy and a small defiant fragment of its outside. Neither recognizes the legitimacy of the other's discourse; for the university considers its other to be incompetent, whilst the part of this other – admittedly a very small part – that has seized and learnt to manipulate the weaponry of philosophical strife, considers the voice of the university to be irremediably tainted by servility.

Little progress can be made in interpreting this conflict so long as one remains attached to idealistic notions of 'controversy' or 'debate'. The constitution of debates is the dominant mode of pacification employed by the university: the validation of certain manageable conflicts within the context of institutionalization, moderation, and the indefinite deferral of consequences. What is transcendental to academic debate is submission to socio-economic power. It might even be fair to suggest that it is Schopenhauer who first spoils the possibility of debate in this case; that Heidegger, for instance, is already provoked. The famous story about Schopenhauer setting his lectures at the same times as Hegel would be an example of this; a dramatization of the relation of exclusion that is at least as basic to the university as dialogue. Anybody who dismisses this gesture as mere perversity is lending implicit credence to the notion that the university gives each a chance to speak, providing a neutral space for the encounter of divergent types of thought. Schopenhauer does not take any such suggestion of academic impartiality seriously:

> the state has at all times interfered in the philosophical disputations of the universities and has taken sides, no matter whether it was a question of Realists and Nominalists, or Aristotelians and Ramists, or Cartesians and Aristotelians, of Christian Wolf, Kant, Fichte, Hegel, or anything else [Sch VII 187].

Furthermore, the intervention of the state is a perpetually operative force that is immanent to the institution itself. University philosophy polices itself as part of its sordid flirtation with state power:

> It never occurs to a professor of philosophy to examine a new system that appears to see whether it is true; but he at once tests it merely to see whether it can be brought into harmony with the doctrines of established religion, with government plans, and with the prevailing views of the times. After all this he decides its fate [Sch VII 167].

By precipitating a non-dialogical collision with Hegel, Schopenhauer certainly demonstrated a measure of tactical ineptitude, but not strategic blindness. For it is difficult to imagine that anyone would want to suggest that an impartial space for the discussion of atheistic philosophy was available at the University of Berlin during the early 1820s. The power of Schopenhauer's diagnosis is that it is able to attend simultaneously to both the metaphysical conflict between philosophy and monotheism and the institutional forestalling of this conflict. This amphibiousness invests his critique of optimism with an enduring energy of dissent. Optimism is the general form of apology; at once the key to the metaphysical commitments of theology and the protection of these commitments from vigorous interrogation. Monotheism, with its description of the world as the creation of a benevolent God, or at least, of a God that defines the highest conception of the good, jusifies an all pervasive optimistic framework for which *being is worthy of protection*. For the optimist revolt, critique, and every form of negativity must be conditioned by a projected positivity; one criticizes in order to consolidate a more certain edifice of knowledge, one revolts in order to establish a more stable and comfortable society, one struggles against reality in order to release being into the full positivity which is its due. All of which inevitably slows things down a great deal, because, unless one has a persuasive plan of the future, negativity is de-legitimated by a prior apologetic dogma. The suggestion is always that 'at least this is better than nothing', a slogan that some Leibnizian demon has probably scrawled above the gates of Hell (not that I have any argument with Hell).

Whilst speculative thought is the logic of social progress, a realization of freedom by means of a gradual absorption of conditions into the collective subject of political action, pessimism is the affect process of unconditional revolt. The most bleak speculative reasoning still retains a commitment to the reality of progressive development, even if this is momentarily frozen into the implicit truth of an agonizing contradiction. If Adorno creates particular difficulties for such a contention it is because he creates equivalent difficulties for speculative thought, partly because he is abnormally sensitive to the irreducible ethnocentrism involved in Hegel's thinking, an ethnocentrism which is related to, although ultimately more interesting than, the colonial triumphalism of his philosophy of history. Its basic character is a terror of regression to a primitiveness that would forsake the laborious advances of one's

'The death of sound philosophy' 13

Occidental ancestors, and this is in turn a symptom of the wretched Western nihilism that insists one has an immense amount to lose. That our history has been in any way beneficial is something Schopenhauer vigorously repudiates, and his vehement anti-historicism (which Nietzsche comes to massively overhaul) has at least this merit: it sets itself firmly against one of the basic apologetic motifs of Occidental societies. After all, we cannot use the word history without meaning a singular process that one population has inflicted on several others, as well as upon its own non-servile virtualities, a process that has combined gruesome accident with sustained atrocity.

The speculative model of revolution is one of 'taking over', the pessimistic model is one of escape; on the one hand the overthrow of oppression-as-exploitation, and on the other the overthrow of oppression-as-confinement. Employing an ultimately untenable distinction it could be said that at the level of social description these models are at least as complimentary as they are exclusive; the extraction of labour power and the inhibition of free movement have been complicit in the domestication of the human animal since the beginning of settled agriculture. But at the level of strategy a certain bifurcation begins to emerge, leading Deleuze and Guattari, for instance, to tease apart a Western and an Eastern model of revolution, the latter being based on a block of partially repressed nomad desire, oriented to the dissolution of sedentary space and the liquidation of the state[3]. Of course, insofar as one is concerned with anything like a directly applicable concrete programme, Schopenhauer has little to offer; what is known of his politics has a definite reactionary slant, and he does not seem to have grasped either the chronic exterminatory tendencies of settled societies, or their deep arbitrariness. The alternative he proposes is one of departure in the mode of renunciation, which is to say, he lacked a nomadology, or failed to explore the delirial antilogic that leads out of the maze. This is a claim at the same level as that which accuses Hegel of lacking a convincing account of the specifically modern dominion of commodity production, and helps to explain the impulse to the concrete associated with Nietzsche and with Marx.

Pessimism is not a value logically separable from an independent metaphysics, because the logical value of identity is itself a comfort of which pessimism destitutes us, whilst a metaphysics of the will subverts the autonomy or separability of value questions. In this sense, pessimism is the first truly transcendental critique, operated against being, and in particular against the highest being, by the impersonal negativity of time or denial. Schopenhauerians and Hegelians can travel a considerable distance together in submitting being unsparingly to its abolition in time, although, in the end, speculative thought exhibits a fear of regression that looks to a pessimistic perpective like an anti-primitivist ideology, serving the interests of pseudo-progressive Western societies. Marx's famous appeal to the working class in the *Communist Manifesto* that they have 'nothing to lose but their chains' is open to both a speculative and a pessimistic interpretation, and it is perhaps the latter that unleashes its most uncompromising force.

*

Part of Kant's legacy is that no important philosopher since his time has considered traditional theism to be theoretically defensible. Kant's *Critique of Pure Reason* methodically dismantles the structure of argument for the existence of God that had been painstakingly constructed by the scholastic and early modern philosophers, the most important pillars of which had been the ontological, cosmological, and teleological proofs, all of which Kant showed to be radically untenable. Although no significant philosopher has contested Kant's thorough demolition of these apologetic arguments, they have responded to it in a number of distinct ways. Kant's own path was the re-foundation of theistic belief in faith guided by moral necessity. Religion became subordinate to the immediate evidence of moral law. The post-Kantian idealists, amongst whom the most notable are, of course, Fichte, Schelling, and Hegel, all sought to reconstruct theology on the basis of speculative reason for which the imagery of Christian monotheism served as something between ornamentation and evidence of a groping historical anticipation. For these thinkers the authority of the Kantian text had become inestimably more authoritative than Judaeo-Christian scripture, whatever their pious declarations to the contrary. Jacobi, Kierkegaard, and others sought an ultra-fideism in which the absurdity of religious belief was transmuted into a positive challenge, whilst Schopenhauer, followed by Nietzsche, concluded that philosophy must become savagely atheistic.

Schopenhauer was not a reluctant atheist. He considered

monotheism to be not merely erroneous, but grotesque. Many elements are involved in this judgement, but the most important, both for his thought and later for Nietzsche's, is the violent repudiation of the massively anthropocentric tendency of such faiths (which he interpreted antisemitically). A central and insistent tenet of Schopenhauer's philosophy is that intellect, personality, and consciousness are extremely superficial and derivative characteristics of complex nervous-systems, and are thus radically untypical of the nature of the cosmos, which is driven by impersonal and unconscious forces. Even in the human being personality was nothing but an ephemeral foam, almost incidental to its basic life-functions, and instrumental in the service of these latter. Furthermore, the personality was not a reason for celebration, but rather a wound, or a gore-spattered cell in which the futile horror of existence was exhibited as squalid suffering, and occasionally, in a few select specimens, as tragedy. The notion of a personal God was therefore a monstrous perversion born of egoism and blindness, an attempted justification of individuated conscious existence that pandered to the miserable vanity of those in flight from the only possibility of redemption: the annihilation of self. In contradistinction from Kant, therefore, Schopenhauer considered theism to be the apotheosis of immorality; a wretched attachment to the principle of personal identity.

Nietzsche wholeheartedly subscribed to the basic tenets of Schopenhauer's diagnosis, but sought to deepen his cosmology, and to jettison the residual egoism that lay in its continued obsession with redemption. Nietzsche no longer considered the sufferings of the self to be a serious objection to the basic cosmic processes that underpinned it. Where Schopenhauer had depicted the unconscious striving of nature as a 'will-to-live', whose most sophisticated form is the egoism of the individuated human animal, Nietzsche re-named this fundamental drive the 'will-to-power', for which survival is a mere tool. For Nietzsche, life is thought of as a means in the service of an unconscious trans-individual creative energy. Mankind as a whole is nothing but a resource for creation, a dissolving slag to be expended in the generation of something more beautiful than itself. The end of humanity does not lie within itself, but in a planetary artistic experiment about which nothing can be decided in advance, and which can only be provisionally labelled 'overman'. For overman is not a superior model of man, but that which is beyond man; the creative surpassing of humanity.

Nietzsche read Christianity as the nadir of humanistic slave-morality, the most abject and impoverishing attempt to protect the existent human type from the ruthless impulses of an unconscious artistic process that passed through and beyond them. The mixture of continuity and discontinuity connecting Nietzsche's atheism with Schopenhauer's is encapsulated in Nietzsche's maxim, 'man is something to be overcome.'

*

Nietzschean atheology is relentless antihumanism, which has led to it being confused with another (quasi-)antihumanistic philosophy: the 'deconstruction' of Jacques Derrida, a philosopher who has exercised a hegemonic power over Bataille-reception in recent years. The immediate roots of deconstruction lie in the phenomenology of Husserl and Heidegger, and with the later work of Heidegger, in particular, it has an almost total intimacy. The dominant motif of this entire current of thought is 'presencing', or *Anwesenheit*, the event through which the phenomenon is given, associated with the operation of language. The axial insight of the later Heidegger and then Derrida – an insight that displaces Kant's critique whilst remaining structurally analogous to it – is that presencing has been traditionally conceived on the model of presence. This is to say, the origin of the phenomenon has been conceived on the basis of the phenomenon itself, so that presencing is thought through that which it constitutes, or, as both Heidegger and Derrida come to conclude, fails to constitute. Derrida's well-known terms 'writing', 'text', 'differance', etc., refer to a process of the constitution of presence that is never consummated, an interminable generative non-presence. He often describes this process in terms that echo, in an anaemic fashion, Nietzsche's will-to-power; an insatiable creative drive, perpetually dissolving its products back into itself in an artistic frenzy without end. But such resonances do not indicate any substantive philosophical relation. The phenomenological tradition, with its fetish of awareness, is quite alien to the philosophies of the energetic unconscious that flow in a tightly compacted series from Kant, through Schopenhauer and Nietzsche, to Freud. There is an immense gulf between Nietzsche's aggressive genealogies that wreck unity on zero, and Derrida's deconstructed phenomenology that interminably probes the border between presence and absence.

Deconstructive readings are undertaken almost exclusively

against the most elementary structures of signification; the binary distinction. Such readings focus upon a text whose conceptual architecture is of this dichotomous or oppositional kind, the claim being that this is in any case an ubiquitous characteristic of Western writing. The binary order of the concept is considered to be the ultimate basis of the myth of phenomenality; the imposition of a spurious clarity, distinctness, and coherence whose principle is the logical law of the excluded middle. For Derrida, in superficial agreement with Hegel's phenomenology of reason, identity and negation are both modes of presence. Derrida's twist is to suggest that the excluded middle, or the difference between identity and non-identity, is never successfully excluded, but is rather subject to a failed repression. The reason for this, to outline it very sketchily, rests on a principle shared by thinkers as various as Spinoza, Hegel, and Saussure, that presence is a contrastive concept. To be present is to have been rigorously differentiated from non-presence, which means that differentiation itself – since it is the condition of presence – is unpresentable. Since difference or non-presence cannot be lucidly represented it is impossible for anything to be rigorously distinguished from it, which means that the conditions of presence are unrealizable. The task of deconstructive reading is the recovery of the written difference, which Derrida calls the trace, and which interferes with the constitution of identity and difference as lucid concepts. The procedure of deconstruction is to first reverse the traditional value hierarchy encrusted in the opposition of terms, and then to explicitly mark a third term, one that has been deployed within the text inconsistently. This third term derives its value from both sides of the opposition; operating as a partially concealed pseudo-concept with incoherent predicates. This term will be a name for presencing or writing, and its discovery consummates a given deconstruction.

Although Derrida's work can be rather baffling at first, especially since his prose style has inherited a considerable dosage of Teutonic inelegance and obscurity, the implications of his machinery of reading for Nietzsche's atheological programme are quite straightforward. He considers atheism to be at best a tactical step on the way to the deconstruction of theology, and in effect even this is a step he seems uninterested in. But even if Derrida were subject to an anti-theistic inclination he could only be driven by his 'philosophy' to search for that which institutes the difference between the presence and absence of God, something like

Schelling's 'Absolute' or Heidegger's 'Being', a search which is scarcely distinguishable from moves long familiar to radical theologians. Heidegger himself saw no contradiction between such a position and a continuing adherence to what is perhaps the most ideologically compromised variant of Christian belief, southern German Roman Catholicism.

Before examining Nietzsche's irreducibility to deconstruction a little more carefully, it is worth briefly introducing the arguments of Jean-François Lyotard, who even in his early 'Nietzschean' stage is caught up in a quasi-deconstructionist position on the question of atheism. There is no doubt that during the period ending in 1974 with *Économie libidinale* Lyotard is far closer to Nietzsche's thought than Derrida has ever been, a symptom of which is Lyotard's attachment to psychoanalytical rather than phenomenological modes of enquiry. Nevertheless, even at this stage of his work, Lyotard disavows the space of atheism with a finality easily comparable with Derrida's. He considers atheism to be reactive, repeating a gesture of negation that belongs to theology rather than to the impulsions of an energetic unconscious which, as Freud argues, knows no negativity. What Nietzschean thought requires, he suggests, is a disinvestment of monotheism and not a critique of it. Christianity should not be attacked but abandoned, since atheism merely perpetuates the memory traces that foster the depressive states of *ressentiment* and disgust. Lyotard seeks to persuade his readers that the thought of the death of God merely dampens libidinal intensities if it is treated as anything other than a matter of indifference. God should bore us into forgetting rather than provoking us into revolt.

What Derrida and Lyotard share, and where they both diverge from Nietzsche, is the supposition that atheism is an instance of negation, rather than a transmutation or transvaluation of its sense. For Nietzsche it is facile to accuse atheism of having a recourse to a notion of negativity which is itself essentially theological, because to do so is to remain passively within a socio-historically realized theological space that continues to organize the meanings of all terms. Negation is re-forged in the celebration of the death of God, to mean the way in which God is not, and this is a sense which is incommensurate with the negation that was permitted within theology and the metaphysics conditioned by it. To say 'there is no God' is not to express a proposition in a pre-established logical syntax, but to begin thinking again, in a way that is radically new, and therefore utterly experimental. Zero is fatally discovered beneath the scabrous crust of logical negativity. It is obscurantism of the most tediously familiar kind to suggest that the 'nothing' of nihilism is an indissolubly theological concept. The *nihil* is not a concept at all, but rather immensity and fate. Nietzsche describes atheism as an open horizon, as a loss of inhibition. The 'a-' of atheism is privative only in the sense of a collapsing dam.

Deconstruction is the systematic closure of the negative within its logico-structural sense. All uses, references, connotations of the negative are referred back to a bilateral opposition as if to an inescapable destination, so that every 'de-', 'un-', 'dis-', or 'anti-' is speculatively imprisoned within the mirror space of the concept. If we were to follow deconstruction to the letter here it would follow that atheism, antihumanism, and antilogic, far from being virulent pestilential swamps, had no force except through their determinate relations to their enemies, which had thus always already bilateralized them into docility. As for deconstruction 'itself', ah, it likes to suffer!

Such logicization of the negative leads to Derrida 'thinking' loss as irreducible suspension, delay, or differance, in which decision is paralysed between the postponement of an identity and its replacement. Suspension does not resolve itself into annihilation, but only into a trace or remnant that has always been distanced from plenitude (rather than deriving from it), so that differance is only loss in the (non)sense of irreparable expenditure insofar as this can be described as the insistence of an unapproachable possibility, which is to say, under the aegis of a fundamental domestication. In *Freud and the Scene of Writing* Derrida is overt in his commensuration of differance with the reality principle, reading both as instances of the regulation of discharges. Differance channels the descent of affective quanta, re-routing them into a detour (which has always already begun) in order that their efflux can be adapted to the exigency of repetition. In a peculiar series of moves Derrida brands desire with a metaphysical inclination (shifting it from an energetic to a phenomenological register), which then allows him to transcendentalize repression by aligning it with the impossibility of pure presence, and to implicitly juggle the thought of repression so that it becomes the repression of the acknowledgement of the necessity of repression (repression of writing-as-repression-of-impossible-inclination)[4]. Thus he redoubles the epistemo-contemplative terms of diagnosis, valorizes the martyrdom of the ego, changes the signs of psychoanalysis whilst reinforcing its secondary-process politics, attempts the elimination of all possible reference to a material, sacrificial, and generative unconscious that is beyond phenomenological recuperation, and, in general, produces one of the most coherent apologetics of libidinal vivisection ever written, all garbed in a spuriously subversive rhetoric.

In terms of the social dissemination of his discourse Derrida is perhaps our Hegel; an assimilator in the service of 'the great tradition' of authoritarian reason and toothless academic professionalism (facilitated by the sophistication of problems into the philosophical stratosphere). Like Hegel he is obsessed by the reference of all things to the concept, by oppositional relations (both profess to resist, re-direct, struggle against them), representation, dependency, the saturating prevalence of *logos*, and capture. Their thinking also shares the unattractive characteristic of thriving upon the frustration of rupture and the sentimental pathos of overwhelming inheritance. Both conceive and practise 'revolt' as a strategy of intelligent conservation. Both write in a ghoulish technical jargon squirming within a tortured syntax. Indeed, the most basic lesson Derrida learns from Heidegger – almost certainly unconsciously – is how to save the socio-political prestige which Hegel attains for philosophy (the reserve of secondary-process apologetic) from the ludicrously over-emphatic idealism of speculative thought. The strategy adopted in both cases is essentially Kantian; if there is something you want to protect, attack it with measured vigour yourself, thus investing it with replenished force, and pre-empting its annihilation. If it is Heidegger who is the most successful practitioner of such *conquest as the transfer of defensive responsibility*, Derrida still remains his most eager disciple. Thus it is that the 'text of Western metaphysics' finds itself subject to a general 'destruction', 'deconstruction', or restorative critique, which – amongst other things – fabricates 'it' into a totality, rescues it from its own decrepit self-legitimations, generalizes its effects across other texts, reinforces its institutional reproduction, solidifies its monopolistic relation to truth, confirms all but the most preposterous narratives of its teleological dignity, nourishes its hierophantic power of intimidation, smothers its real enemies beneath a blizzard of pseudo-irritations (its 'unsaid' or 'margins'), keeps its political prisoners locked up, repeats its lobotomizing stylistic traits and sociological complacency, and, in the end, begins to mutter once more about an unnamable God. Deconstruction is like capital; managed and reluctant change.

An important instance of pseudo-contact is found in Derrida's discussion of Nietzsche and femininity in *Spurs* – a text that serves as a supplement to Heidegger's interpretation of *The Will to Power as Art*. This reading marks out some traits of Nietzsche's sexuality, a sexuality of and as writing, indicating a web of relations to the history and structure of logocentric metaphysics. The condensation of these remarks into a pointed proposition, a stylate form that is more frequent in Derrida's texts than many of his commentators imply, might generate something like this:

> Nietzsche's textuality is worked by a repressed lesbian stratum that subverts the traditional logic of truth and appearance.

According to Derrida the system of repression that partially dominates Nietzsche's writing is orchestrated by a principle of castration, having two moments, articulated as follows:

1 He was, he dreaded this castrated woman.
2 He was, he dreaded this castrating woman [Spu 101].

Castration is determined in thought as a plenitude threatened by absence, of a plus and minus distributed by the law of the excluded middle. It is thus the fundamental psychological repercussion of metaphysics. Freud suggests in many places that it is this structure, structure itself in its purest state, that has governed the construction of gender within Western history. Because castration is a matter of the distribution of a moment of pure and ultimate lack it is readily associated with a problematic of disappropriation. Derrida reads this difference between having and not-having as itself regulated by a more primordial propriative movement that cannot be characterized either by plenitude or lack. He takes this propriative difference to be a moment of deconstructive lesbian excess that he expresses in the phrase: 'He was, he loved this affirming woman' [Spu 101]. In Nietzsche's text – as the unstable principle of its unfurling – can be found the figure of woman in love with herself.

The 'logic' of these movements closely parallels that of Heidegger's *The Will to Power as Art* lectures, for which the collapse of the truth/appearance opposition at the end of Nietzsche's *How the True World at Last Became a Fable* is celebrated as the breakdown of a repressive and unreformable dyadic scheme – a *Herausdrehen*, a twisting-out or writhing-free of metaphysics. Derrida somewhat surreptitiously inserts a figure of lesbian desire into this problematic – against the grain of the ponderous masculinity of Heideggerian prose – in order to mark the auto-affection of nonidentity, or the asymmetric other of the Phallus in touch with her (non)self.

The compromises that box-in this intervention are legion, since once again it is a difference between presence and absence that finally orchestrates it. That it retains a certain seductiveness stems from the fact that it partially captures a shift from bilateral reflection to unilateral propulsion that is profoundly consonant with Nietzsche's thinking, even though this shift is crushed into the border-zone at the edge of a phenomenological determination of plenitude. Zero or the *sacred* is retained within the constriction of profane negativity, and religious fate is interpreted through the technical prowess of philosophy.

*

At the end of a note from the late spring of 1888, numbered 811 in the compilation entitled 'The Will to Power', Nietzsche argues that a woman's aesthetics, biased towards the question of receptivity, have dominated our understanding of art. He suggests that one should not demand of the artist, who gives, that he *becomes a woman*, and receives. The production of art is characterized as masculine, whilst the reception of art, including the entire history of aesthetics, and even philosophy as a whole, is allotted to the feminine. Even though this unstable construction is a blatant efflorescence out of repression – since it collapses profligacy onto the polar terms of an exchange relation (constituting reciprocal or bilateral gender identities) – it allows us to pursue Nietzsche's thinking about art into the inhuman squandering that guides and ruins it.

Nietzsche provides us with some further markers into this abyss earlier in the same note, where he describes the artistic condition as follows:

> the extreme sharpness of certain senses, so they understand a quite different sign-language – and create one – the condition that seems to be a part of many nervous disorders-; extreme mobility that turns into an extreme urge to communicate; the

> desire to speak on the part of everything that knows how to give signs-; a need to get rid of oneself, as it were, through signs and gestures; ability to speak of oneself through a hundred speech media – an explosive condition. One must first think of this condition as a compulsion and urge to get rid of the exuberance of inner tension through muscular activity and movements of all kinds; then as an involutary co-ordination between this movement and the inner processes (images, thoughts, desires) – as a kind of automatism of the whole muscular system impelled by strong stimuli from within-; inability to prevent reaction; the system of inhibition suspended, as it were [N III 716].

And later:

> the compulsion to imitate: an extreme irritability through which a given model becomes contagious – a state is guessed on the basis of signs and immediately depicted – An image, rising up within, immediately turns into a movement of the limbs – a certain suspension of the will – (Schopenhauer!!!) A kind of deafness and blindness towards the external world – the realm of admitted stimuli is rigorously delimited [N III 716].

The artistic process is thus likened to a contagion and a nervous illness, an explosion of abreactive gestures with their associated intensities. The inhibition to this outflow collapses, but the admission of new material is sharply reduced. In other words, the powers of absorption are suppressed; anorexia is coupled with logorrhea, or extreme volubility, and art is thought on the basis of a violent wasting disease.

There is a peculiar economic model at work here, in which a disequilibrium between expenditure and income is pushed towards its extreme. From a bourgeois perspective what we are faced with is the ultimate form of dangerous madness; a process of anti-accumulation that is totally out of control. There are obvious difficulties in grasping the possibility of this economy due to the industrial tendency which denies that it could be basic. Chronic squandering violates the reciprocity which governs the logics of both Artistotle and Hegel since it is incompatible with the principle that determination equals negation, according to which every loss is correlated with an associated gain. Both Aristotelians and Hegelians can become competent accountants, accepting the logical basis of double entry book-keeping (which is why bourgeois and Marxist economists are so often able to understand each other very easily). Nietzsche's remarks, on the contrary, tend to depart from intelligible human economy from the first. The demand in *The Will to Power as Art* that 'one ought not to demand of the artist, who gives, that he should become a woman' [N III 716] evokes an episode from the history of 'how the true world at last became a fable':

> Progress of the idea, it becomes more delicate, seductive, unattainable, it becomes a woman, it becomes Christian [N II 963].

If this conjunction is read as saying 'it becomes a woman, and *therefore* becomes Christian' we can append much of Nietzsche's often ferociously anti-feminine rhetoric to this phrase. For instance, in another note gathered under the heading of *The Will to Power as Art* from about this time, he writes: 'What pleases all pious women, old or young? a saint with beautiful legs, still young, still an idiot' [N III 756]. The problem with such a reading is that Christianity is an identitarian monotheism, insulated against zero, and a privileged graveyard of the sacred; burying the vortex of vulvo-cosmic dissolution beneath the monument of eternal being. Nietzsche is not trapped at the edge of a deconstruction, oscillating between presence and absence, but is rather scrabbling at the secondary-process security of partial unity; fending-off zero with the detritus of logical negation.

If, as Derrida indicates, the pious woman is Nietzsche's synonym for the castrato, we can see that this figure is the opposite of the artist within a heavily revised delirium of wastage. A castrate capital that can only gorge itself and accumulate opposes the delirious anorexic maniac who throws away everything he has. But here we are back to reciprocal determination and double-entry book-keeping; the condition of impossibility for art, in other words absolute capitalism. Castration distils a pure piety of engorgement that drives the artist into a proletarian destitution.

Nietzsche is not unaware of this predicament, and in the passage that immediately precedes 'How the true world at last became a fable' in *Twilight of the Idols* he writes:

> To separate the world into the 'true' and the 'apparent', be it in the Christian fashion, or in that of Kant (a cunning Christian to the end) is only a suggestion of decadence – a symptom of

declining life ... That the artist treasures appearance above reality is no objection to this proposition. Because here, 'appearance' means reality *once again*, only selected, strengthened, corrected... [N II 961].

The story traced by 'How the true world at last became a fable' is that of our history, but it is a superficial process when compared to the pre-history that provides its resources and genealogical sense. The pre-historical narrative leads up to the events which the historical narrative presupposes, the suppression of the Dionysian impulse and its spontaneous flow of unredeemed expenditure into a rationality of conservation and opposition. This dawning of history is traced more fully in the note numbered #584 in *The Will to Power*, a text of sustained power, including this one small fragment:

And behold, suddenly the world fell apart into a 'true' world and an 'apparent' world: and precisely the world that man's reason had devised for him to live and settle in was discredited. Instead of employing the forms as a tool for making the world manageable and calculable, the deranged acuity of philosophers divined that in these categories is presented the concept of the world to which the one in which man lives does not correspond – the means were misunderstood as measures of value, even as a condemnation of their real intention – The intention was to deceive oneself in a useful way; the means, the invention of formulas and signs by means of which one could reduce the confusing multiplicity to a purposive and manageable schema [N III 726-7].

Where accumulative reason has instituted 'truth' and 'appearance' as unsurpassable finalities or pure concepts, the artist understands appearance as reality 'once again' (*noch einmal*). Reality returns in appearance like the ripple of a shock-wave; opening wider and wider domains for migration. Since reality is itself the stimulus for such migrations they will become progressively more devastating, as this stimulus becomes progressively 'selected, strengthened, corrected' or, to abbreviate, 'intensified'. Here at last – where nothing is last – is the convulsion of zero, eternal recurrence, the libidinal motor of Nietzsche's economics.

Nietzsche's economy of the artistic process, or Dionysian economy, is built beneath the Vesuvian antilogic of eternal recurrence. Such an economy is a perpetual re-emergence of inhuman squandering; an inappropriable excess messily exhibited in the transfiguration of negation into profligate zero. It is intrinsic to desire that it always has fresh and – when unmutilated by repression – increasingly sophisticated constructions to waste. A Dionysian economy is, indeed, a slash and burn agriculture of solar stock, in which the negative limit of each conceptual dyad is reconstituted as an intensification of the positive; as an increasing virulence of difference. The delirium of squandering flows from this inevitability that logical negation never arrives, even though zero impacts. In other words, the thought of eternal recurrence is this: that the abolition of integrated being in the process of desire, or unconstrained wastage, corresponds to an intensification of plague and not a (logically intelligible) negation of assets. Epidemic difference is only enhanced by the spasmodic aberration from itself.

A Dionysian economy is the flux of impersonal desire, perpetually re-energized in the pulse of recurrence, in the upsurge of new realities. These resurgent waves of intensity are situated at the 'point' which patriarchal productivism had reserved for its limit; at the end of each becoming a woman (which are misconstrued as specific negations). Desire could thus be said to be nothing but becoming a woman at different levels of intensity, although of course, it is always possible to become a pious woman, to begin a history, love masculinity, and accumulate, because to become a woman is to depart from reality, and no one loves fables more than the church. But reality drifts upon zero, and can be abandoned over and over again. In the lesbian depths of the unconscious, desires for/as feminizing spasms of remigration are without limit.

Everything populating the desolate wastes of the unconscious is lesbian; difference sprawled upon zero, multiplicity strewn across positive vulvic space. Masculinity is nothing but a shoddy bunk-hole from death. Socio-historically phallus and castration might be serious enough, but cosmologically they merely distract from zero; staking out a meticulously constructed poverty and organizing its logical displacement. If deconstruction spent less time playing with its willy maybe it could cross the line ...

Chapter 2

The curse of the sun

> It is the green parts of the plants of the solid earth and the seas which endlessly operate the appropriation of an important part of the sun's luminous energy. It is in this way that light – the sun – produces us, animates us, and engenders our excess. This excess, this animation are the effect of the light (we are basically nothing but an effect of the sun) [VII 10].
>
> The solar ray *that we are* recovers in the end its nature and the sense of the sun: it is necessary that it gives itself, *loses itself without reckoning* [VII 10].
>
> The peoples of ancient Mexico united man with the glory of the universe: the sun was the fruit of a sacrificial madness ... [VII 192].

There is no philosophical story more famous than that narrated in the Seventh Book of Plato's *Republic*, in which Socrates tells Glaucon of a peculiar dream. It begins in the depths of a 'sort of subterranean cavern' [PCD 747], in which fettered humans are buried from the sun, their heads constrained, to prevent them seeing anything but shadows cast upon a wall by a fire. The ascent through various levels of illusion to the naked light of the sun is the most powerful myth of the philosophical project, but it is also the account of a political struggle, in which Socrates anticipates his death. The denizens of the cave violently defend their own benightedness, to such an extent that Socrates asks: 'if it were possible to lay hands on and to kill the man who tried to release them and lead them up, would they not kill him?' [PCD 749]. Glaucon immediately concurs with this suggestion. Such violence is not unilateral. The philosopher, after all, has an interest in the sun that is not purely a matter of knowledge. To have witnessed the sun is a gain and an entitlement; a supra-terrestrial invitation (however reluctantly accepted) to rule:

> So our cities will be governed by us and you with waking minds, and not, as most cities now which are inhabited and ruled darkly as in a dream by men who fight one another for shadows and wrangle for office as if that were a great good, when the truth is that the city in which those who are to rule are least eager to hold office must needs be best administered and most free from dissension, and the state that gets the contrary type of ruler will be the opposite of this [PCD 752].

Light, desire, and politics are tangled together in this story; knotted in the darkness. For there is still something Promethean about Socrates; an attempt to extract power from the sun. (Bataille says: 'The eagle is at one and the same time the animal of Zeus and that of Prometheus, which is to say that Prometheus is himself an eagle (Atheus-Prometheus), going to steal fire from heaven' [II 40].)

To gaze upon the sun directly, without the intervention of screens, reflections, or metaphors – 'to look upon the sun itself and see its true nature, not by reflections in water or phantasms of it in an alien setting, but in and by itself in its own place' [PCD 748] – has been the European aspiration most relentlessly harmonized with the valorization of truth. Any aspiration or wish is the reconstruction of a desire (drive) at the level of representation, but the longing for unimpeded vision of the sun is something more; a teleological consolidation of representation as such. The sun is the pure illumination that would be simultaneous with truth, the perfect solidarity of knowing with the real, the identity of exteriority and its manifestation. To contemplate the sun would be the definitive confirmation of enlightenment.

Gazing into the golden rage of the sun shreds vision into scraps of light and darkness. A white sun is congealed from patches of light, floating ephemerally at the edge of blindness. This is the illuminating sun, giving what we can keep, the sun whose outpourings are acquired by the body as nutrition, and by the eye as (assimilable) sensation. Plato's sun is of this kind; a distilled sun, a sun which is the very essence of purity, the metaphor of beauty, truth, and goodness. Throughout the cold months, when nature seems to wither and retreat, one awaits the return of this sun in its full radiance. The bounty of the autumn seems to pay homage to it, as the ancients also did. Mixed with this nourishing radiance, as its very heart, is the other sun, the deeper one, dark and contagious, provoking a howl from Bataille: 'the sun is black' [III 75]. From this second sun – the sun of malediction – we receive not illumination but disease, for whatever it squanders on us we are fated to squander in turn. The sensations we drink from the black sun afflict us as ruinous passion, skewering our senses upon the drive to waste ourselves. If 'in the final analysis the sun is the sole object of literary description' [II 140] this is due less to its illuminative radiance than to its virulence, to the unassimilable 'fact' that 'the sun is nothing but death' [III 81]. How far from Socrates – and his hopes of gain – are Bataille's words: 'the sickness of being vomits a black sun of spittle' [IV 15].

> In order to succeed in describing the notion of the sun in the spirit of one who must necessarily emasculate it in consequence of the incapacity of the eyes, one must say that this sun has poetically the sense of mathematical serenity and the elevation of the spirit. In contrast if, despite everything, one fixes upon it with sufficient obstinacy, it supposes a certain madness and the notion changes its sense because, in the light, it is not production that appears, but refuse [*le déchet*], which is to say combustion, well enough expressed, psychologically, by the horror which is released from an incandescent arc-light [I 231].

Incandescence is not enlightening, but the indelicate philosophical instrument of 'presence' has atrophied our eyes to such an extent that the dense materiality of light scarcely impinges on our intelligence. Even Plato acknowledges that the impact of light is (at first) pain, because of 'the dazzle and glitter of the light' [PCD 748]. Phenomenology has systematically erased even this concession. Yet it is far from obvious why an absence/presence opposition should be thought the most appropriate grid for registering the impact of intense radiation. It is as if we were still ancient Hellenes, interpreting vision as an outward movement of perception, rather than as a subtilized retinal wounding, inflicted by exogenous energies.

*

Everything begins for us with the sun, because (we shall come to see) even the cavern, the labyrinth, has been spawned by it. In a sense the origin is light, but this must be thought carefully. Our bodies have sucked upon the sun long before we open our eyes, just as our eyes are congealed droplets of the sun before copulating with its outpourings. The flow of dependency is quite 'clear' (lethal): 'The afflux of solar energy at a critical point of its consequences is humanity' [VII 14]. The eye is not an origin, but an expenditure.

The first text in the *Oeuvres Complètes* is Bataille's earliest published book: *The Story of the Eye*. It first appeared – under the pseudonym of Lord Auch – in 1928, which roughly places it amongst a group of early writings including *The Solar Anus* (1931), *Rotten Sun* (1930, quoted above), and the posthumously published *The Pineal Eye* (manuscripts dated variously 1927 and 1931). The common theme of these writings is the submission of vision to a solar trajectory that escapes it, dashing representational discourse upon a darkness that is inextricable from its own historical aspiration.

The Story [Histoire] of the Eye is both the story and the history of the eye, as also *The Pineal Eye* is a fiction and a history. Every history is a story, which does not mean that the story escapes history, or is anything other than history consummating itself in a blindness which occupies the place of its proper representation. *The Story of the Eye* climaxes with the excision of a priest's eye, which is 'made to slip' [*glisser*] into the vulva of the book's 'heroine' Simone, once by her own hand, and once by that of Sir Edmond (an English *roué*). In this way the dark thirst which is the subterranean drive of the sun obliterates vision, drinking it down into the nocturnal labyrinth of the flesh.

Similarly, in *The Pineal Eye*, the opening of 'an eye especially for the sun' – appropriate to its ferocious apex at noon – invites an obliteration; blinding and shattering descent. The truth of the sun at the peak of its prodigal glory is *the necessity of useless waste*, where the celestial and the base conspire in the eclipse of rational moderation. By concluding the movement of ascent that is synonymous with humanity, and providing vision with the verticality that is its due, the pineal eye crowns the epoch of reason; opening directly onto the heavens (where it is instantaneously enucleated by the deluge of searing filth which is the sun's *truth*):

> I represented the eye at the summit of the skull to myself as a horrible volcano in eruption, with exactly the murky and comic

character which attaches to the rear and its excretions. But the eye is without doubt the symbol of the dazzling sun, and the one I imagined at the summit of my skull was necessarily inflamed, being dedicated to the contemplation of the sun at its maximum burst [*éclat*] [II 14].

The fecal eye of the sun is also torn from its volcanic entrails and the pain of a man who tears out his own eyes with his fingers is no more absurd than that anal setting of the sun [II 28].

The perfect identity between representation and its object – 'blind sun or blinding sun, it matters little' [II 14] – is thought consistently in these early texts as the direct gaze; an Icarian collapse into the sun which consummates apprehension only by translating it into the register of the intolerable. In the copulation with the sun – which is no more a gratification than a representation – subject and object fuse at the level of their profound consistency, exhibiting (in blindness) that they were never what they were.

The unconscious – like time – is oblivious to contradiction, as Freud argues. There is only the primary process (Bataille's sun), except from the optic of the secondary process (representation) which – at the level of the primary process – is still the primary process. This is a logically unmanageable dazzling, quite useless from the perspective of reason, which seeks to differentiate action on the basis of reality. This libidinal consistency, which is (must be) alogically the *same* as the sun, is the thread of Ariadne, tangled in the labyrinth of impure difference. At the beginning of *The Solar Anus* Bataille notes that:

> Ever since phrases have *circulated* in brains absorbed in thought, a total identification has been produced, since each phrase connects one thing to another by means of *copulas*; and it would all be visibly connected if one could discover in a single glance the line, in all its entirety, left by Ariadne's thread, leading thought through its own labyrinth [I 81].

All human endeavour is built upon the sun, in the same way that a dam is built upon a river, but that there could be a solar society in a stronger sense – a society whose gaze was fixed upon the death-core of the sun – seems at first to be an impossibility. Is it not the precise negation of sociality to respond to the 'will for glory [that exists in us which would that we live like suns, *squandering our goods and our life*' [VII 193]? Without doubt any closed social system would obliterate itself if it migrated too far into the searing heart of its solar agitation, unpicking the primary repression of its foundation. It is nevertheless possible for a society to persist at the measure of the sun, on condition that a basic aggressivity displaces its sumptuary furore from itself, so that it washes against its neighbours as an incendiary rage. It is such a tendency that Bataille discovers in the civilization of the Aztecs, whose sacrificial order was perpetuated by means of military violence. In *The Accursed Share* – his great work of solar sociology – he remarks of the Aztecs that:

> The priests killed their victims upon the top of pyramids. They laid them on a stone altar and stabbed them in the chest with an obsidian knife. They tore out the heart – still beating – and lifted it up to the sun. Most of the victims were prisoners of war, justifying the idea that wars were necessary to the life of the sun: wars having the sense of consumption, not that of conquest, and the Mexicans thought that, if they ceased, the sun would cease to blaze [VII 55].

What unfolds beneath Bataille's scrutiny cannot be an apology for the Aztecs or even an explanation. What is at stake in his reading of their culture is an economic intimacy, or thread of solar complicity, the pursuit of genealogical lineages that weave all societies onto the savage root-stock of the stars. The raw energy that stabbed the Aztecs into their ferocities is also that which – regulated by the apparatus of an accumulative culture – drives Bataille in his researches. The energetic trajectory that transects and gnaws his entrails is the molten terrain of a dark communion, binding him to everything that has ever convulsed upon the Earth.

It is precisely the senseless horror of Aztec civilization that gives it a peculiar universality; expressing as it does the unavowable source of social impetus. 'The sun itself was to their eyes the expression of sacrifice' [VII 52], and their energies were dedicated to a carnage without purpose, whereby they realized the truth of the sun upon the earth. It seems to Western eyes as though their hunger for blood were indefensible, based upon ludicrous myths, and exemplifying at the extreme a human capacity to be perverted by untruth. If the culture of the Aztecs had been rooted in an arbitrary mythological vision such a reading might be sustained, but for Bataille the thirst for annihilation is the same as the sun. It is not a desire which man directs towards the sun, but the solar trajectory itself, the sun as the unconscious subject of terrestrial history. It is only because of this unsurpassable dominion of the sun that '[f]or the common and uncultivated consciousness the sun is the image of glory. The sun radiates: glory is represented as similarly luminous, and radiating' [VII 189], such that 'the analogy of a sacrificial death in the flames to the solar burst is the response of man to the splendour of the universe' [VII 193], since 'human sacrifice is the acute moment of a contest opposing to the real order and duration the movement of a violence without measure' [VII 317].

Belonging alongside 'sacrifice' in Bataille's work is the word 'expenditure', *dépense*. This word operates in a network of thought that he describes as general or solar economy: the economics of excess, outlined most fully in the same shaggy and beautiful 'theoretical' work – *The Accursed Share* – in which he writes: 'the radiation of the sun is distinguished by its unilateral character: *it loses itself without reckoning, without counterpart. Solar economy* is founded upon this principle' [VII 10]. It is because the sun squanders itself upon us without return that 'The sum of energy produced is always superior to that which was necessary to its production' [VII 9] since 'we are ultimately nothing but an effect of the sun' [VII 10]. Excess or surplus always precedes production, work, seriousness, exchange, and lack. Need is never given, it must be constructed out of luxuriance. The primordial task of life is not to produce or survive, but to consume the clogging floods of riches – of energy – pouring down upon it. He states this boldly in his magnificent line: 'The world ... is sick with wealth' [VII 15]. Expenditure, or sacrificial consumption, is not an appeal, an exchange, or a negotiation, but an uninhibited wastage that returns energy to its solar trajectory, releasing it back into the movement of dissipation that the terrestrial system – culminating in restricted human economies – momentarily arrests. Voluptuary destruction is the only end of energy, a process of liquidation that can be suspended by the acumulative efforts whose zenith form is that of the capitalist bourgeoisie, but only for a while. For solar economy '[e]xcess is the incontestable point of departure' [VII 12], and excess must, in the end, be spent.

The momentary refusal to participate in the uninhibited flow of luxuriance is the negative of *sovereignty*; a servile *différance*, postponement of the end. The burning passage of energetic dissipation is restrained in the interest of something that is taken to transcend it; a future time, a depredatory class, a moral goal ... Energy is put into the *service* of the future. 'The end of the employment of a tool always has the same sense as the employment of the tool: a utility is assigned to it in its turn – and so on. The stick digs the earth in order to ensure the growth of a plant, the plant is cultivated to be eaten, it is eaten to maintain the life of the one who cultivated it ... The absurdity of an infinite recursion alone justifies the equivalent absurdity of a true end, which does not serve anything' [VII 298].

*

One consequence of the Occidental obsession with transcendence, logicized negation, the purity of distinction, and with 'truth', is a physics that is forever pompously asserting that it is on the verge of completion. The contempt for reality manifested by such pronouncements is unfathomable. What kind of libidinal catastrophe must have occurred in order for a physicist to *smile* when he says that nature's secrets are almost exhausted? If these comments were not such obvious examples of megalomaniac derangement, and thus themselves laughable, it would be impossible to imagine a more gruesome vision than that of the cosmos stretched out beneath the impertinently probing fingers of grinning apes. Yet if one looks for superficiality with sufficient brutal passion, when one is prepared to pay enough to systematically isolate it, it is scarcely surprising that one will find a little. This is certainly an achievement of sorts; one has found a region of stupidity, one has manipulated it, but this is all. Unfortunately, the delicacy to acknowledge this – as Newton so eloquently did when he famously compared science to beach-combing on the shore of an immeasurable ocean (= 0) – requires a certain minimum of taste, of *noblesse*.

Physicalistic science is a highly concrete, sophisticated, and relatively utile philosophy of inertia. Its domain extends to everything obedient to God (he is dead, yet the clay still trembles). Within this domain lie many tracts that have momentarily escaped cultivation; 'facts of spirit' for example, along with constellations of docility of all kinds, but these are not sites of resistance. Science is queen wherever there is legitimacy; perhaps *terra firma* as a whole belongs to her. No one would hastily dispute her rights, but the ocean is insurrection (and the land – it is whispered – floats).

Even after the infantile hyperbole of the scientific completion myth has been set aside, there is still a question concerning the *success* of science that remains untouched. It cannot be seriously doubted that philosophy has been *damaged* by science, for it has even come to anticipate its extinction. It has now reached the stage where it has lost all confidence in its power to know, where envy has totally replaced parental pride, and where the stylistic consequences of its bad conscience have devastated its discourse to the point of illegibility. For at least a century, and perhaps for two, the major effort of the philosophers has simply been to *keep the scientists out*. How much defensiveness, pathetic mimicry, crude self-deception, crypto-theological obscurantism, and intellectual poverty is marked by the name of their recent and morbid offspring *die Geisteswissenschaften*.

The first and most basic source of this generalized neurosis amongst the practitioners and dependents of philosophy is their incomprehension of quite *how* it was that 'they' gave birth to the sciences. They tend to think that they were always *bad scientists*, or at least, immature ones. 'If only we had been better at maths' they mutter under their breath, as they take a mournfully nostalgic pleasure in the fact that as calculators Newton and Leibniz still seemed to be 'neck and neck'.

What is lost to such melancholy is the fact that philosophy does not relate to science as a prototype, but as a motor. It was the basic source of investigative libido before being supplanted by the arms industry, and if science has not yet been completely dissolved into a process of technical manufacture, the difference is only a flux of inexplict philosophy. For philosophy is a machine which transforms the prospect of thought into excitation; a generator. 'Why is this so hard to see?' one foolishly asks. The answer quickly dawns: *the scholars*.

Scholarship is the subordination of culture to the metrics of work. It tends inexorably to predictable forms of quantitative inflation; those that stem directly from an investment in relatively abstracted productivity. Scholars have an inordinate respect for long books, and have a terrible *rancune* against those that attempt to cheat on them. They cannot bear to imagine that short-cuts are possible, that specialism is not an inevitability, that learning need not be stoically *endured*. They cannot bear writers *allegro*, and when they read such texts – and even pretend to revere them – the result is (this is not a description without generosity) 'unappetizing'.

Scholars do not write to be read, but to be measured. They want it to be known that they have worked hard. Thus far has the ethic of industry come.

*

Curiosity has imperilled itself in its questioning, it has even harmed itself. That it has not traversed its history triumphantly is only one of the many certainties that it suffers from. It is all too obvious that the Russian roulette of the interrogative mode has led to its near extinction; maimed in the brain by the rigorous slug of the natural sciences. For the responses it has provoked have usually lacked even the bitter solace of *aporia*. To some the world is beginning to seem a crudely intelligible place; a desert of simplicity, dotted with the stripped bones of inquisitiveness.

What if curiosity was worth more than comprehension? This is not such an impossible thought to entertain. Nor is it unreasonable to ask after the necessity that has led the *motor* of thought to be subordinated to its *consequences*. Resolution could only be desirable if there existed an interest superseding thought. Otherwise it should be merely a means, the end of which is the promotion of enigma and confusion. That thought has to tolerate solutions is simply an unfortunate necessity. Perhaps not even that.

Curiosity is a desire; a dynamic impulse abolished by petrification. It would be an idiocy – although an all too familiar one – to try to preserve it in the formaldehyde of obscurantism and mystique. For an eternal mystery is as devastating to curiosity as any certainty could be. The ideology of thought's exterminators is dogmatism, it scarcely matters of which kind.

It is not the ability to preserve riddles that has value, but the ability to engender them. Any text that persists as an acquisition after coming to a comfortable end has the character of a leech, nourishing itself on the blood of problematic, and returning only repulsive inertia. The fertility of a text, on the contrary, is its *inachievement*, its premature termination, its inconclusiveness. Such a text is always too brief, and instead of a draining anaesthetic attachment there is the *sting*.

This book is not of that kind, it slows Bataille down, driving his fleet madness into a swamp of metaphysics and pseudo-science. My refusal to surrender the sun to the denizens of observatories – and the unseemly tussle that results – makes my relation to Bataille somewhat problematic, wrecking large tracts of my text. My relation to scientific knowledge, on the other hand, is nothing less than a scandal. What I offer is a web of half-choked ravings that vaunts its incompetence, exploiting the meticulous conceptual fabrications of positive knowledge as a resource for delirium, appealing only to the indolent, the maladapted, and the psychologically diseased. I would like to think that if due to some collective spiritual seism the natural sciences were to become strictly unintelligible to us, and were read instead as a poetics of the sacred, the consequence would resonate with the text that follows. At least disorder grows.

*

Disorder always increases in a closed system (such as the universe), because nature is indifferent to her composition. The bedrock state of a system which is in conformity with the chance distribution of its elements has been called 'entropy', a term that summarizes the conclusions of Carnot, Clausius, and their successors concerning thermic engines and the science of heat[5]. With the concept of entropy everything changes. Natural processes are no longer eternal clockwork machines, they are either extinct (*Wärmetod*) or tendential. Mechanisms are subordinated to motors; to thermic difference, energy flux, reservoir, and sump. Order is an evanescent chance, a deviation from disorder, a disequilibrium. Negative disorder – negentropy – is an energetic resource, and chance is the potentiation of the power supply. *Macht, puissance*, as potential for the degradation of energy, as the fluidification of matter/energy, as the possibility of release towards the unregulated or anarchic abyss into which energy pours, as the death of God. Upstream and downstream; the reserve and its dissipation. Order is not law but power, and power is aberration. For Nietzsche, for Freud, and then for Bataille, this is the background against which desire is to be thought. The mega-motor.

There is no difference between desire and the sun: sexuality is not psychological but cosmo-illogical. 'Sexual activity escapes at least during a flash from the bogging-down of energy, prolonging the movement of the sun' [VII 11]. A cosmological theory of desire emerges from the ashes of physicalism. This is to presuppose, of course, that idealism, spiritualism, dialectical materialism (shoddy idealism), and similar alternatives have been discarded in a preliminary and rigorously atheological gesture. Libidinal materialism, or the theory of unconditional (non-teleological) desire, is nothing but a scorch-mark from the expository diagnosis of the physicalistic prejudice.

The basic problem with physicalistic thinking is easy to formulate; it remains implicitly theological. Regression to a first cause is an inescapable consequence of the physicalistic position, which thus remains bound to the old theological matrix, even after the throne has been evacuated by a tremulous deicide. The physicalistic contention is that matter receives its impulsion or determination from without; through the combination of an essential lawfulness that transcends the particular entity and the influence of external bodies or forces. Any 'intrinsic' process (such as decay) results from the expression of natural laws, whilst all extrinsic process results from the passive communication of an original cosmic fatality (probabilistic physics makes no essential difference here, since the mathematical – hence formal and extrinsic – determination of probability is no less rigorous than that of causal necessity). Physical matter is therefore unambiguously passive, exhausted by the dual characteristics of transmitting alien forces and decaying according to the universally legislated exigencies of its composition.

There is a sense in which scientific materialism has not yet begun, because it has not registered the distance between its representational object and the real matter/energy matrix, insofar as such materiality is irreducible in principle to the form of the concept. This irrecoverable other of intellectual prehension can be designated as 'chaos' (order = 0), or, to use a terminology in harmony with Boltzmann's thermodynamics, as *absolutely improbable negentropy*. Lest it be thought that this is an irresponsible sub-philosophical notion brought to scientific materialism from without, let me quote a profound fable narrated by Boltzmann (and attributed to his 'old assistant, Dr Schuetz') in his 1895 essay 'On certain questions of the theory of gases':

> We assume that the whole universe is, and rests for ever, in thermal equilibrium. The probability that one (only one) part of the universe is in a certain state, is the smaller the further this state is from thermal equilibrium; but this probability is greater, the greater the universe is. If we assume the universe great enough we can make the probability of one relatively small part being in any given state (however far from the thermal equilibrium), as great as we please. We can also make the

probability great that, though the whole universe is in thermal equilibrium, our world is in its present state [B III 543-4].

It should first be noted that the account Boltzmann gives here is quite possibly the only conceivable physicalistic atheism, at least, if the second law of thermodynamics is to be maintained. It suggests that the thermal disequilibrium which constitutes the energetic positivity (negentropy or 'H-value') of our region of the universe might be not only possible, but even probable, if the universe were large enough. Thus the reality of negentropy would be adequately explained probabilistically, without the need for theological postulates of any kind.

Boltzmann's account introduces a conceptual differentiation between probable and improbable negentropy, the latter − were it to exist − posing an implicit *problem* for thermodynamics. It is, indeed, a notion of absolutely improbable negentropy that Boltzmann quite reasonably attributes to the critics of the second law, and his speculative cosmology is designed precisely to demonstrate the reducibility of all *regional improbability* or deviation to *general probability* or equilibrium (statistical lawfulness). General or absolute improbability would be the character of a universe whose enigmatic positivity was stastico-physically irresolvable. This is not to say that the empirical demonstration of absolutely improbable negentropy could ever *disprove* general statistical mechanics, since no level of improbability can be strictly intolerable to such a perspective. From the perspective of natural science the re-formulation of cosmology on the basis of a general chaotics could only be an *arbitrary* step, with a variable degree of probabilistic persuasiveness (something suspiciously akin to a religion).

In his argument with Zermelo[6], Boltzmann develops the ideas sketched in the text already cited, although the fundamental thought remains the same. High H-values or negentropies are probabilistic aberrations and do not, for this reason, violate any mechanical law. Boltzmann insists that 'vanishingly few' [*verschwindend wenig*] cases of high or ascending H-value are to be expected according to the second law, but that the multiplication of probability by time ('t') can justify any H-value if 't' is given a high enough value. It is worth expanding upon the concept of time at work here, since what is at stake is the dynamic of permutation and not merely an abstract duration, whatever that might be. Even the heat-death condition of minimal H-values are still reservoirs of energy, even though this energy is fully degraded or entropic. Degraded energy has lost its potential to accomplish work, but nevertheless remains in a state of restless mutation. The fact that such mutation is, from a probabilistic perspective, highly unlikely to register a significant change in H-value, does not mean that it ceases to run through perpetual permutation. The time function thus generates a quantitatively definable permutational fecundity for a constant energy reservoir, i.e. the sum of cosmological permutation, or potential transformation of H-value, is equal to energy multiplied by time. The improbability of high H-values can be expressed as the expected proportion of such values within a range of permutations of a given magnitude.

Boltzmann writes: 'In any case, one can arrive again at a large hump in the H-curve as long as the time of movement is extended enough, indeed, if this extension is protracted satisfactorily even the old condition must recur (and obviously in the mathematical sense this must occur infinitely often, given an infinitely long duration of movement)' [B III 569].

It can be argued that when $t = \infty$ any possible H-value becomes probable, and perhaps even necessary. Such an argument actually depends upon the source of transformation being what is called in statistical theory 'ergodic', which means that it is non-preferential in relation to possible random occurrences. It does not seem as if the cosmological rendering of Nietzsche's eternal recurrence, for instance, is based upon an ergodic source. But there is no need to enter into questions about infinity in order to follow Boltzmann's argument, since any finite H-value compatible with the physical limits of the universe becomes probable at a certain finite value 't'. Superficially it might seem as if even this formulation seems to imply a level of ergodism, since it is conceivable that impoverished cycles of mechanical repetition repeated indefinitely would allow a large 't' value whilst excluding the possibility of high H-values. This argument, an extreme version of Poincaré's[7], is actually non-pertinent to Boltzmann's position, since Boltzmann is seeking to explain the existence, and the possible repetition, of actual rather than hypothetical negentropy. More importantly, however, a narrowly mechanical – rather than probabilistic – explanation for the reproduction of negentropy would seem to directly violate the second law, which is based upon a rupturing of the reciprocity between ascending and descending H-values. In other words, the second law requires that it makes more sense to talk about high H-value humps than about low H-value troughs, since thermal equilibrium does not tend to another state.

Boltzmann's own interpretation of this non-reciprocity takes the form of a fascinating and somewhat naturalized variant of Kantianism. He argues that the departure from troughs of thermal equilibrium occurs in periods of time so extended that they escape observational techniques and thus do not fulfill the epistemological conditions of being objects of possible experience. In his words: 'the length of this period makes a mockery of all observability [*Beobachtbarkeit*]' [B III 571]. And: 'All objections raised against the mechanical appearance of nature are . . . objectless and rest upon errors' [B III 576]. Speculation upon natural processes deviating from the entropic tendency are thus dialectical in a Kantian sense, whilst only those processes following the entropic tendency concern legitimate objects of possible experience. On a pedantic note, it seems to me that Boltzmann is rigorously entitled only to argue that it is 'vanishingly improbable' that a negentropic process could be observed.

For Kant's timeless thing-in-itself Boltzmann substitutes vast stretches of time characterized by maximum entropy or thermal equilibrium, and thus by minimal H-values, whilst Kant's phenomenon is transformed by Boltzmann in order to rest upon an energetic foundation of negentropy, thermal dis-equilibrium, or high H-values. Both the 'phenomenal' and 'noumenal' stretches of Boltzmann's cosmological time are characterized by the conservation of energy and atomic particles, even in an equilibriated state. Time must be ejected into transcendence, and thought as a pure form organizing the permutational metamorphosis of elements, in order for the probabilistic emergence of negentropic humps to be possible. It is fundamental to Boltzmann's argument that positive deviations in H-value are equally possible at any time, time being an indifferent grid.

Libidinal matter is that which resists a relation of reciprocal transcendence against time, and departs from the rigorous passivity of physical substance without recourse to dualistic, idealistic, or theistic conceptuality. It implies a process of mutation which is simultaneously devoid of agency and irreducible to the causal chain. This process has been designated in many ways. I shall follow Schopenhauer, Nietzsche, and Freud in provisionally entitling it 'drive' (*Trieb*). Drive is that which explains, rather than presupposing, the cause/effect couple of classical physics. It is the dynamic instituting of effectiveness, and is thus proto-physical. This implies that drives are the irruptive dynamics of matter in advance of natural law. The 'science' of drives, which has been named 'libidinal economy', is thus foundational for physics, as Schopenhauer meticulously demonstrates.

A libidinal energetics is not a transformation of intentional theories of desire, of desire understood as lack, as transcendence, as dialectic. Such notions are best left to the theologians. It is, rather, a transformation of thermodynamics, or a struggle over the sense of 'energy'. For it is in the field of energetic research that the resources for a materialist theory of desire have been slowly (and blindly) composed:

1 Chance. Entropy is the core of a probabilistic engine, the absence of law as an automatic drive. The compositions of energy are not determinations but differentiations, since all order flows from improbability. Thus a revolution in the conception of identities, now derived from chance as a function of differentiation, hence quantitative, non-absolute, impermanent. Energy pours downstream automatically, 'guided' only by chance, and this is even what 'work' now means (freed from its Hegelian pathos), a function of play, unbinding, becoming.
2 Tendency. The movement from the improbable to the probable is an automatic directionality; an impulsion. Entropy is not a telos, since it is not represented, intentionally motivating, or determinate. It nevertheless allows power, tension, and drive to be grasped as uni-directional, quantitative, and irresistible forces. Teleological schemes are no longer necessary to the understanding of tendential processes, and it is no longer necessary to be patient with them, they are superfluous.
3 Energy. Everywhere only a quantitative vocabulary. Fresh-air after two millennia of asphyxiating ontologies. Essences dissolve into impermanent configurations of energy. 'Being' is indistinguishable from its effectiveness as the unconscious motor of temporalization, permutational dynamism. The nature of the intelligible cosmos is energetic improbability, a differentiation from entropy.
4 Information. The laborious pieties of the *Geisteswissenschaften*; signs, thoughts, ideologies, cultures, dreams, all of these suddenly intelligible as natural forces, as negentropies. A whole

series of pseudo-problems *positively* collapsed. What is the relation between mind and body? Is language natural or conventional? How does an idea correspond to an object? What articulates passion with conception? All signals are negentropies, and negentropy is an energetic tendency.

The thermospasm is reality as undilute chaos. It is where we all came from. The death-drive is the longing to return there ('it' itself), just as salmon would return upstream to perish at the origin. Thermospasm is howl, annihilating intensity, a peak of improbability. Energetic matter has a *tendency*, a *Todestrieb*. The current scientific sense of this movement is a perpetual degradation of energy or dissipation of difference. Upstream is the reservoir of negentropy, uneven distribution, thermic disequilibrium. Downstream is Tohu Bohu, statistical disorder, indifference, *Wärmetod*. The second law of thermodynamics tells us that disorder must increase, that regional increases in negentropy still imply an aggregate increase in entropy. Life is able to deviate from death only because it also propagates it, and the propagation of disorder is always more successful than the deviation. Degradation 'profits' out of life. Any process of organization is necessarily aberrational within the general economy, a mere complexity or detour in the inexorable death-flow, a current in the informational motor, energy cascading downstream, dissipation. There are no closed systems, no stable codes, no recuperable origins. There is only the thermospasmic shock wave, tendential energy flux, degradation of energy. A receipt of information – of intensity – carried downstream.

*

Libidinal materialism (Nietzsche) is not, however, a thermodynamics. This is because it does not distinguish between power and energy, or between negentropy and energy. It no longer conceives the level of entropy as a predicate of any substantial or subsistent being. In contrast to the energy of physical thermodynamics, libidinal energy is chaotic, or pre-ontological. Thus Nietzsche's devastating attacks of the notions of 'being', 'thing-in-itself', of a substratum separable from its effects, etc. Where thermodynamics begins with an ontology of energy, of particles (Boltzmann), of space/time, and then interprets distributions and entropy levels as attributes of energy, libidinal materialism accepts only chaos and composition. 'Being' as an effect of the composition of chaos, of the *'approximation of a world of becoming to a world of being'* [N III 895]. With the libidinal reformulation of being as composition 'one acquires degrees of being, one loses that which *has* being' [N III 627]. The effect of 'being' is derivative from process, 'because we have to be stable in our beliefs if we are to prosper, we have made the 'real' world a world not of change and becoming, but one of being' [N III 556].

The great axes of Nietzsche's thought trace out the space of a libidinal energetics. Firstly: a concerted questioning of the logico-mathematical conception of the same, equal, or identical, *die Gleichheit*, which is dissolved into a general energetics of compositions; of types, varieties, species, regularities. The power to conserve, transmit, circulate, and enhance compositions, the power that is assimilated in the marking, reserving, and appropriating of compositions, and the power released in the disinhibition, dissipation, and Dionysian unleashing of compositions. Beyond essentializing philosophies lies art, as the irrepressible flux of compositions, the interchange between excitation and communication.

Secondly: a figure of eternal recurrence, stretched between a thermodynamic baseline (Boltzmann's theory of eternal recurrence) and a libidinal summit, a theoretical machine for transmuting ontologico-scientific discoveries into excitations. First the scientific figure: recurrence as a theory of energetic forces and their permutation; chance, tendency, energy, and information. In the play of *anarchic* combinations and redistributions forces *tend* to the exhaustion of their *reserve* of possible states, inclining to the circle, a figure of affirmation and intoxication, as well as a teaching, message, or signal. A 'sea of forces flowing and rushing together, eternally changing, eternally flooding back, with tremendous years of recurrence, with an ebb and a flood of its forms; out of the simplest forms striving towards the most complex, out of the stillest, most rigid, coldest forms towards the hottest, most turbulent, most self-contradictory, and then returning home to the simple out of this abundance .·. . without goal, unless the joy of the circle is itself a goal; without will, unless a ring feels good will towards itself – do you want a *name* for this world?' [N III 917]. Then the libidinal peak; the recurrence of impetus in the ascent through compositional strata, always *noch einmal*, once again, and never ceiling, horizon, achieved essence: 'would you be the ebb of this great flow' [N II 279].

Thirdly: a general theory of hierarchies, of order as rank-order (composition). There are no longer any transcendental limits; Schopenhauer's 'grades of objectification' are decapitated, thus depolarized, opened into intensive sequences in both directions. Kant is defeated, as transcendental/empirical difference is collapsed into the scales (but it takes a long time for such events to reach us). History returns (what could timelessness mean now?) '[T]o speak of oppositions, where there are only gradations and a multiplicitous delicacy of steps' [N II 589].

Fourthly: a diagnosis of nihilism, of the hyperbolic of desire. Recurrence is the return of compositional impetus across the scales, the insatiability of creative drive. This is 'Dionysian pessimism'; the recurrence of stimulus (pain) and the exultation of its overcoming. For the exhausted ones, the *Schlechtweggekommenen*, this is intolerable, for they are stricken with '[w]eariness, which would reach the end with one leap, with a death leap, a poor unknowing weariness, which would not will once more; it is that which created all gods and after-worlds' [N II 298]. Plato first, then Christianity, feeding on human inertia like a monstrous leech, creating humanity (the terminal animal). Nihilism completes itself in principle at once, God is conceived; a final being, a cessation of becoming, an ultimate thing beyond which nothing can be desired.

*

Freud, too, is an energeticist (although reading Lacan and his semiological ilk one would never suspect it). He does not conceive desire as lack, representation, or intention, but as dissipative energetic flow, inhibited by the damming and channelling apparatus of the secondary process (domain of the reality principle). Pleasure does not correspond to the realization of a goal, it is rather that unpleasure is primary excitation or tension which is relieved by the equilibriating flux of sexual behaviour (there is no goal, only zero); 'unpleasure corresponds to an *increase* in the quantity of excitation and pleasure to a *diminution*' [F III 218]. This compulsion to zero is – notoriously – ambivalent in Freud's text: 'the mental apparatus endeavours to keep the quantity of excitation present in it as low as possible or at least to keep it constant' [F III 219]. Far from being a discrediting confusion, however, such ambivalence is the exact symptom of rigorous adherence to the reality of desire; expressing the unilateral impact of zero within the order of identitarian representation.

Psychoanalysis, as the science of the unconscious, is born in the determination of that which suffers repression as the consequence of a transgression against the imperative of survival. It is the pursuit of this repressed threat to the ego which carries Freud along the profound arch of thought from sexuality to the death drive. At first (in the period up to the First World War) the attempt to explicitly formulate the site of the most irremediable collision between survival and desire leads Freud to his famous reading of the Oedipus myth and the sense of the Father's law, since it is the competition with the Father – arising as a correlate of the infant's incestual longing for the mother – that first brings the relation between desire and survival to a crisis. Later, in the formulation of the death drive, the sacrificial character of desire is thought even more immediately, so that desire is not merely integrated structurally with a threat to existence within the oedipal triangle, but is rather related to death by the intrinsic tendency of its own economy. The intensity of the affect is now thought as inherently oriented to its own extinction, as a differentiation from death or the inorganic that is from its beginning a compulsion to return. But despite recognizing that the conscious self is a modulation of the drives, so that all psychical energy stems from the unconscious (from which ego-energy is borrowed), Freud seems to remain committed to the *right* of the reality principle, and its representative the ego, and thus to accept a survival (or adaptation) imperative as the principle of therapeutic practice. It is because of this basic prejudice against the claims of desire that psychoanalysis has always had a tendency to degenerate into a technology of repression that subtilizes, and therefore reinforces, the authority of the ego. In the terms both of the reality principle and the conservative moment of psychoanalysis, desire is a negative pressure working against the conservation of life, a dangerous internal onslaught against the self, tending with inexorable force towards the immolation of the individual and his civilization.

Metapsychology is solar pyschology. At the heart of Freud's *Beyond the Pleasure Principle* he sketches out his dazzling cosmic insight:

> It would be in contradiction to the conservative nature of the drives if the goal of life were a state of things which had never

yet been attained. On the contrary, it must be an *old* state of things, an initial state from which the living entity has at one time or another departed and to which it is striving to return by the mazings [*Umwege*] along which its development leads... For a long time, perhaps, living substance was thus being constantly created afresh and easily dying, till decisive external influences altered in such a way as to make ever more complicated mazings [*immer komplizierteren Umwegen*] before reaching its aim of death. These mazings [*Umwege*] to death, faithfully kept to by the conservative drives, would thus present us today with the picture of the phenomena of life [F III 248].

Life is ejected from the energy-blank and smeared as a crust upon chaotic zero, a mould upon death. This crust is also a maze – a complex exit back to the energy base-line – and the complexity of the maze is life trying to escape from out of itself, being nothing but escape from itself, from which it tries to escape: maze-wanderer. That is to say, life is itself the maze of its route to death; a tangle of mazings [*Umwege*] which trace a unilateral deviation from blank. What is the source of the 'decisive external influences' that propel the mazings of life, if not the sun?

*

The most profound word to emerge from the military history of recent times is 'overkill'; a term that registers something from the infernal core of desire. Superficially it is irrelevant whether one is killed by a slingshot or by a stupendous quantity of high-explosive, napalm, and white phosphorous, and in this sense overkill is merely an economic term signifying an unnecessary wastage of weaponry. Yet the Vietnam war – in whose scorched soil this word was germinated – was not merely the culmination of a series of military and industrial tendencies leading to the quantification of destructive power on a monetary basis, it was also a decisive point of intersection between pharmacology and the technology of violence. Whilst a systematic tendency to overkill meant that ordnance was wasted on the already charred and blasted corpses of the Vietnamese, a subterranean displacement of overkill meant that the demoralized soldiers of America's conscript army were 'wasted' ('blitzed', 'bombed-out') on heroin, marijuana and LSD. This intersection implies (as can be traced by a systematic linguistic ambivalence) that the absolute lack of restraint – even according to the most cynical criteria – in the burning, dismemberment, and general obliteration of life, was the obscure heart of an introjected craving; of a desire that found its echo in the hyperbolic dimension of war.

Is it not obvious that the hyper-comprehensive annihilation so liberally distributed by the US war-machine throughout south-east Asia became a powerful (if displaced) object of Western envy? Almost everything that has happened in the mass domains of non-institutional pharmacology, sexuality, and electric music in the wake of this conflict attests strongly to such a longing. What is desired is that one be 'wiped out'. After the explicit emergence of an overkill craving, destruction can no longer be referred to any orthodox determination of the death drive (as Nirvana-principle), because death is only the base-line from which an exorbitantly 'masochistic' demand departs. Death is to the thirst for overkill what survival is to a conventional notion of Thanatos: minimal satiation. Desiring to die, like desiring to breathe, is a hollow affirmation of the inevitable. It is only with overkill that desire distances itself from fate sufficiently to generate an intensive magnitude of excitation. Thus, in Freud's energetic model of the nervous-system there are two economies that contribute to psychical excitation. There is the quantitatively stable energy reservoir deployed by the psyche in the various investments constituting its objects of love (including the ego), and there is the 'general economy' of traumatic fusion with alterity that floods the nervous-system with potentially catastrophic quantities of alien excitation. It was Freud's recognition of this second economy, and its role in the genesis of 1914–18 war neuroses (stemming largely from the effects of continuous and overwhelming artillery barrages) that was fundamental to the discovery of the death-drive. If such a traumatic economy is readily susceptible to the thought of overkill, it is because trauma is consequential upon an open-ended series of magnitudes within which lethality can be located at an *arbitrary degree*.

It is because the second law of thermodynamics proclaims that entropy always increases in a closed system that life is only able to augment order *locally*, within an open system from which disorder can be 'exported'. The space in which such localization takes place is not thematized by thermodynamic models, but treated as one of their presuppositions. It is implicitly conceived as homogeneous extension, extrinsic to the distributions which occupy it. Bataille, on the contrary, thinks space (rather than assuming it). The base topic associated with such thinking can be summarized under the title 'labyrinth', and will be investigated in some detail later in this book. For the moment, however, the issue is a more elementary one: that of theorizing the relation between the closed field of the cosmic energy reservoir (0), and the local pool of non-equilibrium economy, open to exchange.

It is tempting to understand the difference between 'general' and 'restricted' economy as commensurate with that between 'closed' and 'open' systems. In both cases the former terms seem to refer to the total field of energy exchange, and the latter to the differentiated regions within such a field. A translation of this kind is not wholly inappropriate, but it simplifies the situation excessively. That which circulates in an economy of the kind Bataille describes is less a 'content' with a general and a local intelligibility than the capacity for relative isolation or restriction as such. There is a sense (that of scientific objectivism) in which utility presupposes negative entropy, but abstract order of this kind is quite different from the 'canalization' [VII 467] which is utility's basic characteristic. The quasi-autonomous territories which inhibit the concrete universalization of the second thermodynamic law are not conditions of 'composition' as Bataille uses this term, they are composition as such. In other words, composition is simultaneous with the real differentiation 'of' space.

It is thus that Bataille extracts 'production' from the idealist schemas which continue to operate within Marx's analysis, those lending the critique of political economy a marked humanist tendency. Work is not an origin, sublating divine creation into historical concretion, but an impersonal potential to exploit (release) energy. The humanized exploitation of class societies is not without a prototype, since surplus production is only possible because of the solar inheritance it pillages. Bataille's solar economics is inscribed within the lacuna in Marxism opened by the absence of a theory of excess, and describes the truly primitive (impersonal) accumulation of resources. Such cosmic-historical economy is axiomatized by the formula that '*the energy produced is superior to the energy necessary to its production*' [VII 466], and maps out the main-sequence of terrestrial development, from which the convulsions of civilization are an aberration.

Strictly speaking, the libidinal main-sequence, impersonal accumulation, or primary (solar) inhibition, emerges simultaneously with life, and persists in a more or less naked state up until the beginning of sedentary agriculture, sometime after the last ice-age. Life is simply the name we give to the surface-effects of the main-sequence. Compared to the violently erratic libidinal processes that follow it, the main-sequence seems remarkably stable. Nevertheless, libido departs from its pre-history only because it has already become unstable within it, and even though the preponderant part of the main-sequence occurs within a geological time-span, the evidence of a basic tendency to the geometric acceleration of the process is unmistakable.

The main-sequence is a burning cycle, which can be understood as a physico-chemical volatilization of the planetary crust, a complexification of the energy-cycle, or, more generally, as a dilation of the solar-economic circuits that compose organic matter, knitting it into a fabric that includes an ever-increasing proportion of the ('inorganic') energetic and geo-chemical planetary infrastructure. Of course, the distinction between the organic and the inorganic is without final usefulness, because organic matter is only a name for that fragment of inorganic material that has been woven into meta-stable regional compositions. If a negative prefix is to be used, it would be more accurate to place it on the side of life, since the difference is unilateral, with inorganic matter proving itself to be non-exclusive, or indifferent to its organization, whereas life necessarily operates on the basis of selection and filtering functions.

When colloidal matter enters the main-sequence it begins to differentiate two tendencies, which Freud characterized at a higher level with a distinction between 'φ' and 'ψ', or communication and isolation (immanence/transcendence, death and confusion)[8]. Organic libido emerges with the gradual differentiation of what seem superficially to be two groups of drives (Freud does not describe them as such until later). A progressive tendency isolates or 'individuates' the organism, first by nucleation (prokaryotes to eukaryotes), and then through the isolation of a germ-line, dividing the protoplasm into 'generative cells' and 'somatic cells'. This is the archaic form of Freud's 'Eros'; on the one hand a tension between soma and generation, and on the other a conservation of dissipative forces within an economy of the species, leading ultimately to sexuality. But this erotic or speciating tendency is perpetually endangered by a regressive tendency that leads to dissolution (Thanatos).

The 'φ' or communication tendency accentuates the various 'interactions' between biological matter and its 'outside', and is thus equivalent to a lowering of the organic barrier threshold, essential to photo-reactivity, assimilation, cybernetic regulation, nutrition, etc. This is the complex of organic functions which Bataille associates with primary immanence. The 'ψ' or isolation tendency is the inhibition of exchange, a raising of the barrier threshold that generates a measure of invariant stability, the conservation of code, controlled expenditure of bio-energetic reserves, etc. The combined operation of these tendencies effects a selective distribution in the degree of fusion between the organism and its environment (a difference that is not given but produced), which precariously stabilizes a level of composition. The maximum state of φ (φ^{max}) is equivalent to the complete dissolution of the organism, at which point its persistence would be a matter of unrestricted chance, free-floating at the edge of zero. At any other level of φ the organism sustains a measure of integration, and what we call 'the organism' is only this variable cohesiveness, or intensity: the real basis of Bataille's 'transcendence'; the maze-fringe of death.

Isolation or transcendence (ψ) is an intensive quantity, since it lacks pre-given extensive co-ordinates. In other words, there is no logico-mathematical apparatus appropriate to the emergence of ψ, since ψ 'is itself' the basic measure of identifiability or equivalence. Communication (φ) escapes both identity and equivalence because it is indifferentiation or uninhibited flow; the intensive zero, energy-blank, silence, death. Only differentiation from φ ($d\varphi = \psi$) is able to function as a resource, storing energy, and precipitating compositions (forms, behaviours, signs). The intensive quantity ψ is therefore the basis and currency of extensive accumulation.

Bataille's economics is based on the principle that extensive exchange ($\psi_1 \rightarrow \psi_2$) is primitively accumulative. The extensive exchange is comprised of two intensive transitions: an expenditure ($\psi \rightarrow \varphi$) and an acquisition ($\varphi \rightarrow \psi$), with the latter always exceeding the requirement of replacement, so that $\psi_1 < \psi_2$. Bataille's emphasis on this point leaves little room for misunderstanding: '*the energy that the plant appropriates to its mode of life is superior to the energy strictly necessary to that mode of life*' [VII 466], '*the appropriated energy produced by its life is superior to the energy strictly necessary to its life*' [VII 466]. 'It is of the essence of life to produce more energy than that expended in order to live. In other words, the biochemical processes are able to be envisaged as accumulations and expenditures of energy: all accumulation requires an expense (functional energy, displacement, combat, work) but the latter is always inferior to the former' [VII 473]. More technically: $\psi_1 \rightarrow \psi_2 = d\phi \rightarrow d+n\phi$.

*

Marx entitled his basic project 'the critique of political economy', which is something similar to what some might now call a 'double reading' in that – interpreting the accounts that the bourgeoisie give of their economic regime – Marx found that the word 'labour' was being used in two different senses. On one hand it was being used to designate the value imparted by workers to the commodities they produce, and on the other hand, it was being used to designate a 'cost of production' or price of labour to an employer. With the ascent of the Ricardian school the tradition of political economy had reached broad agreement that the price of a commodity on the market depended upon the quantity of labour invested in its production, but if workers are being paid for their labour, which then adds to the value of the product, it is impossible to detect any opening for profit in the production and trading of goods. Marx's basic insight was that being paid for one's labour, and the value of labour, were not at all the same thing. He coined the term 'labour-power' [*Arbeitskraft*] for the object of transaction between worker and employer, and kept the word 'labour' [*Arbeit*] solely for the value produced in the commodity. Having thus distinguished the concepts of 'labour' and 'labour-power' the next step was to explore the possibility that labour-power might function as a commodity like any other, trading at a price set by the quantity of labour it had taken to produce. The difference between the capacity for work and the quantity of work necessary to reproduce that capacity would unlock the great mystery of the origin of profit. If labour were traded in an undistorted market with complete cynicism it should command a price exactly equal to the cost of its subsistence and reproduction at the minimal possible level of existence, just as any other commodity traded in such a market should tend towards a price approximating to the cost of the minimal quantity of labour time needed for its manufacture. Marx thus speculated that the average price of labour within the economy as a whole should remain broadly equivalent to the subsistence costs of human life. Thus:

Value of labour − Price of labour = Profit

But why is it that labour-power comes to trade itself at a price barely adequate to its subsistence? There is a twofold answer to this, the first historical and the second systematic, although such separation is possible only as a theoretical abstraction. Both of these interlocking arguments are accounts of the excess of labour, or of the saturation of the labour market:

1 In the section of *Capital* entitled 'The So-called Primitive Accumulation' Marx attempts to grasp the inheritance of capital, and is led to examine a series of processes which are associated with the events in English history which are usually designated by the word 'enclosure'. Broadly speaking the mass urbanization of the European peasantry, which separated larger and larger slices of the population from autonomous economic activity, was achieved by a more or less violent expulsion from the land:

> The prelude of the revolution that laid the foundation of the capitalist mode of production, was played in the last third of the 15th, and the first decade of the 16th century. A mass of free proletarians was hurled on the labour-market by the breaking-up of the bands of feudal retainers, who, as Sir James Steuart well says, 'everywhere uselessly filled house and castle.' Although the royal power, itself a product of bourgeois development, in its strife after absolute sovereignty forcibly hastened on the dissolution of these bands of retainers, it was by no means the sole cause of it. In insolent conflict with king and parliament, the great feudal lords created an incomparably larger proletariat by the forcible driving of the peasantry from the land, to which the latter had the same feudal rights as the lord himself, and by the usurpation of the common lands. The rapid rise of the Flemish wool manufacturers, and the corresponding rise in the price of wool in England, gave the direct impulse to these evictions. The old nobility had been devoured by the great feudal wars. The new nobility was the child of its time, for which money was the power of all powers. Transformation of arable land into sheep-walks was, therefore, its cry [Cap 672].

Urbanization is thus in one respect a negative phenomenon; a type of internal exile. In the language of liberal ideology the peasantry is thus 'freed' from its ties to agrarian production. *Liberté!*

2 The labour market is historically saturated by the expropriation of the peasantry, but it is also able to generate such an excess from out of an intrinsic dynamic. In other words, capital creates unemployment due to a basic tendency to overproduction. The pressure of competition forces capital to constantly decrease its costs by increasing the productivity of labour-power. In order to understand this process it is necessary to understand two crucial distinctions that are fundamental to Marx's theory. Firstly, the distinction between 'use value' and 'exchange value', which is the distinction between the utility of a product and its price. Every commodity must have both a use value and an exchange value, but there is only a very tenuous and indirect connection between these two aspects. An increase in productivity is a change in the ratio between these facets of the commodity, so that use values become cheaper, and labour power can be transformed into a progressively greater sum of utility. Marx seeks to demonstrate that this transformation is bound up with another, which has greater consequence to the functioning of the economy, and which is formulated by means of a distinction between 'fixed capital' and 'variable capital'. Fixed capital is basically what the business world calls 'plant'. It is the quantity of capital that must be spent on factors other than (direct) labour in order to employ labour productively. As these factors are consumed in the process of production their value is transferred to the product, and thus recovered upon the sale of the product, but they do not – in an undistorted market – yield any surplus or profit. Variable capital, on the other hand, is the quantity of capital spent on the labour consumed in the production process. It is capital functioning as the immediate utilization of labour power, or the extraction of surplus value. It is this part of capital, therefore, that generates profit. Marx calls the ratio of variable capital to fixed capital the organic composition of capital, and argues that the relative increase in use values, or improvements in productivity, are – given an undistorted labour market – associated with a relative increase in the proportion of fixed capital, and thus a decrease in profit.

*

The problems that have bedevilled Marxian theory can be crudely grouped into two types. Firstly, there is the empirical evidence of increasing metropolitan profit and wage rates, often somewhat hastily interpreted as a violation of Marx's theory. In fact, the problem is a different though associated one: the absence of a free-market in labour. Put most simply, there has never been 'capitalism' as an achieved system, but only the *tendency* for increasing commodification, including variable degrees of labour commodification. There has always been a bureaucratic-cooperative element of political intervention in the development of bourgeois economies, restraining the more nihilistic potentialies of competition. The individualization of capital blocks that Marx thought would lead to a war of mutual annihilation has been replaced by systematic state-supported cartelling, completely distorting price structures in all industrial economies.

The second problem is also associated with a state-capital complex, and is that of 'bureaucratic socialism' or 'red' totalitarianism. The revolutions carried out in Marx's name have not led to significant changes in the basic patterns of working life, except where a population was suffering from a surplus exploitation compounded out of colonialism and fascism, and this can be transformed into 'normal' exploitation, inefficiently supervised by an authoritarian state apparatus. Marxism – it is widely held – has failed in practice.

Both of these types of problem are irrelevant to the Marxism of Bataille, because they stem, respectively, from theoretical and practical economism; from the implicit assumption that socialism should be an enhanced system of production, that capitalism is too cynical, immoral, and wasteful, that revolution is a means to replace one economic order with a more efficient one, and that a socialist regime should administer the public accumulation of productive resources. For Bataille, on the contrary, 'capital' is not a cohesive or formalizable system, but the tyranny of good (the more or less thorough rationalization of consumption in the interests of accumulation), revolution is not a means but an absolute end, and society collapses towards post-bourgeois community not through growth, but in sacrificial festivity.

Beyond political economy there is general economy, and the basic thought at its heart is that of the absolute primacy of wastage, since 'everything is rich which is to the measure of the universe' [VII 23]. Bataille insists that all terrestrial economic systems are particular elements within a general energy system, founded upon the unilateral discharge of solar radiation[9]. The sun's energy is squandered *for nothing* (= 0), and the circulation of this energy within particular economies can only suspend its final resolution into useless wastage. All energy must ultimately be spent pointlessly and unreservedly, the only questions being where, when, and in whose name this useless discharge will occur. Even more crucially, this discharge or terminal consumption – which Bataille calls 'expenditure' (*dépense*) – is *the problem* of economics, since on the level of the general energy system 'resources' are always in excess, and consumption is liable to relapse into a secondary (terrestrial) productivity, which Bataille calls 'rational consumption'. The world is thus perpetually choked or poisoned by its own riches, stimulated to develop mechanisms for the elimination of excess: '*it is not necessity but its contrary, "luxury", which poses the fundamental problems of living matter and mankind*' [VII 21]. In order to solve the problem of excess it is necessary that consumption overspills its rational or reproductive form to achieve a condition of pure or unredeemed loss, passing over into sacrificial ecstasy or 'sovereignty'.

Bataille interprets all natural and cultural development upon the earth to be side-effects of the evolution of death, because it is only in death that life becomes an echo of the sun, realizing its inevitable destiny, which is pure loss. This basic conception founds a materialist theory of culture far freer of idealist residues than the representational accounts of the dominant Marxist and psycho-analytical traditions, since it does not depend upon the mediation of a metaphysically articulated subject for its integration into the economic substrate. Culture is immediately economic, not because it is traversed by ideological currents that a Cartesian pineal gland or dialectical miracle translates from intelligibility into praxis, but because it is the haunt of literary possibilities that constantly threaten to transform the energy expended in its inscription into an unredeemed negative at the level of production. Poetry, Bataille asserts, is a 'holocaust of words'. A culture can never express or represent (serve) capital production, it can compromise itself in relation to capital only by abasing itself before the philistinism of the bougeoisie, whose 'culture' has no characteristics beyond those of abject restraint, and self-denigration. Capital is precisely and exhaustively the definitive anti-culture.

Capitalism, then, is (the projection of) the most extreme possible refusal of expenditure. Bataille accepts Weber's conclusions concerning the relationship between the evolution of capital accumulation and the development of Protestantism, seeing the Reformation critique of Catholicism as essentially a critique of religion insofar as it 'functions' as a means of economic consumption, or as a drain for the excess of social production. The Protestant repudiation of indulgences – as well as its rejection of lavish cathedral building and the entire socio-economic apparatus allied to the doctrine of salvation through 'works' – is the cultural precondition for the economy closing upon itself and taking its modern form. Bourgeois society is thus the first civilization to totally exclude expenditure in principle, opposed to the conspicuous extravagance of aristocracy and church, and replacing both with the rational or reproductive consumption of commodities. It is this constitutive principle of bourgeois economy that leads inevitably to chronic overproduction crisis, and its symptomatic redundancies of labour and capital. It is not that capital production 'invents' the crisis which comes to be named 'market saturation', it is rather that capital production is the systematic repudiation of overproduction *as a problem*. To acknowledge the necessity of a stringent (although perpetually displaced) limit to the absorption of surplus production is already to exceed the terms in which the bourgeoisie or administrative class can formulate its economic dilemmas. A capital economy is thus one that is regulated as if the problem of consumption could be derived in principle from that of production, so that it would always be determinable as an insufficiency of demand (during the period roughly between 1930 and 1980 this has typically led to quasi-Keynesian solutions nucleated upon US armaments spending). Bataille, in contrast, does not see a problem for production in the perpetual reproduction of excess, but rather, in a manner marking the most radical discontinuity in respect to classical political economy, sees production itself as intrinsically problematic *precisely insofar as it succeeds*.

Chapter 3

Transgression

This is the freedom of the void which rises to a passion and takes shape in the world; while still remaining theoretical, it takes shape in the Hindu fanaticism of pure contemplation, but when it turns to actual practice, it takes shape in religion and politics alike as the fanaticism of destruction – the destruction of the whole subsisting social order – as the elimination of individuals who are objects of suspicion to any social order, and the annihilation of any organization which tries to rise anew from the ruins [H VII].

the republic being permanently menaced from the outside by the despots surrounding it, the means to its preservation cannot be imagined as *moral means*, for the republic will preserve itself only by war, and nothing is less moral than war. I ask how one will be able to demonstrate that in a state rendered *immoral* by its obligations, it is essential that the individual be *moral*? I will go further: it is a very good thing he is not. The Greek lawgivers perfectly appreciated the capital necessity of corrupting the member citizens in order that, their *moral dissolution* coming into conflict with the establishment and its values, there would result the *insurrection* that is always indispensible to a political system of perfect happiness which, like republican government, must necessarily excite the hatred and envy of all its foreign neighbours. Insurrection, thought these sage legislators, is not at all a *moral* condition; however, it has got to be a republic's permanent condition. Hence it would be no less absurd than dangerous to require that those who are to ensure the perpetual *immoral* subversion of the established order themselves be *moral* beings: for the state of a moral man is one of tranquillity and peace, the state of an *immoral* man is one of perpetual unrest that pushes him to, and identifies him with, the necessary insurrection in which the republican must always keep the government of which he is a member [S III 498].

We have no true pleasure except in expending uselessly, as if a wound opens in us [X 170].

the most unavowable aspects of our pleasures connect us the most solidly [IV 218].

It has often been suggested – not least by Sartre – that Bataille replaces dialectic and revolution with the paralysed revolt of transgression. It is transgression that opens the way to tragic communication, the exultation in the utter immolation of order that consummates and ruins humanity in a sacrifice without limits. Bataille is a philosopher not of indifference, but of evil, of an evil that will always be the name for those processes that flagrantly violate all human utility, all accumulative reason, all stability and all sense. He considers Nietzsche to have amply demonstrated that the criteria of the good: self-identity, permanence, benevolence, and transcendent individuality, are ultimately rooted in the preservative impulses of a peculiarly sordid, inert, and cowardly species of animals. Despite his pseudo-sovereignty, the Occidental God – as the guarantor of the good – has always been the ideal instrument of human reactivity, the numbingly anti-experimental principle of utilitarian calculus. To defy God, in a celebration of evil, is to threaten mankind with adventures that they have been determined to outlaw.

The Kantian cultural revolution is associated with a deepened usage of juridical discourse in philosophy. Transcendental philosophy equates knowing with legislation, displacing the previously dominant axis of argumentation – extended between scepticism and belief – with one organized in terms of legitimacy and illegitimacy. The sense of logic, for example, undergoes a massive – if largely subterranean – shift; from evident truth to necessary rule. The metaphysical errors which Kant critiques are formally described as crimes, and more specifically, as violations of rights. The subject is divided into faculties, with strictly demarcated domains of legitimate sovereignty, beyond which their exercise is a transgression. Most important to Kant are the reciprocal injustices of reason and understanding, with his First Critique detailing the trespasses of reason upon the understanding, or theory, and his

Second Critique defending reason against theoretical incursions into its proper domain; that of moral legislation. The lower faculties of sensation, and, to a lesser extent, imagination, are of more indirect concern, since they are branded as incorrigible reprobates; corrupted by their insinuation into the swamp of the body.

Kant initiated the modern tradition of insidious theism by shielding God from theoretical investigation, whilst maintaining the moral necessity of his existence. God was exiled into a space of pure practical reason, simultaneously protected against intellectual transgression and underwriting moral law. In his *Critique of Judgement* Kant describes the moral impossibility of a world without God, and the fate of one attempting to live according to it, in the following terms:

> Deceit, violence, and envy will always be rife around him, although he himself is honest, peaceable, and benevolent; and the other righteous men he meets in the world, no matter how deserving they may be of happiness, will be subjected by nature, which takes no heed of such deserts, to all the evils of want, disease, and untimely death, just as are the other animals of the earth. And so it will continue to be until one wide grave engulfs them all – just and unjust, there is no distinction in the grave – and hurls them back into the abyss of the aimless chaos of matter from which they were taken – they that were able to believe themselves the final end of creation [K X 415–16].

This passage might be from Sade's *Justine: the Misfortunes of Virtue*, reminding us that the age of Kant is tangled with that of Sade, a writer who explored the exacerbation of transgression, rather than its juridical resolution. Where Kant consolidated the modern pact between philosophy and the state, Sade fused literature with crime in the dungeons of both old and new regimes. Sade insisted upon reasoning about God repeating original sin, but even after obliterating him with a blizzard of theoretical discourse his hunger for atheological aggression remained insatiable. Sade does not seek to negotiate with God or the state, but to ceaselessly resist their possibility. Accordingly, his political pamphlets do not appeal for improved institutions, but only for the restless vigilance of armed masses in the streets. 'Abstract negation' or 'negative freedom' are

Hegel's expressions for this sterilizing resistance which erases the position of the subject. It could equally be described as real death.

Bataille's engagement with Sade is prolonged and intense, but also sporadic, consisting of articles and essays which never reach the pitch of intimacy characterizing *Sur Nietzsche*. After Nietzsche, however, it is Sade who comes closest to such an intimacy, and – like Nietzsche – accompanies Bataille throughout the entire length of his textual voyage, with an intellectual solidarity so great that it touches upon a complete erasure of distinction. Sade plays an important role in luring Bataille's discussion of eroticism into its abyssal (non)sense, because his writing is baked to charcoal in the sacred. No writer fathoms more profoundly the utter inutility of the erotic impulse, nor its sacrilegious and insurrectionary fury. 'Sade consecrated interminable works to the affirmation of unacceptable values: according to him life is the search for pleasure, and pleasure is proportional to the destruction of life. In other words, life attains the highest degree of intensity in a monstrous negation of its principle' [X 179].

The orgies, massacres, and blasphemies of the Sadean text knit almost seamlessly onto Bataille's obsession with an intolerable sacrificial wastage vomited into the suppurating cavity of the divine. Bataille finds in these texts 'the *excessive* negation of the principle upon which life rests' [X 168], a pitch of voluptuary intensity at which eroticism passes unreservedly into the sacred. Compared to the Sade-interpretations of Blanchot, for instance, despite complex affinities and inter-textual communications, there is a ravine as great as any that could be imagined; an incommensurability of thought insinuated into a common and inevitable vocabulary. 'Negation', 'crime', 'atheism', 'revolt', are words that Bataille associates with a heterogeneity so repugnant to elevated thought that its repression must be presupposed in the origination of any possible speculation, whereas for Blanchot these are words that belong to reason itself, at least, from the moment that it is permitted to find itself in the solitude of literature. It is only our inertia and our hypocrisy – as Blanchot suggests with an insidious power – that protect us from the latent fury of reason. Unlike Blanchot, Bataille does not emphasize the ruthless consistency of enlightenment rationalism in Sade's writings, even though he acknowledges that Sade seems 'to have been the most consequential representative of XVIIIth century French materialism' [I 337]. 'By definition, *excess* is external to reason' [X 168], he remarks in one discussion of Sade, and it is an incitement to criminality, rather than an exultant rationality that he detects in passages such as this:

> atheism is the one system of all those prone to reason. As we gradually proceeded to our enlightenment, we came more and more to feel that, motion being inherent in matter, the prime mover existed only as an illusion, and that all that exists having to be in motion, the motor was useless; we sensed that this chimerical divinity, prudently invented by the earliest legislators, was, in their hands, simply one more means to enthrall us, and that, reserving unto themselves the right to make the phantom speak, they knew very well how to get him to say nothing but what would shore up the preposterous laws whereby they declared they served us [S III 482].

Either believe in God and adore him, or disbelieve and demobilize, for it is as senseless to rage against omnipotence as inexistence. Thus it is that Sade's opponents take the two strands of his defiance to be mutually contradicting, to cancel each other, and – once *aufhebt* – expressing either a futile rage flung into the void, or a desperate plea for reconciliation. 'Blasphemy is never logical. If an omnipotent God exists, the blasphemer can only be damaging himself by insulting him; if he does not exist, there is no one there to insult', writes Hayman [Hay 31]. After all, how can one revolt against a fiction? It is perhaps a symptom of fixation or regression, an unresolved infantilism in any case, for affect to be detached so completely from an acknowledged reality.

In a world divided between theistic enthusiasts and secularist depressives there is little patience for the atheist who nurtures a passionate hatred for God. The mixture of naturalism and blasphemy that characterizes the Sadean text occupies the space of our blindness, to which Bataille's writings are not unreasonably assimilated. If there is contradiction here it is one that is coextensive with the unconscious; the consequence of a revolt incommensurate with the ontological weight of its object. That God has wrought such loathesomeness without even having existed only exacerbates the hatred pitched against him. An atheism that does not hunger for God's blood is an inanity, and the anaemic feebleness of secular rationalism has so little appeal that it approximates to an argument for his existence. What is suggested by the Sadean furore is that anyone who does not exult at the thought of driving nails through the limbs of the Nazarene is something less than an atheist; merely a disappointed slave.

Amongst the diseases Bataille shares with Nietzsche is the insistence that the death of God is not an epistemic conviction, but a crime. It is no less worthy of cathedrals than the tyrant it abolished, and whose grave it continues to desecrate. Indeed, such new cathedrals are inextricable from the unholy festivities of desecration which resound through them, as the texts of Sade, Nietzsche, and Bataille themselves illustrate.

The illimitable criminality driving Bataille's writing's provokes no hint of repentence within it, but that does not make him a pagan, which is to say juridically: unfit to plead. Lacking the slightest interest in justification, innocence is not an aspiration he nourishes. He is closer to Satan than to Pan, propelled by a defiant culpability. Bataille is altogether too morbid to be a pagan, and yet, despite what is in part a reactive relation to Christianity, the thought of necessary crime is an interpretation of the tragic, and of *hubris*. Tragic fate is the necessity that the forbidden happen, and happen as the forbidden. Quoting what he takes to be a latent popular maxim, Bataille writes that 'the prohibition is there to be violated' [X 67]. He associates this subterranean collective insight with an 'indifference to logic' [X 67] at the root of social regulation, since '[t]he violation committed is not of a nature to suppress the possibility and the sense of the emotion opposed to it: it is even the justification and the source' [X 67]. One of his formulae for this effective paradox is the 'violat[ion of] prohibition . . . according to a rule' [X 75]. Such a violation is not so much provoked by prohibition, as it is compelled by an inexorable process to which prohibition is a response. This thought is commonly expressed within his writings in terms of the economic inevitability of evil, and also, occasionally, as the eruption of transgression.

As an overt theme, 'transgression' is nothing like as dominant within Bataille's writings as is often suggested, and it is only with extraordinary arbitrariness that he can be described as a 'philosopher of transgression'. If it were not for the sustained discussion to be found in *Eroticism* it is unlikely that this term would have come to be read as anything more than the marginal elaboration of a more basic problem (that of expenditure, consumption, or sacrifice). Nevertheless, criminal variations analagous to transgression are prolifically distributed throughout his writings, and lend themselves with apparent ease to a measure of formulation.

In a broadly Nietzschean fashion, Bataille understands law as the imperative to the preservation of discrete being. Law summarizes conditions of existence, and shares its arbitrariness with the survival of the human race. The servility of a legal existence is that of an unconditional one (of existence for its own sake); involving the submission of consumption to its reproduction, and eventually to its complete normative suppression within an obsessional productivism. The word Bataille usually employs to mark the preserve of law is 'discontinuity', which is broadly synonymous with 'transcendence'; Bataille's thought of discontinuity is more intricate than his fluent deployment of the word might indicate. It is the condition for transcendent illusion or ideality, and precisely for this reason it cannot be grasped by a transcendent apparatus, by the inter-knitted series of conceptions involving negation, logical distinction, simple disjunction, essential difference, etc.

Discontinuity is not ontologically grounded (in the fashion of a Leibnizean monad for instance), but positively fabricated in the same process that amasses resources for its disposal. Accumulation does not presuppose a subject or individual, but rather founds one. This is because any possible self – or relative isolation – is only ever precipitated as a precarious digression within a general economy, perpetually renegotiated across the scale of energy flows. The relative autonomy of the organism is not an ontological given but a material achievement which – even at its apex – remains quite incommensurable with the notion of an individual soul or personality. It is in large part because death attests so strongly to this fact that theology has monotonously demanded its systematic effacement.

Because isolation is – in an abnormal sense – 'quantitative', quantity cannot be conceived arithmetically on the basis of discretion. Base, general, or solar economics – which are amongst Bataille's names for economics at the level of emergent discontinuities – cannot be organized by any prior conceptual matrix. The distinctions between quantity/quality, degree/kind, analogue/digital, etc., which typically manage economic thought, are all dependent upon the prior acceptance of discontinuity or derivative articulation. It is obvious that the economics or energetics which Bataille associates with base cosmology cannot be identified with any kind of physicalistic theory, since the logical and mathematical concepts underlying any such theory are devastated by the radical interrogation of simple difference. With the operation of a sufficiently delicate materialist apparatus general economy can in large measure be thought, but in the end its fragmentary and ironic character stems from a delirial genesis in the violation of articulate lucidity.

The solar source of all terrestrial resources commits them to an abysmal generosity, which Bataille calls 'glory'. This is perhaps best understood as a contagious profligacy, according to which all inhibition, accumulation, and reservation is destined to fail. The infrastructure of the terrestrial process inheres in the obstructive character of the earth, in its mere bulk as a momentary arrest of solar energy flow, which lends itself to hypostatization. When the silting-up of energy upon the surface of the planet is interpreted by its complex consequences as rigid utility, a productivist civilization is initiated, whose culture involves a history of ontology, and a moral order. Systemic limits to growth require that the inevitable re-commencement of the solar trajectory scorches jagged perforations through such civilizations. The resultant ruptures cannot be securely assimilated to a meta-social homeostatic mechanism, because they have an immoderate, epidemic tendency. Bataille writes of 'the virulence of death' [X 70]. Expenditure is irreducibly ruinous because it is not merely useless, but also contagious. Nothing is more infectious than the passion for collapse. Predominant amongst the incendiary and epidemic gashes which contravene the interests of mankind are eroticism, base religion, inutile criminality, and war.

*

In *The Accursed Share* Bataille outlines a number of social responses to the unsublatable wave of senseless wastage welling up beneath human endeavour, which he draws from a variety of cultures and epochs. These include the potlatch of the sub-arctic tribes, the sacrificial cult of the Aztecs, the monastic extravagance of the Tibetans, the martial ardour of Islam, and the architectural debauch of hegemonic Catholicism. Reform Christianity alone – attuned to the emergent bourgeois order – is based upon a relentless refusal of sumptuary consumption. It is with Protestantism that theology accomplishes itself in the thoroughgoing rationalization of religion, marking the ideological triumph of the good, and propelling humanity into unprecedented extremities of affluence and catastrophe. It is also with Protestantism that the transgressive outlets of society are de-ritualized and exposed to effective condemnation, a tendency which leads to the terrible exhibitions of atrocity associated with the writings of the Maquis de Sade at the end of the eighteenth century, anticipated already, over three centuries before, with the life of Gilles de Rais.

Bataille describes his 1959 study of Gilles de Rais as a tragedy, and its subject as a 'sacred monster', who 'owed his enduring glory to his crimes' [X 277]. The bare facts are quite rapidly outlined. Gilles de Rais was born towards the end of the year 1404, inheriting the 'fortune, name, and arms of Rais' [X 345] due to a complicated dynastic intrigue involving his parents Guy de Laval, and Marie de Craon. Even by the standards of his times and rank de Rais dissipated vast tranches of his wealth with abnormal extravagance, in Bataille's words 'he liquidated an immense fortune without reckoning' [X 279]. At the battle of Orleans he fought alongside Jeanne d'Arc, 'acquiring renown as "a truly valiant knight in arms" which survived right up to the point of his condemnation to infamy' [X 354]. It has been suggested that the two warriors were friends, but Bataille expresses reservations about this hypothesis [X 356]. On the 30th May 1431 Jeanne d'Arc was burnt by the English. In the years 1432-3 de Rais began to murder children. His preferred victims were males, with an average age of eleven years, although there was occasional variation in sex, and considerable variation in age [X 426]. At least thirty-five murders are well established, although the number was almost certainly a great deal higher; the figures suggested at his trial ranged up to two hundred.

In a somewhat inelegant passage from this study Bataille recapitulates the (quasi-Weberian) general economic background to his researches:

> We accumulate wealth in the prospect of a continual expansion, but in societies different from ours the prevalent principle was the contrary one of wasting or losing wealth, of giving or destroying it. Accumulated wealth has the same sense as *work*; wealth wasted or destroyed in tribal *potlatch* has the contrary sense of *play*. Accumulated wealth has nothing but a subordinate value, but wealth that is wasted or destroyed has, to the eyes of

> those who waste it, or destroy it, a *sovereign* value: it serves nothing ulterior; only this wastage itself, or this fascinating destruction. Its *present* sense: its wastage, or the gift that one makes of it, is its final reason for being, and it is due to this that its sense is not able to be put off, and must be *in the instant*. But it is consumed *in that instant*. This can be magnificent: those who know how to appreciate consumption are dazzled, but nothing remains of it [X 321-2].

The tragedy of de Rais, which Bataille extends to the nobility as a whole, was that of living the transition from sumptuary to rational sociality. He was dedicated by birth to the reckless militarism of the French aristocracy, which Bataille summarizes in the formula: 'In the same way that the man without privilege is reduced to a worker, the one who is privileged must wage war' [X 314]. He is emphatic on this point: 'The feudal world ... is not able to be separated from the lack of measure [*démesure*], which is the principle of wars' [X 318], and also: 'primitively war seems to be a luxury' [X 78]. That honour and prestige is incommensurable with the calculations of utility is an insistent theme in Bataille's work, as pertinent to the interpretation of potlatch amongst the Tlingit as to the blood-hunger and extravagance of Europe's medieval nobility. The context of Christianity and courtly love should not mislead us here.

> The paradox of the middle ages demanded that the warrior elite did not speak the language of force and combat. Their mode of speech was often sickly-sweet. But we shouldn't fool ourselves: the goodwill of the ancient French was a cynical lie. Even the poetry that the nobles of the fourteenth and sixteenth centuries affected to love was in every sense a deception: before everything the great lords loved war, their attitude differed little from that of the German Berzerkers, whose dreams were dominated by horrors and slaughter [X 303–4].

The feudal aristocracy held open a wound in the social body, through which excess production was haemorrhaged into utter loss. In part this wastage was accomplished by the hypertrophic luxuriance of their leisured and parasitic existence, which echoed that of the church, but more important was the ceaseless ebb and flow of military confrontation, into which life and treasure could be poured without limit. De Rais embraced this dark heart of the feudal world with peculiar ardour. Bataille writes of 'his entire – his mad – incarnation of the spirit of feudalism which, in all of its movement, proceeded from the games that the Berzerkers played: he was tethered to war by an affinity that succeeded in marking out a taste for cruel voluptuousities. He had no place in the world, if not the one that war gave him' [X 317]. He continues: 'Such wars required intoxication, they required the vertigo and the giddiness of those that birth had consecrated to them. War precipitated its elect into assaults, or suffocated them in dark obsessions' [X 317].

During the fourteenth and fifteenth centuries the epoch of feudal warfaring reached a crescendo, due to exactly the same processes that were leading to its utilitarian reconstruction. Power was being steadily centralized in the hands of the monarchy, and changes in military technology effected a gradual shift in the social composition of the military apparatus. In particular Bataille points to the way in which the development of archery supplanted the dominant role of heavy cavalry, and to the fact that with the increasing importance of arrows and pikes came an accentuation of military discipline. War became increasingly rationalized and subjected to scientific direction. This evolution was not rapid, but de Rais was personally touched by it. The battle of Lagny in 1432 was the last to plunge him into the heat of conflict, after which his position as a marshal of France – which he had occupied since July 1429 – detached him from the military cutting-edge. Bataille's interpretation of these tendencies is emphatic: '[A]t the instant where royal politics and intelligence alters, the feudal world no longer exists. Neither intelligence nor calculation is noble. It is not noble to calculate, not even to reflect, and no philosopher has been able to incarnate the essence of nobility' [X 318].

War is progressively disinvested by the voluptuary movement passing through the nobility, increasingly becoming an instrument of rational statecraft, calculatively manipulated by the sovereign. A process was underway that would lead eventually to the tightly regimented military machines of renaissance Europe, led by professional officers, and directed operationally in accordance with political pragmatics. Bataille considers this transition from warlord to prince to be crucial in de Rais' case:

> To the eyes of Gilles war is a game. But that view becomes less and less true: to the extent that it ceases to predominate even amongst the privileged. Increasingly, therefore, war becomes a

general misfortune: at the same time it becomes the *work* of a great number. The general situation deteriorates: it becomes more complex, the misfortune even reaching the privileged, who become ever less avid for war, and for games, seeing in the end that the moment has come to lend space to problems of reason [X 315].

Where the church erected cathedrals in a disfigured celebration of the death of God, the nobility built fortresses to glorify and to accentuate the economy of war. Their fortresses were tumours of aggressive autonomy; hard membranes correlative with an acute disequilibrium of force. Within the fortress social excess is concentrated to its maximum tension, before being siphoned-off into the furious wastage of the battle-field. It was into his fortresses that de Rais retreated, withdrawing from a society in which he had become nothing, in order to bury himself in darkness and atrocity. The children of the surrounding areas disappeared into these fortresses, in the same way that the surplus production of the local peasantry had always done, except now the focus of consumption had ceased to be the exterior social spectacle of colliding armies, involuting instead into a sequence of secret killings. Rather than a staging post for excess, the heart of the fortress became its terminus; the site of a hidden and unholy participation in the nihilating voracity which Bataille calls 'the solar anus', or the black sun.

Perhaps one short passage will suffice in lieu of detailing these crimes. Early in his study Bataille remarks:

> His crimes responded to the immense disorder which inflamed him, and in which he was lost. We even know, by means of the criminal's confession, which the scribes of the court copied down whilst listening to him, that it was not pleasure that was essential. Certainly he sat astride the chest of the victim and in that fashion, playing with himself [se maniant], he would spill his sperm upon the dying one; but what was important to him was less sexual enjoyment than the vision of death at work. He loved to look: opening a body, cutting a throat, detaching limbs, he loved the sight of blood [X 278].

Amongst the problematic features of this passage is the fact that it involves an oxymoron in the terms of Bataille's writings, because the prevailing sense of 'work' in these texts is exactly that of a resistance to death. He describes work as the process that binds energy into the form of the resource, or utile object, inhibiting its tendency to dissipation. This difficulty is exacerbated by the central role allocated to vision in Gilles' atrocities. Work constrains the slippage towards death, but it conspires with visibility. Scopic representation and utility are mutually sustained by objectivity, which Bataille – unlike Kant – understands as transcendence; the crystallization of *things* from out of the continuum of immanent flow. The ultimate inanity of Gilles' aberration is attested by the fact that it is not the taste or smell of death he seeks, but its sight. ('Seeking' itself is the scopic form of craving.)

Gilles' passion is sublime, in that it is an attempt to delect in death (noumenon), and like Kant's sublime it requires a 'safe place' for its possibility, which in both cases is that of representation as such. Of all sensory modalities vision is the coldest and most distant, the one most conducive to the idealist illusions which de-materialize irritation and precipitate the phantasm of autonomous subjectivity. Vision is so pregnant with incipient rationalization that it tends to involve an inherent negative reflex, exaggerating its difference from touch. This is why scopophiliac investments are not libidinal tropisms like any other, but compromises; coaxing drives into the domesticated state associated with representation, and by this means constraining them to teleology. For desire to occupy the schema of approximation to a condition that is represented as its telos is consequential upon the visualization of its activating irritation. Impulse is thus lured into the trap of negativity, aspiration, and dependence upon the reality principle; exactly the complex which Bataille summarizes consistently as transcendence.

I hope that it is not mere timidity on my part that leads to this reservation. It would be the shoddiest domestication to suggest that some theoretical comfort were possible here. After all, it is certainly not Rais' ferocity that inhibits his full complicity with the sun.

If transgression appears as the negation of law, it is only because law is coextensive with the unachievable negation of solar flow, just as base matter is deemed negative because it exhibits no resistance to death. Nevertheless, insofar as crime receives its formulation in the court-room it is quite properly understood as a speculative development of legality, as Hegel demonstrates so meticulously in his *Philosophy of Right*. Such an apprehension of crime through the optic of the trial is no merely empirical projection, but a bias rooted in the juridical advantage of existence. Death has no representatives. Which is to say that transgression has no subject. There is only the sad wreck who Nietzsche calls 'the pale criminal', de Rais at his trial for instance, terrified of Satan, separated from his crimes by an unnavigable gulf of oblivion. The truth of transgression, at once utterly simple and yet ungraspable, is that evil does not survive to be judged.

Transgression is not mere criminality, insofar as this latter involves private utility or the occupation by a subject of the site of proscribed action. It is rather the effective genealogy of law, operating at a level of community more basic than the social order which is simultaneous with legality. Transgression is only judged *as such* in the course of a regression to a pre-historical option which was decided by the institution of justice. At this point the sedimentation of energy upon the crust of the earth becomes normatively reinforced by an affirmation of social persistence. Nietzsche explores exactly this issue in section nine of the second essay of his *Genealogy of Morals*, in which he describes the primitive response to transgression:

> 'Punishment' at this level of civilization is simply a copy, a *mimus*, of the normal attitude toward a hated, disarmed, prostrated enemy, who has lost not only every right and protection, but all hope of quarter as well; it is thus the rights of war and the victory celebration of the *vae victis* in all their mercilessness and cruelty – which explains why it is that war itself (including the warlike sacrificial cult) has provided all the *forms* that punishment has assumed throughout history [N II 813].

War is irreducibly alien to a collision of rights, so that it is war that bears down on the one who violates right as such. Transgression is not a misdemeanour, even if this is the necessary form of its social interpretation. It is rather a solar barbarism, resonant with that of the berserkers, and of all those who fathom an abysmal inhumanity on the battle-field. No tragedy without an Agamemnon, or some other mad beast of war, whose nemesis pre-empts the discourse of the juridical institution, and whose death is thus marked by a peculiar intimacy. Bataille writes:

> *Tragedy is the impotence of reason* ... This does not signify that

Tragedy has rights against reason. In truth, it is not possible for a right to belong to something contrary to reason. For how could a *right* be opposed to reason? Human violence however, which has the power to go against reason, is tragic, and must, if possible, be suppressed: at least it cannot be ignored or despised. It is in speaking of Gilles de Rais that I come to say this, for he differs from all those for whom crime is a personal matter. The crimes of Gilles de Rais are those of the world in which they are committed, and these ripped throats are exposed by the convulsive movements of such a world [X 319].

*

However difficult or repellent the matter at stake might be, we can scarcely avoid the search for the sense of transgression, which is the requirement of relating it to the Kantianism which forms our philosophical actuality. It is because Kant completes the understanding of the difference between laws and cases that his involvement is already implict in any attempt to judge crimes. (Hegel will of course suggest that to merely understand justice is still insufficient, and that it remains to justify it.) Our world recoils from meaningless crime even more forcefully than Rais', since modernity is in large part the necessity that death testifies, even if it is in the guise of a 'problematic concept'; serving as a limit to the understanding. Knowing must be articulated with death, and the philosophical vocabulary of the modern age is adapted to this task, examples including: limit, *Aufhebung*, *Indifferenz*, differance, etc. Bataille locates the word 'sacrifice' in this series, in which its specific function is to mark the immanent or base continuity between death and knowing, a continuity which is correlative to the failure of transcendence, and is here described as 'tragedy', or 'the impotence of reason'.

Tragedy – or the repulsion of discursive appropriation from death – effects a sporadic textual disruption whenever it is registered, since, although the productive usage of language ceases, words still jut-out beyond the splinter fringe of discourse; tracking a positive death-lip as it teeters into collapse. This ragged edge of Bataille's writing marks a disappearing base impulse, communicating with the virological reservoir of violated scription which he calls a 'holocaust of words'. Poetry, laughter, and filth have no meaning. They are unable to commensurate to the defence of a juridical subject. Nor can they be justified, affirmed, or protected.

Rimbaud's ruthless abandonment of poetry has a numbing appropriateness.

The name 'Bataille' could easily mislead us. It might seem, for instance, as if transgression had a defence, a voice. As if evil could be a praxis or a cause. It is in such ways that senseless loss might be neutralized within rationality. There are certainly good reasons for seeking to reconstruct some such 'Bataille'. It is an unfortunate fact that such projects inevitably fail, not because of some 'death of the author', but because of the death that is precisely not that *of* the author, or of anybody else. 'Bataille's' irrelevance is due to a death denuded of all sophistical ornamentation, a death that is the vortex of evil, and as such sufficiently incommensurate with his discourse to be exiled to 'the impossible', only puncturing his text as a dark shaft of inavowable impersonality. Literature is itself a crime.

Law is not exercised upon inert beings, but only upon those whose cooperation can be claimed. Obedience is always at least minimally active. This is why the recipient of a commandment is characterized as an agent, and why lawfulness attests to an implicit sovereignty. Docility in respect of the law is quite different from a surrender, in exactly the way that moralists are different from mystics. Surrender is a deeper evil than any possible action. The very principle of action is an acceptance of justice and responsibility, and any act is – as such – an amelioration of crime, expressing defiance within the syntax of redemption. In stark comparison with action, surrender gnaws away the conditions for salvation. Giving itself up to a wave of erasure, the agent dies into the cosmic reservoir of crime. Beyond the (agentic) pact with Satan lies an irreparable dissolution into forces of darkness, apart from which there is no ecstasy. Surrender is not a submission to an alien agency (devotion to God), but a surrender of agency in general, it is not any kind of consigning of oneself over to another (return to the father), but utter abandonment of self; a dereliction of duty which aggresses against one's birth.

Bataille's reading of Rais is a discourse on evil, or a philosophy of the sublime, and not a poem, a sacrificial denudation, or an effectuation of death. It cannot be sufficiently stressed that evil is never on trial. The same bedrock of human docility that in Rais generates the complex of separations between self and activity, self and victim, culpability and death, is also at work in Bataille's text, producing equivalent transcendent effects. Just as with Rais' pact with the devil, his association with Bataille is contractual, socialized, respectful of identities and norms. It is in accordance with a reconstructive or discurive exigency that a visual theme and the philosophical schema of sublimity, along with the proper names 'Gilles de Rais' and 'Georges Bataille', line up in a testament to transgression. Such reportage might be the ape of glory, but it would be difficult to maintain that it was alien to Rais' case, or that his superstition, vanity, and voyeurism did not work to transform him into a recognizable figure; schematizing him into our world. Rais cannot be innocently resuscitated on the outside of modernity, as if representation was a pure transcendence, qualified to judge the specificity of accumulative sociality. To the extent that we accommodate ourselves to the good, that which is wretched, reserved, and confessional about Rais belongs also to us.

Chapter 4

Easter

In a sense, the world is still, in a fundamental manner, immanence without clear limit (indistinct flowing of being into being, I dream of the unstable presence of waters interior to water). It is so to such an extent that the position, interior to a world, of a 'supreme being', distinct and limited like a thing, is first of all an impoverishment. There is without doubt, in the invention of a 'supreme being', a will to define a value greater than any other. But this desire to grow has as its consequence a diminution [VII 301].

God does not abandon Jesus except fictitiously [VI 85].

*

I wiped the blade against my jeans and walked into the bar. It was mid-afternoon, very hot and still. The bar was deserted. I ordered a whisky. The barman looked at the blood and asked:
'God?'
'Yeah.'
'S'pose it's time someone finished that hypocritical little punk, always bragging about his old man's power . . .'
He smiled crookedly, insinuatingly, a slight nausea shuddered through me. I replied weakly:
'It was kind of sick, he didn't fight back or anything, just kept trying to touch me and shit, like one of those dogs that try to fuck your leg. Something in me snapped, the whingeing had ground me down too low. I really hated that sanctimonious little creep.'
'So you snuffed him?'
'Yeah, I've killed him, knifed the life out of him, once I started I got frenzied, it was an ecstasy, I never knew I could hate so much.'
I felt very calm, slightly light-headed. The whisky tasted good,

vaporizing in my throat. We were silent for a few moments.
The barman looked at me levelly, the edge of his eyes twitching slightly with anxiety:
'There'll be trouble though, don'tcha think?'
'I don't give a shit, the threats are all used up, I just don't give a shit.'
'You know what they say about his old man? Ruthless bastard they say. Cruel . . .'
'I just hope I've hurt him, if he even exists.'
'Woulden wanna cross him merself,' he muttered.
I wanted to say 'yeah, well that's where we differ', but the energy for it wasn't there. The fan rotated languidly, casting spidery shadows across the room. We sat in silence a little longer. The barman broke first:
'So God's dead?'
'If that's who he was. That fucking kid lied all the time. I just hope it's true this time.'
The barman worked at one of his teeth with his tongue, uneasily:
'It's kindova big crime though, isn't it? You know how it is, when one of the cops goes down and everything's dropped 'til they find the guy who did it. I mean, you're not just breaking a law, your breaking LAW.'
I scraped my finger along my jeans, and suspended it over the bar, so that a thick clot of blood fell down into my whisky, and dissolved. I smiled:
'Maybe it's a big crime,' I mused vaguely 'but maybe it's nothing at all . . .'
'. . . and we have killed him' writes Nietzsche, but – destituted of community – I crave a little time with him on my own.

In perfect communion I lick the dagger foamed with God's blood.

*

This book was supposed to be finished at Easter, like God.
It will take longer.
God sighs, he can't get it together, time is passing, he is losing all sense for time. Crucifixion passes like an agitating dream. Nails, a little blood. None of it seems very serious.
The ants insult me with this faint dribbling of pain. Am I not the creator of a Hell?

*

Christ screams on the cross: 'Father, your parsimony disgusts me, is this a death?' He thinks of the abortion he missed, lying wrapped in bloody rags on the floor of a cheap hostelry. He is excited by the thought of his mother in mortal sin, and of a harsher love than he ever knew. How was it possible for her to forgo the delight of hacking God's fruit from her womb? (That was a chance for *religion*.) 'For, behold, the days are coming in which they shall say, Blessed *are* the barren, and the wombs that never bare, and the paps which never gave suck' [John XXIII:29].

Instead there was 'an odious comedy' [VI 85], this hollow melodrama of Easter.

*

Ash slimed with pain my exultation is unbearable
mother do you still bleed? God asks
his guts forked out into the dust
yellow and fat like insect smear
death always a stranger
and your idiot smile
spawning monstrosity with dulled eyes

*

Eloi, Eloi, lama sabachtani? [Mark XV:34].
There is no answer.
Merely the blank violence of the sun.

*

I am far from intolerant of Nietzsche's aristocratism. It does not seem obvious to me that someone living amongst Christians should feel disposed to democracy. It would be less demeaning if the beasts in the fields were to legislate in one's name.

For this 'reason' I consider myself at war with my society, complying with its ordinances only insofar as these convenience my dominant whim. I acknowledge none of its agents or authorities, except in the way a fox acknowledges the hunt. A state is already a sufficient object for disgust, let alone one that allies itself with the Christian religion.

Not that it is a virile struggle that I wage. I wheeze, massaging my headache, but without hope. I imagine myself old, still alive, somewhat fatter, and a Christian. Sickened, I push on. I see myself kneeling, drooling pieties . . . longing to be saved.

What could more thoroughly demonstrate my unbelief than entertaining such obscenities . . . ?

*

There is only one sane and healthy relation to Christianity; perfect indifference. Mine is not of that kind. My detestation for the Christian faith exhausts my being, and more. I long for its God to exist in order to slake myself as violence upon him. If there are torments coming to me I want them, all of them; God experimenting in cruelty upon me. I want no lethargy in Hell, rather vigour and imagination. Oh yes, it is all very wretched, and if I am grateful to Christianity it is for one thing alone; it has taught me how to *hate*.

God drinks upon the poison of my hate with an erotic ardour, since his ruthless erasure is even more precious to him than it is to me. After tasting deep surrender in his passion to annihilate, how could he relish a return to the sordid world of obedience; to that of his *duty to exist*? Nothing comes to religion later – or more abjectly – than God.

I have not been a theist for a single second of my life. In my first assemblies at primary school, when the theistic idiocy was first wheeled out, I remember thinking: it is natural that adults should lie to you, but is it really necessary for them to insult the intelligence quite this much? As for the longing to believe, nothing could be more alien to me, because nothing is more obvious than the fact that humanity – far from being a creation – is a disease. Why should the absence of a divinity analogical to mankind be more disturbing than the absence of a giant tortoise supporting the world on its back? If pressed, I would be forced to argue that the latter belief offers more consolation, adds greater richness to cosmology, exhibits greater intellectual sophistication. Monotheists are like those dull and uninspired children who *compel* you to patronize them. In the end, one has to ignore them, one cannot stoop far enough to argue, after all, if they are capable of believing such things what are they not capable of believing? An insipid pseudo-religion in the terminal phase of its senescence is perhaps safer than the rejuvenating absurdities into which its disillusioned adherents would undoubtedly stumble.

In the first moment in which I understood what I was being asked to believe I immediately knew *why* I was being asked to do so. Could there be a less subtle, a more brutal way of trying to frighten people into being good? I cannot think of one, however strenuous my attempts. God the father ... what could be less challenging than a psychoanalysis of monotheism? A delusion that refuses to hide itself, to mask or complicate itself, to compromise its tedious insanity; its critics – after scarcely beginning the task of demolition – have always caught themselves yawning. The great defence mechanism of this cult; to be too uninteresting to fight. Morality has clung to inanity with an unmatched fervour, the most hated heretics were always those who threatened to introduce thought, enquiry, or style into religion; to undermine its monotony. To be burnt by the church it sufficed to question the omnibanality of God.

Sometimes I wonder what is to be involved in writing this book. I am not a particularly industrious individual. The protocols of scholarship have always confused me. It is 03:10 in the morning and as I lean against the wall my finger runs across a line in the plaster, a fissure, dissociation . . .

Momentarily I know one thing (alone):

Bataille's most unfailing signature is spiritual disease.

*

I dream of the damnation I have so amply earned, stolen from me by the indolence of God.

Chapter 5
Dead God

Ghost in tears
O dead God
hollow eye
damp moustache
single tooth
O dead God
O dead God
Me
I pursued you
with unfathomable
hatred
and I would die of hatred
as a cloud
is undone [V 121].

I am not a philosopher but a saint, perhaps a madman [V 218n].

Bataille does not transmit a philosophy, but rather a delirious negative evangile: 'death can be *tasted*'. Monotheism has always pre-emptively reconstructed this message: 'you mean it can be known.'

Whatever else Bataille's *Method of Meditation* might be, it is also the violent contamination of Cartesianism. The title itself is compacted from Descartes' *Discourse on Method* and his *Metaphysical Meditations*, perhaps his principal texts. The reference is not incidental, since Descartes is a limit-point of isolation, and in *Inner Experience* Bataille explicitly discusses him in such terms. Descartes sought to know God, and to make use of this knowledge philosophically. In this way a certain theological suppression of religion is consummated, with the philosopher sealing himself definitively within the prison of representation.

Cartesian thinking understands itself ideologically in terms of a 'radical doubt' (in reality wholly spurious), which is designed to serve it as an indisputable starting point for its intellectual productions, thus masking its neo-scholastic apologetic character. The corrosive force of doubt is to be pre-emptively exhausted in the initiation of the modern philosophical project, and thus mastered/ ejected by constructive reason without delay. What is in truth the extreme cowardice of Cartesian doubt – its undisturbed piety – is necessitated by its immediately theological character, since from the perspective of the church the slightest hint of radical interrogation is *suspect*. Such 'doubt' merely replays the sham humility of Christian hope in the secular mode, rendering it epistemological, but maintaining its hypocritical and dogmatic character. Faith takes on the form of certainty in knowing, without ceasing to be inflexibly superstitious.

The Cartesian ego in its function as indubitable foundation serves to equilibriate reason and existence, or rather, carries the inherited and uninterrogated certainty of this equilibrium forward into secular reason. This coherence of existent knowing has always been taken by philosophy to be the evident principle of ontology, or the harmonious reciprocity of knowing/being. From Plato, through the Scholastics, to Descartes and beyond, thought presupposes and confirms existence, just as existence bears witness to its origin in divine ideation. Ontology can only be consummated by a being that is adequate to the highest forms of being – those that are insulated against the processes of corruption or degeneration that bring about a subsidence into non-being – so that it is finally in the divine image (which is, anyway, conveniently anthropoid) that the indestructible soul must be wrought. Only an immortal entity is able to reflectively apprehend pure being, without becoming inevitably lost in the swamp of matter; that dangerous compacted mass of being and annihilation, malignantly metamorphic, infectious, gnawed, and rotten with time.

In keeping with the inherent tendency of all ontology, Descartes' ego is thus an extremity of separation; a capsule-entity stripped of all relations other than those mediated by God, and moving only in strict succession from self, through the divine, to a weakly conceived alterity. It finds an immaculate relation to the profane world through representation, by means of which its being is reserved from the hazards of contact in the very exercise of knowing. It is in accord with such a doctrine that negation is purified of its raw materiality, and is thought as a function of representation, a logical operation, the denial of a thesis by and for a subject whose positivity is repeated indifferently throughout any series of intellectual affirmations or denials.

It is in Descartes' philosophy that doubt is exhibited in its definitively profane sense, as despair transcended by the ego of ontological knowing. This profanation of oceanic despair – the opening of modernity in philosophy – does not subvert scholastic reasoning, but rather fulfills it, since it is the triumph of theology over religion. It is thus that in diagnosing the poverty of modern thinking Bataille is not advocating any variety of squalid historical regression, because the only characteristic of scholastic philosophy worthy of affirmation is its ineffectiveness, rooted in a servile idiocy that has proven to be remarkably tenacious. Despair is not a motif of theology, but a lacuna within it. It is neither disbelief, or doubt, both of which involve an ambivalence in the application of logical signs to an ontologically petrified thesis, but an unknowing so radical that it both escapes the scope of any possible epistemology and lacks all doctrinal intelligibility. Despair cannot be defined as a claim, hesitation, denial, or uncertainty. It is an abandonment, and a plea without conceivable destination; a desertification resulting from the catastrophic disappearance of *the value of being*. Despair is not humble, but hubristic, and it is not pious in the least, but *tragic*.

In *The Birth of Tragedy* Nietzsche indicates that the issue at the core of the tragic is *community*. Despite the earliness of this text – written at a time when Nietzsche still adhered to a Wagnerian exaltation of the nation – the sense of community at work in it is only superficially commensurable with a thought of ethnic, political, or social unity. Tragic community is not the affirmation of a collective identity, but rather the dissolution of all identifiable traits in an uncircumscribable movement of catastrophe and festival; catastrophe of the individuated self, festival of anonymous flow. Sacred communion (as opposed to mere empirical aggregation) cannot be politically restricted, since it does not proceed by means of a controllable process of assemblage, but by the blinding subsidence of autonomy. This takes the form of the sacrifice of the collectively invested individual; the tragic hero, the prince, God. Its emblem, therefore, is not the reverance of the masses (for leader, homeland, culture, race, or creed), but regicide and eruption in the streets.

From the first verse of John's Gospel to Hegel's *Science of Logic*, and beyond, Western history traverses a thanatological plateau. Man is the animal that knows it will die, determined in its essence by a knowledge whose specific mode is an immortalizing sublimation.

In the massively preponderant aggregate the Christian religion has preached not just the contingency of death, but its *impossibility*. God, for instance – insofar as he is shackled to his credibility – is *unable* to die, despite his melodramatically vaunted omnipotence. This is an infacility that is protracted through the angels. Humans are at least permitted a ludicrous pretence at termination (Christ: God pretending to be a man pretending to die), but only the beasts are able to truly expire, perhaps because only they are left alone to do so.

The death of God that Nietzsche outlines is not without a partial anticipation. If humanity's most morbid religion is initiated by an act of God, such an act is surely best described as a botched suicide attempt. It seems likely, as is so often the case, that this was a *gesture*, a plea for attention. The Judaeo-Christian portrait of God is a classic sketch of pathological insecurity. How desperate he is to be loved! So insufficient to himself, and so alone. How sickening to live for ever in this way. Unable to even dream of escaping the smell of oneself. No one hates God as much as God. No one hates anything as much. It is not difficult to imagine his excitement, attending the nihilistic ruin of his cult. The prospect of release at last! Freed of all responsibility to serve as the principle of beings! His emergent superfluity must have welled up in him with the power of sexual crisis, such that it had all suddenly not been.

There are times when one's pity for God becomes overwhelming; nothing has ever had to bear a more ignoble inexistence than he. To not exist *without excuse* (as St Anselm demonstrated), his very essence condemns him for this default. Could there be a more humiliating sinecure? When a replacement for God was sought in the years 1888–9 even Nietzsche – that maniac of compassion – was reluctant to accept the post [N III 1351].

*

The madman. – Have you not heard of that madman who lit a

lantern in the bright morning hours, ran to the market place, and cried incessantly: 'I seek God! I seek God!' – As many of those who did not believe in God were standing around just then, he provoked much laughter. Has he got lost? asked one. Did he lose his way like a child? asked another. Or is he hiding? Is he afraid of us? Has he gone on a voyage? emigrated? – Thus they yelled and laughed.

The madman jumped into their midst and pierced them with his eyes. 'Whither is God?' he cried; 'I will tell you. *We have killed him* – you and I. All of us are his murderers. But how did we do this? How could we drink up the sea? Who gave us the sponge to wipe away the entire horizon? What were we doing when we unchained this earth from its sun? Whither is it moving now? Whither are we moving? Away from all suns? Are we plunging continuously? Backward, sideward, forward, in all directions? Is there still any up or down? Are we not straying as through an infinite nothing? Do we not feel the breath of empty space? Has it not become colder? Is not night continuously closing in on us? Do we not need to light lanterns in the morning? Do we hear nothing as yet of the noise of the gravediggers who are burying God? Do we smell nothing as yet of the divine decomposition? Gods, too, decompose. God remains dead. And we have killed him.

'How shall we comfort ourselves, the murderers of all murderers? What was holiest and mightiest of all that the world has yet owned has bled to death under our knives: who will wipe this blood off us? What water is there for us to clean ourselves? What festivals of atonement, what sacred games shall we have to invent? Is not the greatness of this deed too great for us? Must we not ourselves not become gods simply to appear worthy of it? There has never been a greater deed; and whoever is born after us – for the sake of this deed he will belong to a higher history than all history hitherto.'

Here the madman fell silent and looked again at his listeners; and they, too, were silent and stared at him in astonishment. At last he threw his lantern on the ground, and it broke into pieces and went out. 'I have come too early,' he said then; 'my time is not yet. This tremendous event is still on its way, still wandering; it has not yet reached the ears of men. Lightning and thunder require time; the light of the stars requires time; deeds, though done, still require time to be seen and heard. This deed is still more distant from them than the most distant stars – *and yet they have done it themselves.*'

It has been related that on the same day the madman forced his way into several churches and there struck up his *requiem aeternam deo*. Led out and called to account, he is said to have replied nothing but: 'What after all are these churches now if they are not tombs and sepulchers of God?' [N II 126–8].

God is nowhere to be found, yet there is still so much light! Light that dazzles and maddens; crisp, ruthless light. Space echoes like an immense tomb, yet the stars still burn. Why does the sun take so long to die? Or the moon retain such fidelity to the Earth? Where is the new darkness? The greatest of all unknowings? Is death itself *shy* of us?

The brilliance of God's non-being provokes a wave of cynical laughter. How strange that God's last act should be so entertaining! A good joke, but rather an old one now. It spawned innumerable witticisms that circulated in the market-place; a final testament dissipated amongst the buzz of commodity exchange, but they faded fast. What was the death of God anyway? A slight fizz of exuberance in the stock-market? A moderate lightening of the spirit? A relaxation? The end of a badly-scripted play, greeted by the languid effervescence of cheap champagne?

For a long time there have been more important things to talk about in market-places. The things they save the expensive champagne for. Perhaps they laugh a little at God's demise occasionally, but they are bored by it. Even his taxidermists have deserted him, the best of them at any rate. Those that remain are mostly the otherwise unemployable; the second rate, the incompetent or unenthusiastic. So he deteriorates still, becoming more moth-eaten and absurd. If they laugh at all it is because Jahweh has come to seem so much like a neglected teddy-bear; balding, one arm hanging loose, an eye coming away. When they were children stories about bears had frightened them. Not any more.

There was always something shoddy about this God. Lost on the way to being, and to us. Even lost, for a little while, on the way to death. A stumbler, an unwitting clown, everything he does is botched, improvised, ostentatious; his past a mix of gaucherie and tantrum. Nowhere a hint of precocity, but always retardation, leaving abundant signs of a debilitating learning-difficulty wherever he makes a mark, a *slow* child. (Even the theologians admit to his 'simplicity'.) His diminishing flock rarely ask him about scientific matters any more, few of them dare ask themselves. He long ago dropped out of such classes, to the secret relief of his family. For a while they insisted that he had other gifts – ineffable ones – and (with the blindness of mothers) praised the ageing infant's good nature, which they said had calmed down a lot. One can only smile.

Maybe it is that we brought out the worst in him. For who could doubt God's fear of us? Was he not omniscient? Did he not always see the rusty dagger in our hands? And we were created in his image! (The corporealization of his hatred for himself.) What tatters of self-love remained to him came apart at this sight. To reign over all things, as the archetype of *man*. A piteous enough truth to exhibit.

Few things approximate so closely to infinity as the humorous incommensurability between man and the sum of the universe. To span such a gulf within oneself is to live an idiocy. To be not only an animal, but a *depraved* one: an aborted animal, a sick animal, a delirious animal. Upon first seeing a rabid dog one thinks it is becoming human. This is not a promising basis for divinity.

If he hid from us it was only in attempting to hide his eyes; to block us out. Yet amongst the accidents of his omniscience – or of his inexistence – was included the absence of eyelids. We burnt on his sleep-starved retina like harsh stars. Our deicide crawled like a rash upon his skin. He could only stare at us, and our history ensued; a convulsion of lethal horror.

Of course, he made innumerable attempts at emigration, but who would have him? Who wants a second-hand God? Philosophy provided only a temporary refuge; rebelling eventually against his bad manners. How nostalgic he was of his days as a carpenter, once he had become a tramp.

It is tempting to dredge into our lassitude, seeking another end for God. Might he not have been allowed to retire? The state would surely have granted him a modest pension (does not Kant provide the basis for such a policy?). After all, few would dispute that senile tyrants make wretched victims. It seems scarcely more dignified to kill God than to slaughter a dog when it becomes too old to work. Who, then, is still capable of Nietzsche's generosity? It is rare to find one who takes much pride in slaughtering God these days. More common is a vague feeling of impurity; one has soiled oneself by bothering with something so vile and corrupt. That God was ever permitted residence amongst us is a source of embarrassment, or, at best, of uneasy humour. It is understandable that many should feel vaguely bad about God, was he not a little too vulnerable, old, and pitiful to kill? Should we not greet his inexistence with an impatient 'of course', and turn to more serious things? Do we really lack the delicacy to let God die quietly, on his own, like a dog?

It is true that we probably merited a better God to sacrifice. It is not unreasonable to imagine that a cosmos that spawned a Herakleitus deserved a more dignified ruler than the grumpy old ape of Occidental monotheism. Nevertheless, it is pointless nursing such regrets. They belong to the mournful 'might have beens' of our history; decided long before we had a chance to *shop around* for a God.

*

Bataille ends an early article entitled 'Propositions' with the words: 'the true universality is the death of God' [I 473]. He is insistent, throughout the entire sweep of his work, that the death of God, as announced in Nietzsche's *The Gay Science*, is to be thought of as a religious event, indeed, as the positive end of religion (as zero)[10]. For Bataille – far more than for Nietzsche – the atheology thus engendered is of a specifically Christian character, in that it is rooted in the 'sense' of the crucifixion. Bataille reads the world historical power of Christianity through its quasi-latent content of an absolute sacrifice – that of God himself – which has created a religion of divine suicide. At the same time he considers Christianity to have deformed and obscured this thought, burying it under a theology of redemption. In the development of monotheistic belief man 'tends to substitute for the evident prodigality of the heavens the avidity which constitutes him: it is thus that little by little he effaces the image of celestial reality without sense or pretension and replaces it with a personification (of an anthropomorphic nature) of the *immutable* idea of Good' [I 518]. The subordination of the sacred category of death to the rational category of immorality (perdurant value) is a profanation of religion; the transformation of sacrifice into utility, exchange, and negotiation. A God unable to expend itself utterly is a figure of servility and abjection, bound to persistence with iron chains. 'God the transcendent guarantee of *being* – the service of God abasement before this principle: that *being* persist, be imperishable [IV 167].'

Bataille insists that Nietzsche's thought of the death of God is sacrificial, orgiastic, and festive. Christian belief must pass over not into a complacent scientific utilitarianism, but into the ecstasies of uninhibited wastage. The loss of God is the loss of self, the definitive shattering of the anthropic image, so that the perdurant ego of servile humanity is dissolved into the solar energy flow. Bataille is not remotely interested in being saved, he wants only to touch the extreme, writing that 'I have wanted and found ecstasy' [V 264], an ecstasy that is the experienced loss of being. This is not a matter of dying, but of surviving (momentarily) only through excess, as chance, without guarantees, and without inhibiting the dissipative tide:

> Being is given to us in an *intolerable* surpassing of being, no less intolerable than death. And because, in death, this is withdrawn from us at the same time it is given, we must search for it in the *feeling* of death, in those intolerable moments where it seems that we are dying, because the being in us is only there through excess, when the plenitude of horror and that of joy coincide [III 11-12].

*

God has only one possible *meaning*: Phallus. The God of the ontological argument is Omniphallus, in whom reason, being, authority, and the good coincide. It belongs to the essence of a perfect being that he exist forever. Who could deny that the crucified was well hung? But perhaps one should not laugh about such things, for even if God is a comic, one's willy – and its mythology – has surely to be taken seriously.

As for Jahweh's immense throbbing member, that is a matter of the gravest consequence. Through it he establishes himself as the supreme transcendent object, eternally postponing the black spasm whose result is detumescence and the end of the universe. Were God to ever sacrifice his erection for a taste of death the principle of identity would dissipate into scorched dust, and being would relapse into the dark.

Phallus – as psychoanalysis has always said – is the same as castration. To be an immortal organ of intimidation is to abstain forever from the movement twisted through oblivion and relapse. In *The Solar Anus* Bataille remarks: 'Those in whom the force of eruption is accumulated are necessarily situated below [*en bas*]'

[I 85]. What God must never succumb to is the molten penis of terrestrial coupling, for which logic (of castration) has lost its sense, because nothing remains to separate it from vulvic dissolution.

*

In the final spasm of sexual anguish God bites off his penis and – with his maw dripping blood – mewls like a dying hyena into the void.

*

– Would you like to see my rags? she said.
With both hands gripping the table, I turned towards her. Seated, she lifted a leg high: in order better to open the slit, she drew apart the skin with both hands. Thus the 'rags' of Edwarda gazed at me, hairy and pink, full of life like a repugnant octopus. I stammered softly:
– Why do you do that?
– You see, she said, I am GOD . . . [III 21]

The narrator of *Madame Edwarda* proceeds to kiss the whore's 'rags' as the Christian mystics kiss the wounds of Christ. There can be little doubt that Bataille imagines the vulva as a wound, but this is not because of a negative relation to castration. Far from being an excised penis, the vulva is a complex terrain of contact with death, of exactly the kind castration proscribes. Nor can the flowing wound that breaks open being into communication be one pole of a sexual relation – matched by a plenitude – since this vulvic opening would be sexuality itself, except there is no such thing as sexuality itself.

The ancient Romans are only the most famous example of the arithmetical gratuitousness of zero. When zero is absent it is not missed; no one notices the default of default. Nevertheless, counting systems enriched by zero – and the place-order associated with it – are of massively enhanced sophistication over those in which nothing is missing. Introducing nothing makes an inestimable difference.

Zero is indivisible, so that zero belief cannot be rigorously differentiated from belief in zero. It is in this sense that atheism is a religion. Not that atheism is committed to a specific conviction, quite the opposite; it is precisely the specificity of conviction that it attacks. Understood negatively it denies the false absolute of *theos*, but understood positively it affirms the true absolute marked by the 'privative' a-; the *nihil* from which creation proceeds, the undifferentiable cosmic zero.

When the valet touched the slit he groaned:
– In the name of God [IV 41]!

I drink in your rending
and I spread your naked legs
I open them like a book
where I read that which kills me [IV 14, 161].

I am God
I knock on your head
herr priest
I kill you
I am a cunt [III 158].

Everything has obviously gone wrong for us in order for Plato to begin with One rather than Zero. To take One as originary is to presuppose everything; such as unity, individuation, achieved form, and dogmatic plenitude. The One is the phallomorphic base of Occidental culture, in the sense that Irigaray understands it. It is the mono- of monotheism, and monotheism is condensed irreligion; the definitive patriarchal effacing of intra-uterine indifferentiation (and thus of the primary ripple from out of chaotic zero). The differentiated one is the Father, and his adorers understand nothing of religion. Even in writing the nothing, as Aquinas does, they eclipse it with absolute ego (Him). Nor is it the case that primary immanence is merely crushed with arbitrariness beneath a partially inadequate metaphorics, since – far from being neutral between the sexes – it is precisely because indifferentiation ($= 0$) is sexually unsegmented that it is even more feminine than the mother. The femininity of zero is uncompromised by its indifference, due to the unilateral character of individualizing deviation. Whilst zero is certainly alien to the Father, there is no differentiation from zero. Indeed, zero is so utterly vulvo-uterine that patriarchy is synonymous with irreligion (faith).

Between barter systems and money systems there is a difference strictly analogous to that between Roman arithmetics and the place-value system from India, transmitted by the Arabs to the West. Like zero, money is a redundant operator; adding nothing in order to make things hum. When Marx associates capital with death he is only drawing the final consequence from this correspondence. Surplus value comes out of labour-power, but surplus production comes out of nothing. This is why capital production is the consummating phase of nihilism, the liquidation of theological irreligion, the twilight of the idols. Modernity is virtual thanocracy guided insidiously by zero; the epoch of the death of God. There is no God but (only) zero — indifferentiation without unity — and *nihil* is true religion.

Schopenhauer remarks of the cosmic vulva (= 0):

> We must not even evade it, as the Indians do, by myths and meaningless words, such as reabsorption in *Brahman*, or the *Nirvana* of the Buddhists. On the contrary, we freely acknowledge that what remains after the complete abolition of the will is, for all who are still full of the will, assuredly nothing. But also conversely, to those in whom the will has turned and denied itself, this very real world with all its suns and galaxies, is — nothing [Sch II 508].

Chapter 6

The rage of jealous time

> For thou shalt worship no other god: for the LORD whose name *is* Jealous, *is* a jealous God [Exod XXXIV:14].
>
> For the LORD thy God *is* a consuming fire, *even* a jealous God [Deut IV:24].
>
> 14. Ye shall not go after other gods, of the gods of the people which *are* round about you.
> 15. (For the LORD thy God *is* a jealous God among you) lest the anger of the LORD thy God be kindled against thee, and destroy thee from off the face of the earth [Deut VI].
>
> Therefore thus saith the Lord GOD; Surely in the fire of my jealousy have I spoken against the residue of the heathen [Ezek XXXVI:5].
>
> God *is* jealous, and the LORD revengeth; the LORD revengeth, and *is* furious; the LORD will take vengeance on his adversaries, and he reserveth *wrath* for his enemies [Nah I:2].

Amongst the many partial anticipations of the modern thought of the transcendental in antiquity is the *jealousy* of Jahweh. Extricated from its childish psychological constriction – its commensuration to a personal being – this is one of the few *religious* thoughts to be found in the history of Western monotheism. To refuse to share, to coexist, to tolerate equivalence; these things are ruthlessly divine. In comparison to Jahweh, the God of the Christians is a wheedler; a door to door salesman. It is true, nevertheless, that the genocidal frenzy with which Jahweh asserts his monopoly can disconcert. Squeamishness is not a charge one can fairly bring against him:

> 1. When the Lord thy God shall bring thee into the land whither thou goest to possess it, and hath cast out many nations before

thee, the Hittites, and the Girgashites, and the Amorites, and the Canaanites, and the Perizzites, and the Hivites, and the Jebusites, seven nations greater and mightier than thou;
2. And when the Lord thy God shall deliver them before thee; thou shalt smite them, *and* utterly destroy them; thou shalt make no covenant with them, nor shew mercy unto them:
3. Neither shalt thou make marriages with them; thy daughter thou shalt not give unto his son, nor his daughter shalt thou take unto thy son' [Deut VII].

16. But of the cities of these people, which the Lord thy God doth give thee for an inheritance, thou shalt save alive nothing that breatheth:
17. But thou shalt utterly destroy them; *namely* the Hittites, and the Amorites, the Canaanites, and the Perizzites, the Hivites, and the Jebusites; as the Lord thy God hath commanded thee [Deut XX].

Jealousy is inextricable from paroxystic violence, historically rooted in national chauvinism, before being sublimed into the cosmological intolerance of a divinity. What does it matter who is instrument here? Whether God serves the annihilating designs of a tribe, or the tribe serves to purify the earth of alien gods? There is no antagonism at the origin, but rather a perfect pact between the election of the chosen people and the brutal solitude of the unnameable One.

What the Jews never understood about this God (the Christians understood it even less of course) was the *sovereignty* of this jealous wrath. How could these feverish rages be subordinated to an end beyond themselves, to a mere persistence, as if God – too – was subject to inhibition? A God that held himself in check, submitting the splenetic extravagance of his moods to the exigency of being, would be something far less glorious than the sun (he would be humbled by a mediocre star). Each creature uselessly dispensing with its existence would outstrip his prodigality, deepening by a ratchet-notch his hatred for himself.

Could such a God glimpsing the impossible sovereignty of his fury – time opening as a dark shaft of impersonal loss – and, howling in utter loathing at the servility of self, restrain from scurrying to a squalid death on the cross?

God savours himself, says Eckhart. This is possible, but what he savours is, it seems to me, the hatred which he has for himself, to which none, here on Earth, can be compared (I could say: this hatred is time, but that bothers me. Why should I say time? I feel this hatred when I cry; I analyse nothing) [V 120].

Why should anyone be interested in time? I cannot imagine. The scrawniness of an arm, a finger, the enigma of a face; these things make sense (hurt). Time, on the contrary, is as vacant as a marriage, or God alone in the dark.

At the moment I seize myself in the mire of being, swamped by the detestation of ulterior ends, I AM GOD AND TIME LAUGHS AT THE ETERNAL PRETENTION OF SLAVES. 'This God who leads us beneath his clouds is mad. I know him, I am him' [III 39]. (Bataille recommends that one chant: 'I represent myself covered in blood, broken but transfigured and at one with the world, at once like prey and like a tooth of TIME which kills incessantly and is incessantly killed' [I 557–8].)

*

Jealousy is as inextricable from a movement of abolition as it is essential to the being of God. Time cannot be limited to a property or attribute of divinity, for this would make jealousy posterior to a preliminary legislation of essence. It would, in any case, be impossible for God to resent the absolute wilderness of time, since his hatred must pander to the flow of erasure. Perhaps it is that God mistakes himself for time, until he sees things die without reluctance, and turns upon himself in unfathomable desperation. I AM THAT I AM is already a pre-emptive afflux of incinerating privilege, or it is nothing. In the beginning was the rage, or is it that we imagine God being disappointed by his creation? A surprised God? A bewildered God? His great work gone astray. This is the psychological divinity, taken aback by naughty children, the offended God that we tell our five year olds about. A God without wrath, but only 'righteous anger'. A magistrate. What could such a being fail to botch? But jealousy is not indignation, and at the moment of unfettered rage, when God no longer serves anything, and the molten edge of his wrath delects in the submission of being to sovereign whim, then 'authority no longer belongs to God but to time' [I 471].

Bataille writes of 'the catastrophe of time' because security cannot establish itself, because time is *jealous* of being. It is in his early essay 'Sacrifices' (1936) that he first develops this thought to its rigorous conclusion in incompletion and collapse. No ontology of time is possible, and yet ontology remains the sole foundation for discursive accomplishment. There are only the shattered spars and parodies of philosophy, as ruinous time pounds thought into the embers of an unwitting sacrifice, wreathed in a laughter as cold and nakedly joyous as the void.

> Time is not the synthesis of being and of nothing if being or nothing do not find themselves except in time and are nothing but arbitrarily separated notions. There is not then in effect either being or nothing in isolation, there is time [I 96].

> [T]he existence of things is not able to enclose the death which this existence brings, but is itself projected into the death that encloses it [I 96].

Time is the suicidal jealousy of God, to which each being – even the highest – must fall victim. It is thus the ultimate ocean of immanence, from which nothing can separate itself, and in which everything loses itself irremediably. The black mass of jealous rage swells like a cancer at the core of the universe, or like a volcanic ulceration in the guts of God, and its catastrophic eruption consumes all established things in the acidic lava of impersonality. We say 'time' – and become philosophical – to describe jealousy purifying itself of God (but with God purity collapses also).

> Perhaps there is still passion in God, but it is passion as the dog is the dog when the dog is on a leash. There is no possibility for the passion of God to unchain itself, since God is reason. Perhaps the experience of the mystics is in accord with me, because it shows that from the sacred one must leave a place for an unchaining which receives no limits, since, from the sacred, it is necessary to break every species of boundary, to no longer consider limits either of reason or morality as possible. But, once again, at this moment, is it not evident that God dies? [VII 370].

That jealous time erases all things is in no sense the acknowledgement of a de-materialization, since the only place to escape from matter was God. The thought that matter is not a content of time is perhaps the preeminent shadow of a truth that is 'at once' an impossibility and an abomination (also an ecstasy). As the shockwave of jealousy ejects the universe's lactescent debris from the crater of reason, transcendent matter loses the perfection of its inertia (design), and nature implodes into the spasms of its own laceration. As the destroyer the universe is time, and as the destroyed nature, but in the destruction nature sloughs-off the crust in which it had petrified itself and infests time like rot, regressing to its molten core; base-matter, becoming, flow, energy, immanence, continuity, flame, desire, death. 'Ecstatic time is not able to find itself except in the vision of things that puerile hazard makes brusquely appear: cadavers, nudities, explosions, spilt blood, abysses, bursts of sun and of thunder' [I 471].

There is every reason to resist such insanity, reason is nothing else. Nothing could be more evidently intelligible than the fact that: 'no enterprise has cost a sum of labour greater than that which sought to arrest the flow of time' [I 504]. 'Civilization' is the name we give to this process, a process turned against the total social calamity – the cosmic sickness – inherent to process as such. If the deluge, which is danger in itself, is the final motor of history, it is the great civilizations which are the engines or composite machines, channeling flows and engendering the mirage of function. As with an ant's nest, what emerges in the aggregate is a frenetic immobilism, a literal robotism, converting process into work, and work into the further embalming of process. Everything is set against 'the explosive immensity of time' [I 472]. Insofar as a civilization functions, therefore, it becomes increasingly sclerotic and pyramidalized; rituals, customs, codes, all hardened against the release of unendurable forces that would follow from the melt-down of the energy source (which is pushed further and further upstream, purified).

> The long period stretching from the Ancient empire of Egypt to the bourgeoise monarchy of Orleans – which elevates the obelisk in the square 'to the applause of an immense populace' – has been necessary to man in order to achieve the setting of the most stable limits to the deleterious movement of time. The mocking universe being slowly delivered to the severe *eternity* of its All-Powerful Father, guarantee of deep stability. The slow and obscure movements of history have their place here at the heart and not the periphery of beings and it is the long and inexpiable struggle of God against time that they figure, it is the combat of 'established sovereignty' against the shattering and creative madness of things. Thus history endlessly resumes the response

of the immovable stone to the Herakleitean world of flows and flames [I 505].

This is a movement of synchronization; distilling-out an absolute time to provide a form for history *without impingement*, extrinsically compiling events into manipulable series. Every civilization aspires to a transcendent *Aeon* in which to deposit the functional apparatus of *chronos* without fear of decay. What is dammed-up in the Aeon is the densely material time of rupture and ruthless re-creation, whilst what remains to anaemic chronology is time as the medium of homogeneous, commensurable, and reproducible processes; a domesticated temporality adjusted to work, from which catastrophe has been abstracted-out through sublimation into the infinite. Synchronization is founded upon an immense and precarious stabilization; the petrification of a pure and absolute time, or the completion of time as such (the timeless essence of time). Synchronization has as its basic presupposition the Aeon as final register of events, as the perfectly immaculate scroll upon which creation's unfolding is inscribed, and it is because of this that it corresponds to the servility of God; to his proper function and cosmic duty as book-keeper of the universe. In other words, synchronization has as its condition of possibility the imperative rationality of the divine. Nietzsche tells us that – even after it has occurred – it takes a long time for the death of God to arrive, but that does not mean it is delayed, rather: it unleashes the asynchronicity whose ultimate repression God was. To be too early – *unzeitgemäß* – is not at all to wait. It is to suffer the eruption of real time. Neither is death the arbitrary content of asynchronicity; a subject predicated by it. Death is not extrinsically, but inherently, asynchronous.

*

12. And I saw the dead, small and great, stand before God; and the books were opened: and another book was opened, which is *the book* of life: and the dead were judged out of those things which were written in the books, according to their works.
13. And the sea gave up the dead which were in it; and death and hell delivered up the dead which were in them: and they were judged every man according to their works.
14. And death and hell were cast into the lake of fire. This is the second death.

15. And whosoever was not found written in the book of life was cast into the lake of fire [Rev XX].

But the fearful, and unbelieving, and the abominable, and murderers, and whoremongers, and sorcerors, and idolators, and all liars, shall have their part in the lake which burneth with fire and brimstone: which is the second death [Rev XXI:8].

It seems that something is in fact annihilated. The end and the beginning correspond. At the beginning was God alone. Therefore things will be brought to a point where there is again nothing but God alone. Thus all creatures will be annihilated – voice of Aquinas' heretical interlocutor [A XIV 51].

No text has programmed the thought of death in the Western tradition more fundamentally than chapters XX and XXI of *Revelation*, where its historically dominant topic is established, namely, the 'second death', or terminal fate of the soul (see also Rev II:11, XX:6). Augustine's *City of God*, written between AD 413 and 427, established the orthodox interpretation of these passages. The 'second death' is first mentioned in Book XIII chapter 2 [CG 510], but the decisive text is chapter 12 of the same book, where he remarks:

> the first death consist of two, the death of the soul and the death of the body; so that the first death is the death of the whole person, when the soul is without God and without a body, and undergoes punishment for a time. The second death, on the other hand, is when the soul is without God, but undergoes punishment with the body [CG 522].

He concludes this brief discussion with the words:

> the last or second death, which has no other death to follow it [CG 522].

The second death is thus aligned rigorously with eternal damnation, which is in turn conceived on the basis of the language found in *Revelation* and elsewhere: the *infernal* terminology that has provided the West with its imagery of ultimate torment for two millennia. To die the second time is to burn forever, suspended without cessation in the flames of Hell. This infinitely protracted combustion process transcends the terrestrial arbitrariness of the first death, constituting a limit to the operation of the negative; an unsurpassable incendiary horizon.

As is always the case with Augustine, his account is characterized by its vulgarity, gracelessness, and complete destitution of intelligence. This oafish crudity was to provide a crucial model for later Christian discourses on the subject, and captures very well the essentially brutal nature of the faith, which even the more spirited Christian writers would continue to propagate in the mode of traditional authority. Thus it is that Thomas Aquinas – who demonstrates intellectual and literary powers immeasurably outstripping those of Augustine – places those powers in the service of the Augustinian dogmas, typifying the most noble pattern of orthodox Christian culture: that of sophisticating an inherited spiritual loutishness.

It is Aquinas' stupendous *Summa Theologiae* – an intellectual cathedral that is perhaps the greatest single achievement of Christian civilization – that Bataille parodies in his own *Somme Athéologique* ('everything that one sees is the parody of another, or perhaps the same thing in a deceptive form' [I 81] as he remarks in *The Solar Anus*). It is Aquinas' meticulous construction of the inherited faith in this work that provides the first solid cultural foundations for the exercise of Christian authority, a function analogous to that of Kant in our own age (in which epistemology – or regulated scepticism – comes to replace theology under the impetus of a massive infrastructural transformation of socio-historical production processes). Aquinas began writing the *Summa* in 1265, when he was forty years old, and continued it – with intermittent interruptions – until his death in 1273. Far more than the messy, wildly inconsistent, and arbitrarily compiled text we know as 'the bible', it is the *Summa* that provides a doctrinal basis for hegemonic Christianity, and the return to primary scripture – associated above all with Luther – marks the beginning of an inexorable degeneration process.

The central accomplishment of the *Summa* is that of establishing a rational basis for the Augustinian rantings that had become embedded in the faith, and prominent amongst these is the conception of the 'second death' as eternal torment, bound to the doctrine of the soul's natural immortality (the deepest well-spring of Christian *ressentiment*). The heart of Aquinas' argumentation on this matter is found in the four articles of Question 104 [A XIV 35–55], which is arguably the most important text in the entire sweep of scholastic philosophy.

The position Aquinas inherited from Augustine can scarcely be described as philosophical. It is at most an attempt to construct some semblance of doctrinal consistency on the basis of conscientious but talentless scriptural exigesis conducted in the context of an anti-pagan polemic that aspires to persecutory authority. Not that this in any way compromises Augustine's claim to be exemplary of Judaeo-Christian piety, on the contrary; his rabid intolerance responds perfectly to the dominant tone of monotheistic belief. Nevertheless, one can only sympathize with Aquinas, trying to argue for the rationality of the faith, whilst behind him reverberate deranged barkings such as this:

> But in that last condemnation, although a man does not cease to feel, his feeling is not that of pleasure and delight, nor that of health and tranquillity. What he feels is the anguish of punishment, and so his condition is rightly called death rather than life. The second death is so called because it follows the first, in which there is a separation of natures which cohere together, either God and the soul, or the soul and the body. It can therefore be said of the first death that it is good for the good, bad for the bad; but the second death does not happen to any of the good, and without doubt it is not good for anyone [CG 511].

*

Aquinas' extraordinarily intricate task was to reconstruct the Christian doctrine of death on orthodox grounds (but this time rational ones), without succumbing to the humanistic impiety latent in the notion of the soul's natural immortality. Both Irenaeus and Arnobius had challenged this doctrine, considering it incompatible with the absolute dependence of all created things upon God, and even Augustine himself seems at times to undermine it. Once the natural immortality of the soul is questioned, however, it is but a short step to the thought that the unreformably wicked might be simply extinguished – after an appropriate period of rigorous punishment – rather than eternally tortured: a doctrine that Irenaeus seems to have held, and Arnobius certainly did. This is the extreme heresy of annihilationism, later to be associated with the Socinians (who were vigorously persecuted for it) and other Arians. It was considered so heinous a belief throughout the hegemonic period of Christian domination that professing it was literally suicidal, since it merited a reaction on the scale of atheism itself: torture and death (both first and second, although atheists were no doubt more concerned about the first). D.P. Walker, in his discussion of seventeenth and eighteenth century annihilationism, remarks that: 'atheists and Socinians, who were supposed to believe in the annihilation of the wicked, were generally considered outside the bounds of even the broadest religious tolerance; since they were socially dangerous, it was the business of the state to eliminate them' [DH 4].

It is thus a mark of considerable integrity that Aquinas – some 400 years earlier – insists upon the (limited) plausibility of the annihilationist case. He divides his argument into stages, first affirming God's power to annihilate, and only then denying that this power is in fact exercised by a benevolent being (eternal damnation as the sentimentality of God). He concedes, in the first stage of this argument:

> just as before things existed God had the power of not giving them existence, and thus of not creating, so also once they are created he has the power of not continuing to uphold them in existence; they would then cease to be. That is annihilation [*Quod est eas in nihilum redigere*] [A XIV 49].

Annihilation or – more precisely – the return to nothing, is related to two interconnected concepts of decisive importance to scholastic theology; those of *creation* and *conservation*. The *nihil* of annihilation is the nothing from which creation brings forth the being, since 'what is created comes out of nothing [ex nihilo]' [A VIII 41]. Creation both draws the being out of nothing, and holds it out of nothing, or conserves it. The perpetual conservation of the being is a positive and incessant causation that relates it immediately to God, so that '[w]ere God to annihilate, it would not be through some action, but through cessation from action' [A XIV 51]. Annihilation is thus a *release from action*; a relapse that has a merely negative relation to God. It is the being's own tendency that leads it to annihilation, as soon as God ceases to interfere in the creature's relation with absolute death (which is alien to God, since his relation to nothingness is purely inhibitive). In one sense the being of the creature communes with God as its cause, but as a difference from the *nihil* the tension of the creature relates only to death, and God's participation is that of a third party incidentally impinging upon a communication that escapes him. God and the *nihil* squabble over creation as jealous rivals fight over a shared lover, except that the creature – however much it might respect God – is torn by its desire in quite the other direction, whilst the *nihil* has all the tantalizing indifference that naturally flows from incomparable powers of seduction.

*

The heresy of annihilationism, by ridding itself of the distracting circus of damnation, clarifies the fundamental impetus of Judaeo-Christian monotheism as no other doctrine can. This God is the antagonist of zero, and therefore the fortress of identity, personality, individuation. To be exiled definitively from such a God – to lose his protection – is to relapse into indivisible non-being; decreated into the *nihil*. That annihilationism has failed to have a significant influence upon Christian orthodoxy attests in part to the tenacious privilege that folk religion and superstition have always maintained over intellectual consistency within the churches, but more importantly, it indicates the voluptuary and disciplinary investment in the thought of the eternal torment of the wicked (exemplified by Augustine).

For the pious annihilationist the perpetuation of existence beyond death is conceived as a reward, reserved only for the deserving, more precisely, the good. More profound than the vulgar empiricity of torment, it is non-being that is the true *punishment*. The souls of the wicked are subject to the undifferentiable pole of an absolute judgement; simple extinction. For those who remain stubbornly unenticed by the prospect of the long post-necroid haul under God there is thus a surgical and non-penitentiary alternative.

Like all blocks of reactive libido, annihilationist Christianity mapped a displaced active impulse within itself. Utter dissolution is offered as a lure, but safely imprisoned in a system of ethico-logical exclusion processes; permeable only to that inarticulate ardour which springs from the repressed materiality of the human animal. The taint of evil, or of divine (paternal) disapproval, serves as one barrier screening the ego from the non-image of death. Even more important – because more deeply concealed – is a trap simultaneous with the origin of the logical; that of viewing death from the perspective of God. God – a being – is conceived as thinking both being and its negation with unperturbed mastery, so that non-being is thought through the power of a (supreme) being; as being qualified by absolute impoverishment, and as the inferior pole of a bifurcation within being. Above all, non-being is simply to be thought, and the divine model of logical relatedness secures being in its privileges; adorning it in the robes of methodological presupposition. Death expresses the law, and thus subordinates itself to the highest being. The intellectual neutrality that is thus attributed to God in his comprehension of non-being is the real possibility of a thanatology, or logic of death.

Pious annihilationists are committed not only to the possibility of thanatology, but to its effective existence in the divine intellect, as the absolute pinnacle of reason and justice. For them thanatology is architecturally fundamental to divine law. Such servile annihilation is an eliminative negativity, which can be thought of in two broad ways: either as a formal or as a speculative relation (deconstruction is happy to accept it as either before displacing it). Formal elimination corresponds to a positivity understood as extraneous to its negative qualification, whilst speculative elimination – formalistically (mis)conceived – is the simultaneous inherence and non-inherence of such qualification to positivity. In both cases the content of such a negation is determined by that which is qualified by it, which is the precise definition of elimination. The Spinozistic principle that Hegel enthusiastically embraces as the speculative restlessness germinal in formal reasoning – *Omnis determinatio est negatio* – means that a positivity is determined by its exact elimination, or, in the words attributed to Hegel in the *Zusatz* to his lesser *Logic*: '[t]he foundation of all determinateness is negation' [H VIII 196].

The in- of indetermination can only be read as either the formal negation or the speculative development of determination if it is itself understood as eliminative, which is to say, determinate. Such a move is of course – when fully explicit – Hegelianism itself. Quite different is the indeterminate sense of indeterminate negation, which is not eliminative, but ferocious. Ferocious negation is radically heterogenous in respect to the annihilation it effects, so that it is intrinsic to its definition that it cannot be derived from its eliminative consequences by either formal or speculative logic. Far from being topic neutral, logic is reasoning from the basis of secure existence, which is to say, in the absence of time (Hegel thinks history, but not time). The laws of identity, non-contradiction, or determinate negation attain their rigour only by qualifying itself with respect to metamorphosis: insisting upon the simultaneity of logical relations, or the absence of temporal differentiation (asynchronicity). Such a qualification is constitutive for ideality, whether in the weak (scientific) or the strong (theological) sense. In other words; ideality is nothing other than logical obedience or pure being, and the topic of logic is ontology. It is unfortunate for the logicians that suicide is not a mere decision, but also a technical problem, exemplifying the irreducibly heterogeneous relation between the 'being' and its potential for inexistence (which is never even remotely its own). Such a heterogeneity is attested more generally by the *struggle for oblivion* and the positivity of the sacrificial process. It is the ferocity of death that entangles it in eroticism. 'The sexual act is in time what the tiger is in space' [VII 21]. Unlike a logical negation, death requires a complex occasion: intricate conjunctions, the interpenetration of bodies, turbulent flows. There are innumerable ways to die, but this proliferation of routes out of the maze does not lead to the simplicity of a general negative possibility.

Ferocity is not reflectively determined through the exercise of a negation, indeed, it has no determination at all, but only a real composition generated in a violent collision of heterogeneous elements, whose issue is a complex synthesis. The various negativities consummated in complex syntheses have no logical equivalence, but only real consistency, or, in Bataille's terms, *community*. It is because the realization of expenditure requires the assemblage of a complex synthesis that there is a problem of consumption, finding its inevitable issue in an impossibility, in the sensation of dying or undeath: existence out of excess. Nature, far from being logical, 'is perhaps entirely the excess of itself' [III 219], smeared ash and flame upon zero, and zero is immense.

Chapter 7

Fanged noumenon
(passion of the cyclone)

The supreme concept with which it is customary to begin a transcendental philosophy is the division into the possible and the impossible. But since all division presupposes a concept to be divided, a still higher one is required, and this is the concept of an object in general, taken problematically, without its having been decided whether it is something or nothing [K III 305–6].

what matters is not the enunciation of the wind, but the wind [V 25].

*

Peter Hillmore's report for the *Observer* [5th May 1991, p.23] begins:

> As idle as a painted ship upon a painted ocean. The water is still now, almost unnaturally so as if it was resting from its monumental act of carnage, exhausted by its orgasmic tidal surge.
> Nothing seems to move. The water, so savage last week, now laps gently round the bodies. Half-embedded in the mud and very, very still, a child lies in the water, arms and legs stiffly outstretched, its body bloated by the heat, its face battered and bloody.
> Next to it lies the body of a calf, its eyes wide in final uncomprehending shock. A few yards away in the middle of the road lie the bodies of two dead fish, as if the sea had even turned on its own.

The state of Bangladesh, until 1971 East Pakistan, is nestled in the delta complex of the Ganges and Brahmaputra rivers, and is amongst the poorest as well as the most densely populated regions of the earth. It is a country whose natural inheritance is a mixture of fertility and disaster, and whose people are exposed by their poverty to the unimpeded course of elemental forces; rendered naked before the storms. Since records began in the eighteenth century at least 1.2 million Bangladeshis have been killed by cyclones, as many as half a million in the storm of 1970 alone.

Cyclones are atmospheric machines that transform latent energy into angular momentum in a feed-back process of potentially catastrophic consequence. Their conditions of emergence are a warm water surface, a latitude of at least five or six degrees deviation from the equator (such that the Coriolis effect is operative), a pronounced instability in the air column or a low surface pressure, and the absence or virtual absence of wind shear. When these conditions coexist a cyclone can develop, over a period that normally lasts from four to eight days. A large cyclone transfers 3.5 billion tons of air an hour from the lower to upper atmosphere, and releases energy in the order of 10^{25} ergs every second. At the centre of the cyclone is a still zone of low pressure known as the 'eye' or 'core' which registers no radar echo, and which functions as the immobile motor of the storm's angular momentum or expressed energy[11].

Large cyclones have the impact of immense explosions, and when they strike the coast of Bangladesh they leave a shock-wave in the silt, throwing-up numerous evanescent islands in the shallows of the gulf of Bengal. Due to the general hunger for land, and the richness of the sediment that has been carried down to the sea, these fragile traces are enthusiastically occupied, rice is cultivated upon them, and fish harvested from their shores. It takes no great feat of imagination to envisage the fate of the peasants and fishermen clustered on these insubstantial ripples of earth when the cyclone returns, and instantaneously consumes the tenuous vestiges of previous ravages. The densely inhabited silt traces are not merely flooded, but utterly erased, as everything which had seemed solid is dissolved into the vortex of the storm. The people of the Bangladesh coast are episodically consumed by a harsh truth from which we can momentarily hide. Being a patriarchal faith, or doctrine of identity, the Islamic culture predominant in Bangladesh is no better a preparation for this liquidation than Judaism or Christianity would be. Nevertheless, an annihilation such as that of the cyclone – in which all stability is washed away and loss alone prevails – is not merely a disaster, but religion.

*

Of the 'terrain of pure understanding' Kant says:

> This domain is an island, enclosed by nature itself within unalterable limits. It is the land of truth – enchanting name! – surrounded by a wide and stormy ocean, the native home of illusion, where many a fog bank and many a swiftly melting iceberg give the deceptive appearance of farther shores, deluding the adventurous seafarer ever anew with empty hopes, and engaging him in enterprises which he can never abandon and yet is unable to carry to completion [K III 267–8].

Is not transcendental philosophy a fear of the sea? Something like a dike or a sea-wall?

A longing for the open ocean gnaws at us, as the land is gnawed by the sea. A dark fluidity at the roots of our nature rebels against the security of *terra firma*, provoking a wave of anxiety in which we are submerged, until we feel ourselves drowning, with representation draining away. *Nihil ulterius*

Incipit Kant:

We are not amphibians, but belong upon solid earth. Let us renounce all strange voyages. The age of desire is past. The new humanity I anticipate has no use for enigmatic horizons; it knows the ocean is madness and disease. Let me still your ancient tremors, and replace them with dreams of an iron shore.

Reason in its legitimate function is a defence against the sea, which is also an inhibition of the terrestrial; retarding our tendency to waste painstakingly accumulated resources in futile expeditions, a 'barrier opposed to the expenditure of forces' [II 332] as Bataille describes it. It is a fortified boundary, sealing out everything uncertain, irresolvable, dissolvant, a sea-wall against the unknown, against death. This is a structure continuous with the great land reclamation projects of Frederick II of Hohenstaufen: a matter of drainage, rigorous separation of the wet and the dry, eradication of marshes and ambiguous terrains, rigidification of the soil ('the mosquitos and other stinging insects that make the wilds of America so trying for the savages, may be so many goads to urge these primitive men to drain the marshes and bring light into the dense forests that shut out the air, and, by so doing, as well as by the tillage of the soil, to render their abodes more sanitary' [K X 328]). Such terrestrialism reaches its zenith in Prussia's classic age; in the restriction of policy to continental ambitions. It is thus characterized by a certain hardness; a certain deliberate blindness towards death, as towards everything that flows freely like a wound.

Unlike either Schopenhauer or Nietzsche, who in different ways seek to place themselves outside the ambit of an Occidental history dominated by the monotheistic order of the supreme object, and to connect with the east Asiatic zero that contests it, Bataille seems to resign himself to a struggle *without refuge* against the One. Far more even than Nietzsche, Bataille thinks of zero as a subtraction from One – as the death of God – and approaches it in anguish. In this way he aligns himself with a procedure of immense influence upon the course of European modernity, that of a progressive problematization from unity, harmonized with the dissolution of sedentary community. The most powerful example of such thinking is to be found in the cultural heartland of capital, which is to say, in the critical philosophy initiated by Kant.

*

Bataille 'interrupts' [V 29] *Inner Experience* in order to make a few pages of remarks about Hinduism, in a section which ends with a technical argument designed to reinforce his claim to be no more interested in liberation from rebirth than in any other type of salvation. He compares the asceticism of Hinduism to that of Christianity, distancing himself from both in the name of excess, and pretends to no affinity with 'the naïvety – the purity – of the Hindu' [V 30]. Perhaps most important of all is the affirmation of mess and inadequacy implicit in the words: 'I do not doubt that the Hindus go far into the impossible, but *to the highest degree* they lack that which matters to me; the faculty of expression' [V 31]. It is because he is a writer that Bataille disdains to be a mystic. In what he understands of the Hindu religion – and he lays claim to no intimate knowledge of it – there is one tenet alone to which he unconditionally subscribes: '[o]nly intensity matters' [V 29].

Inner experience translates mysticism into a vagrant vocabulary at the scurf-edge of tradition. As the initial gesture of a *Summa Atheologica*, it begins amongst the ruins of God. Echoing Céline – that other wretched tramp of nihilism – he calls experience 'a voyage to the end of the possible of man' [V 19], and thinks interiority not as the secret recess of the self, but as a plane of contact and contagion. The core of inner experience is not personal identity, but naked intensity, denuded even of oneself, and jutting from the refuse of Christian dogmatics as a broken lurch into the unknown. He insists: 'inner experience is ecstasy' whilst 'ecstasy is . . . communication, opposing itself to the subsidence onto oneself' [V 24].

It is the order of the object that organizes inner experience as private reverie, and as a detachment from relation. Above all it is the God of monotheism − the supreme or absolute being − which reproduces the prison of individuation at the scale of the cosmos. This is why the ecstasy of the unknown, which gnaws away the last landmarks from Bataille's voyage, contests any possible resurrection of theological edifices. As he remarks:

> I hold the apprehension of God, even when formless and without mode . . . for an arrest of the movement which carries us to the more obscure apprehension of the *unknown* . . . [V 17].

An utter intoxication such as this is quite different from its Kantian anticipation, although Kant too contests the right of dogmatic theology to guide his journey:

> Nothing but the sobriety of a critique, at once strict and just, can free us from this dogmatic delusion, which through the lure of an imagined felicity keeps so many in bondage to theories and systems. Such a critique confines all our speculative claims rigidly to the field of possible experience; and it does this not by shallow scoffing at ever-repeated failures or pious sighs over the limits of our reason, but by an effective determining of these limits in accordance with established principles, inscribing *nihil ulterius* on those Pillars of Hercules which nature herself has erected in order that the voyage of our reason may be extended no further than the continuous coastline of experience itself reaches − a coast we cannot leave without venturing upon a shoreless ocean which, after alluring us with ever-deceptive prospects, compels us in the end to abandon as hopeless all this vexatious and tedious endeavour [K IV 392−3].

For Kant it is not enough to have reached the ocean, the shoreless expanse, the *nihil ulterius* as positive zero. He recognizes the ocean as a space of absolute voyage, and thus of hopelessness and waste. Only another shore would redeem it for him, and that is nowhere to be found. Better to remain on dry land than to lose oneself in the desolation of zero. It is for this reason that he says the 'concept of a noumenon is . . . a merely *limiting concept*' [K IV 282].

In this way the Occidental obsession with the object consummates itself in the blind passivity of its nihilism. Beyond experience, it is suggested, there must be thought 'an unknown something' [K III 283], although 'we are unable to comprehend how such noumena can be possible' [K III 281]. More precisely:

> [The noumenon] . . . is not indeed in any way positive, and is not a determinate knowledge of anything, but signifies only the thought of something in general, in which I abstract from everything that belongs to the form of sensible intuition [K III 281].

That no transcendent object is found is an event which retains the sense of a lost or absent object, rather than that of a contact with or through objectlessness. The ocean has no sense except as a failure of the land. Even whilst supposedly knowing nothing of the noumenon, which, we are told, has 'no assignable meaning' [K III 303], one somehow still knows that it would be something other than objectless waste without end, or the void-plane touched upon at zero-intensity. Kant is peculiarly adamant in this respect:

> [W]e cannot think of any way in which such intelligible objects might be given. The problematic thought which leaves open a place for them serves only, like an empty space, for the limitation of empirical principles, without itself containing or revealing any other object of knowledge beyond the sphere of those principles [K III 285].

The noumenon is the absence of the subject, and is thus inaccessible in principle to experience. If there is still a so-called 'noumenal subject' in the opening phase of the critical enterprise it is only because a residue of theological reasoning conceives a stratum of the self which is invulnerable to transition, or synonymous with time as such. This is the 'real' or 'deep' subject, the self or soul, a subject that sloughs-off its empirical instantiation without impairment, the immortal subject of mortality. It only remains for Hegel to rigorously identify this subject with death, with the death necessitated by the allergy of *Geist* to its finitude, to attain a conception of death *for itself*. But this is all still the absence of the subject, even when 'of' is translated into the subjective genitive, and at zero none of it makes any difference.

With Kant death finds its theoretical formulation and utilitarian frame as a quasi-objectivity correlative to capital, and *noumenon* is its name. The effective flotation of this term in philosophy coincided with the emergence of a social order built upon a profound rationalization of excess, or rigorous circumscription of voluptuous lethality. Once enlightenment rationalism begins its dominion ever fewer corpses are left hanging around in public places with each passing year, ever fewer skulls are used as paperweights, and ever fewer paupers perish undisturbed on the streets. Even the graveyards are rationalized and tidied up. It is not surprising, therefore, that with Kant thanatology undergoes the most massive reconstruction in its history. The clerical vultures are purged, or marginalized. Death is no longer to be culturally circulated, injecting a transcendent reference into production, and ensuring superterrestrial interests their rights. Instead death is privatized, withdrawn into interiority, to flicker at the edge of the contract as a narcissistic anxiety without public accreditation. Compared to the immortal soul of capital the death of the individual becomes an empirical triviality, a mere re-allocation of stock.

In the *Analytic of the Sublime* in his Third Critique Kant tentatively raises the possibility that we might taste death – even if only through a 'negative pleasure' – but nowhere does he raise the possibility that death might savage us. Even when positivized as noumenon, death remains locked in the chain of connotations that passes through matter, inertia, femininity, and castration, resting in its pacified theistic sense as toothless resource and malleable clay. There is no place, no domain, for base matter in Kant's thinking, since even auto-generativity in nature is conceived as a regulative analogue of rational willing. One must first unleash the noumenon from its determination as problematic object in order to glimpse that between matter and death there is both a certain identity and an intricate relation, or, in other words: a unilateral difference appending matter to the edge of zero. Not that this complicity has anything to do with the inertia crucial to the mathematical idealization of matter, or with any other kind of mechanical sterility. Matter is no more simply dead than it is *simply* anything else, because simplicity is the operator of the transcendent disjunction between subject and object which effaces base materiality. The death 'proper' to matter is the jagged edge of its impropriety, its teeth.

If death can bite it is not because it retains some fragment of a potency supposedly proper to the object, but because it remains uncaged by the inhibition objectivity entails. Death alone is utterly on the loose, howling as the dark motor of storms and epidemics. After the ruthless abstraction of all life the blank savagery of real time remains, for it is the reality of abstraction itself that is time: the desert, death, and desolator of all things. Bataille writes of 'the ceaseless slippage of everything into nothing. If one wants, time' [V 137], and thinks of himself as 'a tooth of TIME' [I 558]. It could also be said – in a more Nietzschean vein – that zero-becoming has its metaphor in a bird of prey, for which every object is a lamb.

Repression always fails, but nowhere is there a more florid example of such failure than the attempt to bury death quietly on the outskirts of the city and get down to business. Only the encrusted historical superficies of zero are trapped in the clay, distilling death down to its ultimate liquidity, and maximizing its powers of infiltration. Marx notes this filtration process in *Capital*, where he remarks about money/death that it 'does not vanish on dropping out of the circuit of the metamorphosis of a given commodity. It is constantly being precipitated into new places in the arena of circulation vacated by other commodities' [Cap 114]. Dead labour is far harder to control than the live stuff was, which is why the enlightenment project of interring gothic superstition was the royal road to the first truly vampiric civilization, in which death alone comes to rule.

*

Politics is the archaic and inadequate name for something that must pass away into the religious history of capital. There are no effective anti-capitalist interests, but only anti-bourgeois desires in alliance with zero. The notorious asceticism of accumulative Protestantism already prefigures the suicide of the last ruling class, anticipating the definitive surrender of all humanity to death. Marx says in the *Grundrisse*:

> The cult of money has its asceticism, its self-denial, its self-sacrifice – economy and frugality, contempt for mundane, temporal and fleeting pleasures; the chase after the *eternal* treasure. Hence the connection between English puritanism, or also Dutch protestantism, and money making [Gr 232].

Weber remarks: 'this asceticism turned with all its force against one thing: the spontaneous enjoyment of life and all it had to offer'

[PES 166]. This is the initial impulse into capital's religious history; the sacrifice of all dogmatic theology to the ascetic ideal, which is finally consummated in the death of God. The theology of the One, rooted in concrete beliefs and codes that summarize and defend the vital interests of a community, and therefore affiliated to a tenacious anthropomorphism, is gradually corroded down to the impersonal zero of catastrophic religion. In its early stages capital is still a matter of self-control, but after a couple of centuries its rigid ethos withers away, because there is no effective self left to resist it. To quote Weber again:

> Man is dominated by the making of money, by acquisition as the ultimate purpose of his life. Economic acquisition is no longer subordinated to man as the means for the satisfaction of his material needs. This reversal of what we should call the natural relationship, so irrational from a naïve point of view, is evidently as definitely a leading principle of capitalism as it is foreign to all peoples not under capitalistic influence. At the same time it expresses a type of feeling which is closely connected with certain religious ideas [PES 53].

and:

> The capitalistic economy of the present day [1904–5!] is an immense cosmos into which the individual is born, and which presents itself to him, at least as an individual, as an unalterable order of things in which he must live. It forces the individual, in so far as he is involved in the system of market relationships, to conform to capitalistic rules of action. The manufacturer who in the long run acts counter to these norms, will just as inevitably be eliminated from the economic scene as the worker who cannot or will not adapt himself to them will be thrown into the streets without a job [PES 55].

Once the commodity system is established there is no longer a need for an autonomous cultural impetus into the order of the abstract object. Capital attains its own 'angular momentum', perpetuating a run-away whirlwind of dissolution, whose hub is the virtual zero of impersonal metropolitan accumulation. At the peak of its productive prowess the human animal is hurled into a new nakedness, as everything stable is progressively liquidated in the storm.

Bataille associates the unknown with 'a vertiginous movement towards the void' [V 94] which he also describes as 'the rending fall into the void of the heavens' [V 93], collapsing two themes into each other which Kant had strained to keep apart, those of noumenon and intensive zero. It is frequently suggested in the writings of the immediately post-Kantian generation that Kant illegitimately differentiates noumena from each other, and Bataille shares a broadly Schopenhauerian impetus in his response to this issue, but it is not until Nietzsche that the differentiation between noumenon and zero is vigorously interrogated, and even then this is only undertaken in a sporadic and elliptical fashion. It is first of all Bataille, and later Deleuze, who respond to this matter with irresistible tenacity, and thus undercut the phenomenological stumblings that have been the more common retort to the Kantian challenge.

Where Kant resists the conflation of noumenon from zero-intensity, Bataille runs them convulsively into each other. All his writings – irrespective of whether they are marked by a predominantly literary or philosophical character – are cut-up by oblivion, discontinuity, and incompletion. Zero alone cannot be fragmented, divided, or partitioned – being undifferentiability without unity – but the expense of this continuity for discrete being is without limit:

> We are not totally denuded except in going without fraudulence to the unknown. It is the part of the unknown which gives to the experience of God – or of poetry – their great authority. But the unknown demands in the end an empire without division [V 17].

*

In the First Critique Kant differentiates between four divisions of nothing, reciprocally correlated to the four classes of the categories. These are the *ens rationis* or empty concept without object, the *nihil privativum* or empty object of a concept, the *ens imaginarium* or empty intuition without object, and the *nihil negativum* or empty object without concept [K III 306–7]. It is the first of these nothingnesses which applies to the noumenon, as Kant writes:

> To the concepts of all, many, and one there is opposed the concept which cancels everything, that is, *none*. Thus the object of a concept to which no assignable intuition whatsoever corresponds is = nothing. That is, it is a concept without an object (*ens rationis*), like noumena, which cannot be reckoned

among the possibilities, although they must not for that reason be declared to be also impossible . . . [K III 306].

Kant makes the indifferentiating gesture '= nothing' in relation to the noumenon, but only amongst a systematic obliteration of illimitable zero; crushing it under the categories of the object which – according to their four classes – stamp it with inverse features of mathematical unity, semantic definition, substantial reciprocity, and logical identity. It is crucial to the historical force of Bataille's thought of sacrifice that it contests both the general tendency of this Kantian articulation and each of its particular elements. Rather than sharing the features of subtraction, deprivation, impotence, and dialectic, which Kant allots to the four aspects of nothing, sacrifice characterizes zero as undifferentiably pre-unitary, extravagant, unilateral, and impossible.

The noumenon is not primarily an epistemological problem, but a religious one. Bataille writes that 'a sort of rupture – in anguish – leaves us at the limit of tears: thus we lose ourselves, we forget ourselves and communicate with an ungraspable beyond' [V 23]. When he adds that 'the sole truth of man, finally glimpsed, is to be a supplication without response' [V 25], it is not being suggested that a reference to alterity is inherent to experience in a phenomenological fashion, but rather, that experience is immanent to the trajectory of loss or sacrifice, in terms of which it is a real modification or limitation. The relation of the known to the unknown is unilateral not reciprocal, following the pattern of the difference between restricted and general economy. Zero is exploded into general economy, in which '[d]eath is in a sense a deception' [V 83] because there is no privacy at zero, only the undifferentiable cosmic desert, impersonal silence, a landscape touched upon only in the deepest abysses of inhuman affect. 'Despair is simple' Bataille writes, 'it is the absence of all hope, of every *lure*. It is the state of desolate expanses and – I can imagine – of the sun' [V 51]. This is the terrain of immanence or the unknown; positive death as zero-intensity, unilaterally differentiated from ecstasy or naked sensation. It is the whole ramshackle complex associated with the taste of death in Bataille's writings, leading him to remark in *Inner Experience*, for instance: 'I remain in intolerable unknowing, which has no issue other than ecstasy itself' [V 25].

Throughout his writings Bataille implicitly or explicitly repeats a deft materialist gesture, indicating that transcendent dogma does not lie in the positing of an outside to experience, but rather, in the positing of experience as dissociated from its slide into oblivion. Experience can never comprehend or define dissolvant immanence, and the claim that it might can be symptomatologically interpreted as the consequence of a utilitarian reconstruction into objectivity. It is thus that Bataille reiterates Nietzsche's diagnosis concerning the moral basis of epistemology. The very possibility of a problem about the relation between experience and the real – requiring a theory of representation – presupposes the deformation of experience in terms of the 'good', or, in other words, the stable, isolated, and determinate, correlated to the caging of noumenon in the form of the object. In wild variance to the basic presupposition of overt or cunning idealism, experience is not given in reality as knowledge, but as collapse.

Just as Kant domesticates the noumenon by defining it as an object, so he domesticates zero-intensity by conceiving it as pure consciousness. The vestigial traces of the subject/object relation – i.e. of epistemology – constrain the movement of inner experience by substantializing a pole of knowing and a pole known, even at 'pure intuition = 0' [K III 208–9]. It is to refuse such constraint that Bataille insists that: '[e]xperience finishes by attaining the fusion of subject and object, being unknowing subject, like unknown object' [V 21], and remarks of 'oneself' that 'this is not the subject isolated from the world, but a place of communication, fusion of subject and object' [V 21]. In this shift from the transcendental idealist treatment of zero to that of base materialism there is a difference of seismic consequence. The discussion of zero-intensity in Kant's *Schematism*, for instance, is securely framed by an immunized inner-sense, and characterized by the idealistic structures of representation and reversibility:

> Now every sensation has a degree or magnitude whereby, in respect of its representation of an object otherwise remaining the same, it can fill out one and the same time, that is, occupy inner sense more or less completely, down to its cessation in nothingness (= 0 = *negatio*). There therefore exists a relation and connection between reality and negation, or rather a transition from the one to the other, which makes every reality representable as a quantum. The schema of a reality, as the quantity of something insofar as it fills time, is just this continuous and

uniform production of that reality in time as we successively descend from a sensation which has a certain degree to its vanishing point, or progressively ascend from its negation to some magnitude of it [K III 191].

This is a particularly extreme passage, much of which he will later qualify, accepting that 'sensation is not in itself an objective representation' [K III 208], for instance, and also massively problematizing the possibility of empty intuitions. Nevertheless, despite all such subtilizations, Kant never swerves from his stubborn insistence upon thinking zero in terms of the privacy of the individuated subject. This humanist usage of the *nihil privativum* is nowhere illustrated more starkly than in the words:

> from empirical consciousness to pure consciousness a graduated transition is possible, the real in the former completely vanishing and a merely formal *a priori* consciousness of the manifold in space and time remaining [K III 208].

Purity is, of course, a motif of almost inestimable importance throughout the entirety of Kant's critical writings. Of its many functions there is one that can be glimpsed with particularly sharp definition in this passage, which is that of the subjectification of abstraction, or the sublimation of death into a power of the subject. The extinction of the subject is floated speculatively as a representational schema, through which thought seizes an autonomy for itself over against the passivity of sensation. Kant does not deny that pure consciousness is oblivion, death, or the subject in itself – which is to say that it is nothing ($= 0$) – he simply evades the issue, implicitly consigning it to the imagination.

Purity is a negation to the second power, through which death de-realizes even itself. Thinking these negations bilaterally leads to a transcendental idealism and an immaculate morality, whilst echoing them unilaterally leads to a base materialism and a diseased religion. On the one hand the tendency to autonomy is soberly reinforced, on the other it is deliriously ruined. Death is either paralysed by God or drowned in matter.

Kant is no less aware than Bataille that at issue there is a question of continuous flow. In the *Anticipations of Perception* he notes that:

> The property of magnitudes by which no part of them is the smallest possible, that is, by which no part is simple, is called

their continuity . . . Such magnitudes may be called *flowing*, since the synthesis of productive imagination involved in their production is a progression in time, and the continuity of time is ordinarily designated by the term flowing or flowing away [K III 211].

In the end it is the domesticated character of the Kantian notion of time which forestalls the lurch of this thought to a base materialist conclusion. Purity conditions the *a priori*, which hypostasizes time as such, which in turn idealizes intensity. Flow as such is thus fixed as an eternal form of representation, frozen in an endless descent to zero. It is for this reason that Kant has an entirely ahistorical comprehension of intensity, failing to grasp the positive order of its repression: the inhibition of flow (continuity). In other words: he does not raise a problem of the object with sufficient radicality to escape from the cage of epistemology in the direction of a libidinal or base materialism. He does not acknowledge that between the noumenon and zero intensity there is no difference, or that neither are susceptible to isolation. Above all, he nowhere seems to suspect the obvious fact that zero is the primary repressed of monotheistic cultures, so that its intensive impact is historically saturated. Bataille digs demolitionally into the fault-lines of all these evasions in a single comment: 'the extreme is at the end, is nowhere except at the end, like death' [V 57].

*

Bataille's break with Kantian humanism is characterized by a ruthless exactness, as it moves sure-footedly from one fissure of disintegration to another. Continuum is wrested definitively from humanist containment, the order of the object is contested with a profundity at the scale of zero, and interiority is denuded to the point of impersonal intensity. In *Method of Meditation* he replies to critics of *Inner Experience*:

> I understand by *continuum* a continuous medium which is the human collectivity, opposing itself to a rudimentary representation of indivisible and decidedly separated *individuals*.
>
> The critiques that have been made of *Inner Experience* which give to 'torment' an exclusively individual sense reveal the limit, in relation to *continuum*, of the individuals which have made them. That there exists a point of *continuum* where the test of 'torment' is inevitable, is not merely incapable of being denied,

this point, situated at the extreme, defines the human being (the *continuum*) [V 195].

The human animal is the one through which terrestrial excess is haemorrhaged to zero, the animal destined to obliterate itself in history, and sacrifice its nature utterly to the solar storm. Capital breaks us down and reconstructs us, with increasing frequency, as it pursues its energetic fluctuation towards annihilation, driven to the liberation of the sun, whilst the object hurtles into the vaporization of proto-schizophrenic commodification. By tapping into the deep flows of history Bataille ensures that intensity is no longer thought of as anticipated perception, but as the ecstasy of the death of God, delirial dissolution of the One:

> Above all *no more object*. Ecstasy is not love: love is possession to which the object is necessary, at once possessor of the subject, and possessed by it. There is no longer subject = object, but a 'gaping breach' between one and the other and, in the breach, the subject, the object are dissolved, there is passage, communication, but not from the one to the other, *the one* and *the other* have lost distinct existence [V 74].

Desire responds to the cosmic madness pulsed out of the sun, and slides beyond love towards utter communication. This is a final break with Christendom, the disconnection of base flow from the terminal sentimentalism of Western man, nihilism as nakedness before the cyclone. Libido no longer as the energy of love, but as a raw energy that loves only as an accident of impersonal passion. Communion through the storm, no longer through resentment at it. At the level of the secondary process a trickle of relief supplies expresses the actual parsimony of the West in its relation to Bangladesh, but at the stratum of primary desire the West is exacerbated in its virtual generosity; in its cyclone passion (which is not merely a passion for the cyclone).

> Man differs from animal in that he is able to experience certain sensations that wound and melt him to the core. These sensations vary in keeping with the individual and with his specific way of living. But, for example, the sight of blood, the odour of vomit, which arouse in us the dread of death, sometimes introduce us into a kind of nauseous state which hurts more cruelly than pain. Those sensations associated with the supreme giving-way, the final collapse, are unbearable. Are there

not some persons who claim to prefer death to touching an even completely harmless snake? There seems to exist a domain where death signifies not only decrease and disappearance, but the unbearable process by which we disappear *despite ourselves* and everything we can do, even though, *at all costs*, we *must not* disappear. It is precisely this *despite ourselves*, this *at all costs*, which distinguish the moment of extreme joy and of indescribable but miraculous ecstasy. If there is nothing that surpasses our powers and our understanding, if we do not acknowledge something greater than ourselves, greater than we are *despite ourselves*, something which *at all costs must* not be, then we do not reach the *insensate* moment towards which we strive with all that is in our power and which at the same time we exert all our power to stave off [III 11].

Chapter 8
Fluent bodies
(a digression on Miller)

If now the brain and spinal cord together constitute that corporeal *being-for-self* of spirit, the skull and vertebral column form the other extreme of it, an extreme which is separated off, viz. the solid, inert thing [H III 246].

In order to find one's way in a maze of this kind it is unfortunately necessary to resume things historically. The important thing ... is the fundamental and originary division between two principles, spirit and matter. Insofar as that division is established, there is, whatever one says, a superiority of spirit over matter, and spirit harvests all conceivable superiority, that is; on one side the divine, and on the other reason [VII 368].

the whiteness
of the sea
and the paleness of the light
concealed the bones [III 369].

To revert to a naïve question: what 'is' matter? Is it possible that we could receive a message that could respond to this interrogation? There is an anthropocentric conception of messages as transmissions between beings that share a code. According to such a definition the reception of a message depends upon a prior agreement with the sender. One can receive messages from other humans, or from personal beings such as God or angels, as long as there is a pre-established system of significations. If a message is not coded according to the rules of a familiar system it might still be possible to translate it into the terms of such a system, deciphering or interpreting it. It is thus possible for messages to be retrieved from extinct languages, as long as sufficient similarity exists between them and familiar languages for a systematic series of correspondences to be established. Such similarities can be described as the 'formal' or 'structural' properties of the signifying system, distinguished from its 'material' or 'empirical' instantiation.

Methods of structural analysis have the great 'advantage' that they are able to exclude extraneous aspects from consideration, ignoring everything except for the formal relations between the terms – signifiers – of the message. The densely encrustated matter of historical associations, which is the impurity inherent in real transmission, can be washed away from the message like the mud from a fossil. One need not be prejudiced about where the text came from. As for the formal relations that remain; they are also a matter of exclusion: this time the exclusion each term operates upon the others, sublimating itself into a transcendent unity, a pure nexus of articulation.

Developments in the technology of information have lent urgency and concreteness to the study of codes. Techniques have arisen for the translation of messages into codes built out of a single alternative (bilaterized and reciprocal) of 'one' and 'zero'. These are digital codes, according to which messages can be generated by the presence/absence (flow/blockage) of an electric current. Such codes are readily adaptable to machines which can transmit, store, and operate upon information of a logical and mathematical kind, since decimal numbers can be converted into digital ones, and logical functions are easily reproduced by 'logic gates'. With an appropriate coding system any system of symbols can be allotted its digital equivalent; a series of binary digits ('bits') adequate to specify it. A precise quantitative determination can be given for the minimal length for sequences of bits required to recode an alphabet of symbols n: $\log_2 n$.

*

Bataille exhibits no positive interest in the philosophies of structure (to which he was, in any case, scarcely exposed). Like the thermodynamicists and information theorists his concerns lay not with the analysis of discontinuity, but with its explanation, or rather, with the genealogy of its cultural presupposition. Far from being a possible content of articulated signs, Bataille's matter is that which must be repressed as the condition of articulation, whereby immanent continuity is vivisected in transcendence. The importance of structural thought is real, but symptomatological; incarnating matter's positive effacement by utilitarian sociality. In a short early text called *Architecture* he writes:

> each time that *architectural composition* is found elsewhere than in monuments, whether this is in physionomy, costume, music or painting, one is able to infer a taste for *authority*, whether human or divine. The great compositions of certain painters express the will to constrain the spirit to an official ideal. The disappearance of academic construction in painting is, on the contrary, the open road to the expression (and thus even to exultation) in the pychological processes most incompatible with social stability. It is this that explains in large part the lively reactions provoked for over half a century by the progressive transformation of painting, up to then characterized by a sort of dissimulated architectural skeleton [I 171].

Structure, bilateral articulation, reciprocal exclusion, and determinate negation all belong to bones and not to soft tissues. That structure comes to the fore is a matter of the momentary dominion of the profane:

> For primitive people the moment of greatest anguish is the phase of decomposition; when the bones are bare and white they are not intolerable as the putrefying flesh is, food for worms [X 59].

*

The ahistorical, descriptive, and normalizing study of language usage is pragmatics, which can be contrasted with the historical, epidemic, and aberrational experiments in flow summarized as 'libidinal-' or 'base materialism'. Base materialism is the plague of unilateral difference, which is a difference that only operates from out of the undifferentiated. Thinking of this kind is flagrantly inconsistent with the principle of identity. The aberrant phenomena summarized under the label 'spirit', for instance, are spiritually differentiated from matter, whilst remaining materially undifferentiated from it. Similarly, culture is only culturally different from nature, such that the most strenuous deviations from nature leave nature uninterrupted. The human animal rebels unilaterally against its animality, just as life differentiates itself against and within the undifferentiable desert of death. A unilateral difference is the simultaneity of a tendency to separation and a persistence of continuity, which is a thought that cannot be grasped, but only succumbed to in delirium. For any ardent materialism truth is madness.

The dominant tendencies in philosophy are complicit with ordinary language in their supression of unilateral differences, and their insistence upon bilateral or reciprocal relations. Because separation is normally thought of as mutual discontinuity, the world is interpreted as an aggregate of isolated beings, which are extrinsically amalgamated into structures, systems, and societies. Such thinking precludes in principle all possibility of base contact or communion.

Spawned by unilateral difference, the human animal is a hybrid of sentience and pathology; or of differentiated consistency with matter. Knowing that its community with nature sucks it into psychosis and death mankind valorizes its autonomy, whilst cursing the tidal desires that tug it down towards fusional dissolution. Morality is thus the distilled imperative to autonomous integrity, which brands as evil the impulse to skinless contact and the merging of bodies.

Base materialism is compelled to acknowledge that Henry Miller is a 'saint' [XI 46], and that the *Tropic of Cancer* is a sacred book.

*

To an important degree Miller's *Tropic of Cancer* responds to the surrealist culture of 1930s' Paris, especially to the creative practice of 'automatic writing' which entangles literature with sexuality in a guerrilla struggle against repression. The stylistic infelicities and thematic confusions of his writing are inextricable from its force as a seismic upheaval in the history of literature, stemming as they do from his passionate rebellion against the normative regulations of aesthetic and moral censorship. It is precisely the jagged and meandering character of this text that attest to its torrential emancipatory energy; liberating writing from the pedantic bourgeois delicacies that cage literature in the prison of the ego. In the opening pages he insists that: 'I have made a compact with myself not to change a line of what I write. I am not interested in perfecting my thoughts, nor my actions' [TC 19]. The unconscious does not coo sweet lyrics or unroll immaculate and measured prose, it howls and raves like the shackled and tortured beast that our civilization has made of it, and when the fetters are momentarily loosened the unconscious does not thank the ego for this meagre relief, but hisses, spits, and bites, as any wild thing would.

This is not to suggest that Miller is without inhibition. He is, for instance, notorious for his misogyny. It is obvious to anyone reading his books that women frighten him. It is not mere fear that grips him but anxiety; terror of nothing, the horror that patriarchy interprets in terms of castration. Who is in a position to condemn him for this hesitancy at the brink of dissolution? Is it not rather the nakedness of his avowal that triggers an inane and moralistic response? Phallus is the great security of male-dominated culture, and beyond it lies an ocean of loss as desolate as zero. Miller writes: 'if they knew they were thinking about nothing they would go mad' [TC 82]. He quotes his friend Van Norden's anguished comments on the vulva: 'It's an illusion! You get all burned up about nothing ... All that mystery about sex and then you discover that it's nothing – just a blank' [TC 144–5]. His own response is different:

> When I look down into that crack I see an equation sign, the world at balance, a world reduced to zero and no trace of remainder. Not the zero on which Van Norden turned his flashlight, not the empty crack of the prematurely disillusioned man, but an Arabian zero rather, the sign from which spring endless mathematical worlds, the fulcrum which balances the stars and the light dreams and the machines lighter than air and the lightweight limbs and the explosives that produced them [TC 249].

Upon zero or utter continuity everything flows without resistance. There is no possibility of becoming settled, rooted, or established, of instituting stable communities or codes. Names and labels regress to the magmic-pulse of language, sliding in useless digression. According to Freud kissing is included amongst the perversions because it digresses from procreative sexuality, wandering erratically across the cosmic desolation of the unconscious. Zero is the vortex of a becoming inhuman that lures desire out from the cage of man onto the open expanses of death. Not that death as utter digression is the same as the becoming inert of the body. It is first of all the anegoic psychosis of communicative fusion; floating on the far side of all effort.

There are times when Miller, confronted by the oceanic blank of zero, falls back upon the spurious identity of bones, which he associates with Phallic rigidity: 'Animals with a bone in the penis. Hence, *a bone on* ... "Happily", says Gourmont, "the bony structure is lost in man." Happily? Yes, happily. Think of the human race walking around with a bone on' [TC 11]. Which doesn't prevent him remarking two pages later that '[t]here is a bone in my prick six inches long' [TC 13]. A corpse has one preeminent and historically fateful heterogeneous distribution: that between its skeletal structure and its soft tissues. This is apprehended as a difference between what is perdurant, dry, clean, formal, and what is volatile, wet, dirty, and formless. On the basis of this resource Western civilization has been not merely thanatological, but osseological, which is something reaching beyond the fascination with the skeleton – and particularly the skull – that is distributed extremely widely across cultures. Osseology, in its deep sense, is the usage of the difference between the hard and soft parts of the body as a logical operator in the discourse on matter and death. For instance, differentiation between eternal form and perishable substance, celestial purity and terrestrial filth, divine architecture and base flow. The skeleton is thus conceived of as an invisible harmonious essence, an infrastructure beneath the disturbing tides of soft pathology. It is the prototype of intelligible form, contrasted with the decaying mass of the sensible body.

The skeleton is the relatively dead part of an organism, and because of this it is also the part relatively immune to dissolution. Which is another way of saying that the hard parts of an organic body are those most isolated from the communicative general-economic flows of its metabolism, but also the parts it most faithfully transmits into the future. The residues of life follow upon a pre-emptive compromise with death; what remains of life is only the disloyal part of itself.

> The grimacing skeleton that invaded the iconography of the late Middle Ages seems to have been unknown to Greco-Roman antiquity. On the other hand, the cult of the skull goes back to Peking man (440,000 to 220,000 BC). Veneration for skulls is to be found in all primitive religions as well as in all the great religions of antiquity. Cortez's Spaniards, counting the skull-trophies in Mexican temples, found 136,000. The Toltecs cut off the skulls and used them as bowls. The Gauls cut off the heads

of their dead enemies and brought them back to their villages, suspended from the necks of their horses, then nailed them as trophies in front of their houses. In New Caledonia widows kept the skulls of their husbands in baskets [SD 10–11].

There is something treacherous about a skull, that most intimate companion, so indifferently adapted to an inorganic regime, so untouched by the disappearance of flesh. It is the natural emblem of piracy, criminality, and cold betrayal. Perhaps everybody occasionally imagines their skull become a paperweight, or (less modestly) a museum exhibit in some distant time. Such thoughts are a little more cynical than those which capture it shortly after interment; a chamber of heaving maggots and filth. One only glimpses its calcic imperviousness by imaginatively stripping it of our rot, ageing it tastefully, polishing it. In the end one comes to feel that it merely tolerates its momentary participation in us, numbly awaiting the cessation of our tedious biological clamour.

Clearer than all I see my own grinning skull, see the skeleton dancing in the wind, serpents issuing from the rotted tongue and the bloated pages of ecstasy slimed with excrement. And I join my slime, my excrement, my madness, my ecstasy to the great circuit which flows through the subterranean vaults of the flesh. All the unbidden, unwanted, drunken vomit will flow on endlessly through the minds of those to come in the inexhaustible vessel that contains the history of the race. Side by side with the human race there runs another race of beings, the inhuman ones, the race of artists who, goaded by unknown impulses, take the lifeless mass of humanity and by the fever and ferment with which they imbue it turn this soggy dough into bread and the bread into wine and the wine into song. Out of the dead compost and the inert slag they breed a song that contaminates. I see this other race of individuals ransacking the universe, turning everything upside down, their feet always moving in blood and tears, their hands always empty, always clutching and grasping for the beyond, for the god out of reach: slaying everything within reach in order to quiet the monster that gnaws at their vitals. I see that when they tear their hair with the effort to comprehend, to seize this forever unattainable, I see that when they bellow like crazed beasts and rip and gore, I see that this is right, that there is no other path to pursue. A man who belongs to this race must stand up on the high place with gibberish in his mouth and rip out his entrails. It is right and just, because he must! And anything that falls short of this frightening spectacle, anything less shuddering, less terrifying, less mad, less intoxicated, less contaminating, is not art. The rest is counterfeit. The rest is human. The rest belongs to life and lifelessness [TC 255–6].

Washing about the rigid parts of the body are the swirls of ecstasy and filth whose only fidelity is to zero. Not that rigidity and fluidity enter into any kind of opposition within a structure or dialectic. There is no elemental duality at stake here, since this would involve a rigid difference transcending and dominating its terms, as if a typology, signifying system, or patchwork of language-games were extrinsically organizing base flows, in the manner of Wittfogel's hydraulic bureaucracies[12]. The savage truth of delirium is that all ossification – far from being a metaphysical separation from decay – is a unilateral deviation from fluidity, so that even bones, laws, and monuments are crumbled and swept away by the deep flows of the Earth. Far from establishing an eternal *logos* on the model of pure ossification, the tongue rots into a delirial meander of oozing slime and dirt, indistinguishable from the contaminating mess it vomits into the gutters of literature.

There is a boundary of sorts along the banks and shores of the body where fluidity and rigidity meet, but this is not sufficient to authorize the irrigational idol of *rigid differentiation*. It is not difficult to imagine how such an idol might have arisen, of course. Is it not natural to imagine rigidity setting the terms for its contestation? It is almost tautological to conceive liquidity as *giving way*. Nevertheless, differentiation is contested at the scurf-edge of the flow, where sediments of detritus are tugged problematically between solidity and liquification. If fluidity prevails the bank is dissolved, washed away, permeated, flooded; it is only in the momentary constraint of fluids that the fixed channels of an irrigation are realized. However desperately Miller clings at times to his bones, to his bone on, to the mouldering patriarchal infrastructure of his corpse, in the end there is infiltration and collapse into the deluge, into the unsurpassable hydraulic mega-machine: 'I am a writing machine. The last screw has been added. The thing flows. Between me and the machine there is no estrangement. I am the machine . . .' [TC 34].

*

Speaking philosophically, and in accord with common sense, flow is gauged in terms of a fixed grid assembled from space, time, and matter. Flow displaces mass in space over time in a strictly quantifiable fashion, and is therefore – as a concept – *posterior* to the apparatus of its representation. Not only does time function as a dimension of its description, but a deeper temporal prioritization of the representational grid (whether this is idealized or naturalized) locates flow as an empirical content, mapped along axes *achieved in advance*. Becoming is subordinated to a transcendent law, allowing it to be judged, denigrated, and condemned. Compare Miller's words:

> For the fraction of a second perhaps I experienced the utter clarity which the epileptic, it is said, is given to know. In that moment I lost completely the illusion of time and space: the world unfurled its drama simultaneously along a meridian which had no axis. In this sort of hair-trigger eternity I felt that everything was justified, supremely justified; I felt the wars inside me that had left behind this pulp and wrack; I felt the crimes that were seething here to emerge tomorrow in blatant screamers; I felt the misery that was grinding itself out with pestle and mortar, the long dull misery that dribbles away in dirty handkerchiefs. On the meridian of time there is no injustice: there is only the poetry of motion creating the illusion of truth and drama [TC 102].

Even ordinarily time is thought of as a flow, but flows characterize the repressed of thinking. That time is conceived as a river, streaming dissymmetrically from the future into the past, is a representation controlled by a defensive system, simultaneous with mature patriarchy, nucleated upon the ego, and correlated with the generation of a utilitarian hydraulics. A transcendent differentiation rigidifies a stabilized subject/object couple or appropriate synonym; the former as a fixed point of apprehension, the latter as an underlying essence. This double deliquification channels a quantifiable homogeneous substance through a rigid conduit; the transcendent apparatus of *time as such* and the ego, ontology as managed flow.

Nothing of this pompous monolithic architecture can resist the torrent of Miller's prose when it surges most ruthlessly out of zero:

> Yes, I said to myself, I too love everything that flows: rivers,

sewers, lava, semen, blood, bile, words, sentences. I love the amniotic fluid when it spills out of the bag. I love the kidney with its painful gall-stones, its gravel and what-not; I love the urine that pours out scalding and the clap that runs endlessly; I love the words of hysterics and the sentences that flow on like dysentery and mirror all the sick images of the soul; I love the great rivers like the Amazon and the Orinoco, where crazy men like Moravagine float on through dream and legend in an open boat and drown in the blind mouths of the river. I love everything that flows, even the menstrual flow that carries away the seed unfecund. I love scripts that flow, be they hieratic, esoteric, perverse, polymorph, or unilateral. I love everything that flows, everything that has time in it and becoming, which brings us back to the beginning where there is never end: the violence of the prophets, the obscenity that is ecstasy, the wisdom of the fanatic, the priest with his rubber litany, the foul words of the whore, the spittle that floats away in the gutter, the milk of the breast and the bitter honey that pours from the womb, all that is fluid, melting, dissolute and dissolvent, all the pus and dirt that in flowing is purified, that loses its sense of origin, that makes the great circuit towards death and dissolution [TC 258–9].

Between the body and the utterances that traverse it there is not in truth a relation, but rather a repressed continuity. Literature surges and foams wherever bodies diffuse, vomit themselves, melt into each other, and subside into the heaving toxic syrup of solar tides. It does not stem from the architectural design of a transcendent author-god, imprisoned in rigid individuation, but accumulates black and excremental, like a rich silt at the edge of the great impersonal flows. 'Looking into the Seine I see mud and desolation' [TC 70]. If intense literature seems very often to have an autobiographical character – as with Miller – this is not primarily because a life expresses itself, it is far more a matter of an integrated life being haemorrhaged into the laceration of writing, rhythmically dishevelled and coagulated down to an impermanent clotting in the subterranean lava-flows of base culture. 'And when you show me a man who expresses himself perfectly,' writes Miller, 'I will not say that he is not great, but I will say that I am unattracted' [TC 254]. To describe Miller as a writer is not to lend him a personal integrity as one who writes, but to scatter the ashes of his name into the rivers of fluent textuality which nag all personalities to pieces, as they bear their luxuriant froth of words downstream towards chaos and death. 'I feel this river flowing through me,' remarks Miller in the penultimate sentence of the book [TC 318].

None of this has anything to do with metaphor. Metaphor is only an issue where literal and figurative usages can be bilaterally distinguished, where orthodox functions have been diked-up against the currents of digression. To write of the body being traversed by rivers is not mere metaphor, except when the body has been penned into its solidity and rivers have been degraded to drainage ditches. However many rivers have been integrated into urban and industrial sewerage systems, there are still solar rivers, pathological rivers, rivers of sex, madness, literature, and plague which refuse to slumber wretchedly within their banks. The word 'river' in its ordinary usage is an instrument of irrigationist repression, and its aberrant upsurge is not metaphor, but catastrophic erosion.

For so long as we persist as dammed-up reservoirs of labour-power we preserve our humanity, but the rivers flowing into us are an irresistible urge to dissolution, pressing us into the inhumane. Beneath the regulated exchanges of words we howl and gnaw at our fettered limbs. An impersonality as blank and implacable as the sun wells up beneath us, a vermin-hunger for freedom:

> If I am inhuman it is because my world has slopped over its human bounds, because to be human seems like a poor, sorry, miserable affair, limited by the senses, restricted by moralities and codes, defined by platitudes and isms [TC 257].

Humanity is a petrified fiction hiding from zero, a purgatorial imprisonment of dissolution, but to be stricken with sanctity is to bask in death like a reptile in the sun.

God is dead, but immeasurably more importantly, God is death (except 'God' means the fascist ass-hole of the West). The beginning of the secret is that death (= 0) is immense.

*

From birth we are brain-washed into conformity with the cage, taught to accumulate, to shore ourselves up, to fear madness and death. Trapped in a constricting tangle of language routines we tread a narrow circuit in the maze

We are told that chance will not take care of us, and that it is difficult to live
but work and seriousness are slums of delusion
the garbage-heap of individuation has no worth
what is called life at the outer edge of patriarchy is a bleak box of lies, drudgery, and anaesthesia blended with inane agony
what matters about the outside of the box is not just that it is the outside of the box, but that it is immense
what matters is the abyss, the gulf

*

They want us to fear death so much, but we can inhabit it like vermin, it can be our space, in our violent openness to the sacred death will protect us against their exterminations, driven insane by zero, we can knot ourselves into the underworld, communicate through it, cook their heavenly city in our plague.
we can scamper in and out of the maze in a way they cannot understand,
during the first weekend of June
at half-past one on Sunday morning
deep in the crypt of the night
together with a fellow voyager in madness
i crossed the line into death
which is called Hell because the police control heaven

*

Melting shells drunk on our inexistence
torched in the flame of the sacred
we trudged though the burnt and blackened swamps of the shallows
testing the edge of the estuary
dripping brimstone from our boots
an immense ocean of annihilation stretched out before us

*

There has been a revolution in Hell
Satan hangs from a gibbet and rots
wreathed in the howls of anarchy
out there beyond the stars
the cold wind of zero rages without interdiction

Chapter 9
Aborting the human race

[M]an is by nature a political animal. He who is stateless by nature and not just by chance is either subhuman or superhuman, like the man reviled by Homer as 'classless, lawless, heartless'; for being naturally without a state, he is a lover of war and may be compared to an unprotected piece in a game of draughts [Pol 7].

Perceived under the perspective of action, Nietzsche's work is an abortion ... [VI 22].

There is a sense in which Bataille's works – as *works* – are not especially 'difficult'. They are, indeed, no more problematic than the words we use to tranquillize ourselves against love and dying (against the passion to die). One could very easily 'understand' Bataille whilst protracting a decent and productive life. There is even a necessity to do this, which it would be hypocritical to wholly disown. One might avoid being merely interested in these texts, yet it is still possible that the agitation which remained would be dissolved into those little lazinesses and indecencies with which we meagrely spice our domesticity. It is for this reason (reason itself) that I feel I understand Bataille's obsessiveness, his repetition, his reluctance to leave us with what has already been so clearly said. It is for this reason too that any book making it easier to understand Bataille is written *contra* him. The gurus of writing will of course say that we should be quite without regard for 'Bataille', as if the failure of authorialism were properly replaced by a textualist triumph. After all, who would not rather be faced with a life or a production, when the alternative to either is wreckage? How uselessly cruel it is then to suggest that Bataille's repetition is a scream provoked by what becomes its own meaninglessness, and, less even than this, an echoing involution into abortion.

Bataille does not repeat out of a fear that he has been misunderstood, quite the contrary. It is precisely because what he has written might merely be understood that it must perpetually be re-insisted. His thinking is not without a frightening simplicity. It is perhaps even reducible to one question: *what is an end?*

Humans like to have two ends, and to keep them as distinct as possible; blessing *telos* and cursing *terminus*. In this respect a certain zenith is reached in the Kantian practical postulate of immortality, where the perfection of teleological process requires the infinite recession of extinction. One end supplants the other. We are all kantians now (I use the small case advisedly) and it has come to seem almost natural that our history be comprehended as teleological. It is only since Nietzsche that it has come to seem (immanently) terminal.

Repetition can no doubt be accused of wrecking the progression of an *oeuvre*. To repeat is a sign that one has 'lost the thread', and beginning again is the abjection proper to discourse; collapse (violent detumescence?), sentience as return from oblivion. The writer, drunk (if only upon the literary malaise), cannot even remember the contents of the crumpled pages strewn about the waste bin, or the previous paragraph, the previous book, the previous anything. No adequate attempt is made at recovery. The past stinks in its decomposition. One begins again.

What is an end? One shudders perhaps. An end? Are there more than one? Is not the very question a violation of sorts? A ruthless denuding? Should death be pushed so harshly into my awareness? Can she not wait? Is it not permissible to sleep?

If life were a discourse death could wait, but dreams break down, there is repetition. Bataille's text does not anticipate death; it fractures seismically under the impact of oblivion. Each of its waves are broken recollections of the taste of death. Each beginning again – as such and irrespective of its inherent signification – moves under the influence of an unanticipated dying. Waves have no memory. They react afresh each time to the deep ebb that undoes them in darkness, beating to a pulse that eludes them. The absent shingle-hiss of death is discursively manipulated into textual regularity, but this does not erase the multiple beginnings again; marking the contour of each retraction into silence. '[S]omething inside me undid itself' [IV 342], says the anonymous narrator of a short fragment beginning: 'At the start of the degeneration . . .'.

*

What do you want to make of your life? A cruel question, when it is not a naïve one. What is a life if not a definitive unmaking? Whatever the gibberings of profane man, it is not open to us to make anything of ourselves.

*

Telos lends itself to discourse, whilst even the silence of terminus is effaced. Death has no advocates. Even those who align themselves with her do so for other reasons; extreme suffering – for instance – has no end of commentators, each desperate for a pact with the Great Silence. This advantage accruing to survival when it comes to putting one's case is a banal prejudice, but no less an effective one for that. Theoretical biology has been based on nothing else for over a century. Survival will always have rigged any conceivable tribunal, but surely we can agree (Nietzsche laughs) that inevitability is not justice?

In the end – one no longer denies it – there is death, but for the moment one has . . . other ends? There must surely be other ends. Man as an end in himself? We have that of course, some would say we have considerably too much of it. Since zoology has matured enough to adopt its most aberrant specimen – the perverse animal – it is difficult for us not to see preposterous claims to a unique human dignity as a slander against nature. Nevertheless, is it not possible to precipitate the principle of our humanism, distill it down to goodness? Who could be so impudent as to seek something other than goodness? This is surely the very essence of the end, the absolute end, gleaming magnificently in its Platonic rendition: *The Good*. How touchingly naïve this word sounds today.

The Good is the object of rationalized desire, of what had become, by the end of the eighteenth century, *Wille*, will. The word our economists eventually settled for is *preference*, those with more of an ideological bent tend to prefer *choice*. Even after being winkled by psychology from its Platonic niche in the celestial order, the good is still indispensable to concrete reason, as its end and orientation. The good is exactly what – upon reflection – we want. At least, it is what we should want; the intelligibility of educated desire. Our civilization has deluged us with 'goods', at least in its metropolitan heights. Yet, as Freud suggests, we remain discontented by civilization, gnawed by *Unbehagen*. The problem with goodness is less its maldistribution than the fact it is so depressingly tedious. We applaud Mother Theresa without reservation, before succumbing to our yawns (longing for her to be arraigned for a sex-crime, or for a war to break out). Perhaps all righteousness is on the side of the good, but as to the 'good life', wouldn't it be somewhat better to be dead?

Since Schopenhauer in modern times (but already with Augustine) all those who have thought at all about the matter have known that we do not in the slightest want the good. The good is exactly what we don't want, that which is set against our wanting, a barrier, a renunciation. Even the few beleaguered Aristotelians who survive have long since ceased to speak of desire, preferring 'virtue' (the way to a good life no doubt, but one that leaves us perfectly indifferent, or perhaps mildly nauseous). Faced with the option of working towards an ethical community or stealing an illicit kiss we might choose the path of duty, but we would not pretend to be furthering our beatitude.

Argument is no longer necessary to contend that desire is an amoral savagery, there is near unanimity about it, usually in the form of an implicit ego-psychology which acknowledges stoically that sexuality will always be with us, even though it makes us ill. Nevertheless, it is still the case that the fact no one wants what is 'good for us' disturbs us less than it might. What slight perturbation it does cause is usually interpreted as a need for a harsher or more insidious moralization, for more education, greater ideological penetration, a larger police force. When we scare ourselves our sympathies always seem to lie with the passive subject, and not with the wild beast.

Kant remarks in *The Critique of Judgement*:

> As the single being upon earth that possesses understanding, and, consequently, a capacity for setting before himself ends of his deliberate choice, he is titular lord of nature, and, supposing we regard nature as a teleological system, he is born to be its ultimate end. But this is always on the terms that he has the intelligence and the will to give to it and to himself such a reference to ends as can be self-sufficing independently of nature, and, consequently, a final end. Such an end, however, must not be sought in nature [K X 389].

'An end that must not be sought in nature' could mean at least two things. It might, as Kant would no doubt prefer, indicate a distinct ontological stratum – the 'supersensible' – which would be the reserve of ends. Alternatively, it might simply suggest that nature has ends, and of such a kind that far from ends 'being' in some way different from that of nature, being, in nature, comes to an end. For what is it that 'man' understands, if it is not that nature brings 'him' to an end? The human animal has a unique potentiality to not only die with utter futility, but to infiltrate its hypertrophic terminus into the most effervescent currents of natural becoming. Since *homo sapiens* has prowled the earth, nature has adapted to new shadows.

*

However else it is possible to divide Western thinking, one fissure can be teased-open separating the theo-humanists – croaking together in the cramped and malodorous pond of Anthropos – from the wild beasts of the impersonal. The former are characterized by their moral fervour, parochialism, earnestness, phenomenological disposition, and sympathy for folk superstition, the latter by their fatalism, atheism, strangely reptilian exuberance, and extreme sensitivity for what is icy, savage, and alien to mankind. Nietzsche is perhaps the greatest of all anti-humanist writers. At the very least, his writings attest to the most powerful eruption of impersonality in the Occidental world since it was rotted by the blight of the Nazarene. It is possible that Herakleitus was more effortlessly inhuman, and that – beneath the shadow of the cross – Spinoza and Sade occasionally reach a comparable pitch of anegoic coldness, but nowhere outside Nietzsche's texts is there an antipersonalistic war-machine of equivalent ferocity.

It is deliberate ignorance or idiocy in respect of Schopenhauer that allows humanist readings of Nietzsche to proliferate so shamelessly; readings in which a so-called 'superman' prefigures an existential choice for mankind, in which eternal recurrence is a personal – or even ethical – predicament, in which affirmation is an act of voluntary consent, will to power is a psychological description of self-assertion, and values are subjectively legislated idealities.

It should not be necessary to explicitly recollect that, on the basis of his reading of Schopenhauer, Nietzsche assumed the unconsciousness and impersonality of will or desire, and never indicates a regression to a Kantian/humanist understanding of this matter. Nor should it be necessary to re-assert the intrinsic connection between the will and the transcendental problematic of time, inherited from the same source. The same could be said about the obvious reference to Schopenhauer exhibited in the very expression 'will to power', the Schopenhauerian germ for the thought of 'rank-order' in that of 'grades of objectification', the architectonic connection between Schopenhauer and Nietzsche in terms of the history of philosophy, the crucial Schopenhauerian background to Nietzsche's remarks about women, etc. Nietzsche's break with Schopenhauer is of extreme profundity, but it remains a break with Schopenhauer, rather than some kind of ahistorical existential inspiration.

If stressing the importance of Schopenhauer to the entire sweep of Nietzsche's writing were merely to polemicize on behalf of elementary standards of scholarship it would be a piece of academicist moralism of the shoddiest sort. The crucial issue is not that reading Nietzsche without reference to Schopenhauer gets Nietzsche wrong, but that it makes him more humane. Schopenhauer is the great well-spring of the impersonal in post-Kantian thought; the sole member of the immediately succeeding generation to begin vomiting monotheism out of their cosmology in order to attack the superstition of self. The repression of Schopenhauer's thinking is continuous with the co-option of Nietzsche back into the monotheistic/humanistic fold of ontologically grounded subjects, real choices, existential individuation, irreducible persons, ethical norms, and suchlike garbage. Whether or not some kind of tentative antihumanism is then launched on the basis of a quasi-phenomenological or deconstructive gesture is scarcely a matter worthy of great excitement, except for those concerned to choose between Luther and the pope.

*

That finality has been an overt issue throughout the history of modern philosophy has been mainly due to the struggle against the Aristotelian tendencies of scholasticism by the thinkers of the Enlightenment. It is because of this history that finality is normally conceived in terms of an opposition between teleology and mechanism, or between final and efficient causation, since this distinction is the seventeenth and eighteenth century battle-front between the church and modern science. Finality was associated above all with the teleological argument for the existence of God – the argument from design – according to which nature is open to theological interpretation as the approximation to a divine blueprint.

For Aristotle the theological dimension of teleology is closely bound to its libidinal dimension, since desire is understood as a tendency towards an intrinsic perfection whose ultimate keystone is the sufficiency of God. The telos or goal of all striving is something presupposed by activity, such that desire must already have received its potential for realization extrinsically, thus preserving the Platonic association between Eros and subordination. Both the Aristotelian and scholastic usage of teleology is dependent upon the thought of originary perfection or God, subordinating desire to the sufficiency of complete being. In other words, theological time is encompassed by perfection or absolute achievement, which enslaves becoming to a timeless potential of that which becomes. Such a potential is a design, archetype, or plan, existing ideally and eternally in the supreme intellect, and usurping all creativity from nature.

For those familiar with the general tenor of Kant's attempt to harmonize the competing ideologies of established authority and progress, the predominant character of his response to the problem of finality will be something less than shocking. The combination of theoretical agnosticism and practical apologetics, which he employs in the first two critiques in order to legitimate a responsible space for science alongside instituted power, is still operative in the third. The potential of the theologians is smuggled into the *Critique of Judgement* as the possibility of a complete system of science, a regulative idea which derives from the originary perfection of reason. Even though teleology loses its right to dogmatic theorizing, it continues to guide the thought of nature in terms of the infinitely accomplished idea.

In order not to inhibit the development of the sciences Kant denaturalizes teleology, lodging its redoubt in his practical philosophy, and therefore in reason. A rational being or person is to be practically conceived not as a natural entity – a delirious clot of matter – but as an end in itself; imbued *a priori* with a potential for perfect goodness that is only sullied by the pathological factors of its animal existence. The realization of the human perfection that is embryonically presupposed by reason is the endless task of morality, wherein process approximates to the timeless form of its utter accomplishment. It is thus that, like Plato, Aristotle, and the church, Kant thinks of goodness as perfectly instituted in advance, as a supersensibly derived potential.

Schopenhauer seeks to extricate the thought of finality from this theological framework, but his success is strictly limited. Although he eradicates the theological dogma of originary intellect from his philosophy he continues to rely on the notion of Platonic Ideas to interpret natural processes, and thus succumbs in turn to the finalist doctrine of potential, in the form of a Kantian transcendental perfectionism. Schopenhauer, too, deprives desire of creativity, by conceiving all its possible consequences as eternal potentialities of the noumenal will. Desire as the will to life is merely the perpetual re-instantiation of pre-given forms.

Despite the problems to which he succumbs, Schopenhauer's philosophy makes a number of important advances, by initiating a war against the intellectualist interpretation of will, beginning the rigorous separation of affective intensity from phenomenality, and germinating a philosophy of scalar or stratal difference. In three crucial anti-Kantian gestures he argues that 'the *will* always appears as the primary and fundamental thing, and throughout asserts its preeminence over the intellect' [Sch III 231], that '[p]henomenon means representation and nothing more' [Sch I 154] whilst 'we are quite wrong in calling pain and pleasure representations' [Sch I 144], and continually refers to 'the ascending series of animal organizations', 'the scale of animals' [Sch III 327], and more generally to 'grades of the will's objectivity' [Sch I 179], or degrees of '*stimulation or excitement*' [III 240]. In Schopenhauer's philosophy such thinking remains uncomfortably wedded to a series of bilateral disjunctions between the transcendental and the empirical, subject and object, thing in itself and appearance, etc., and is thus martialled under the metaphysical dignity of man, whose nervous-system he describes as 'nature's final product' [Sch III 320]. It nevertheless marks the departure of a voyage in intensity, one that Nietzsche exacerbates beyond the threshold of the irreparable.

*

In his appendix to *The Metaphysics of Sexual Love* Schopenhauer cites the claim in Aristotle's *Politics* that: 'For children of people too old as well as too young leave much to be desired in both a physical and mental regard, and children of those in advanced years are weaklings.' A little later he comments:

> Aristotle, therefore, lays down that a man who is fifty-four years of age should not have any more children, though he may still continue cohabitation for the sake of his health or for any other reason. He does not say how this is to be carried into effect, but he is obviously of the opinion that children conceived when their parents are of such an age should be disposed of by abortion, for he had recommended this a few lines previously [Sch IV 660].

The context for this peculiar remark is a discussion of pederasty, or the libidinal architectonics of classical idealism. The philosophical or academic relation is homoerotic and inter-generational; a restricted pedagogy that mimics the unit of patrilineal reproduction. Schopenhauer's endeavour is to map out a descriptive eugenics that is able to provide biological intelligibility for such a relation, and the consequence – indicated by his Aristotle citation – is his suggestion that pederasty diverts young and old males from procreative sexuality, in order to forestall the racial deterioration that would result from the transmission of their inadequately formed or decrepit sperm. It is thus that a subterranean complicity is exposed between the Idea (or perfect form), patriarchy, and racial hygiene.

Pederasty substitutes for abortion, translating it into the homoerotic bond, and reproducing it in conformity with the dominion of achieved form. The radical abortion of tragedy and irredeemable waste is Socratically sublimated into the service of the Idea, becoming a police function of theistic sociality, within a political economy of managed sperm. There is a superficial preconscious stratum of Nietzsche's writing that harmonizes closely with such a politics, for instance the note numbered 734 in *The Will to Power* which argues:

> Society, as the great trustee of life, is responsible to life itself for every aborted life – it also has to pay for such lives: consequently it ought to prevent them. In numerous cases, society ought to prevent procreation: to this end, it may hold in readiness, without regard to descent, rank, or spirit, the most rigorous means of constraint, deprivation of freedom, in certain circumstances castration [N III 923].

There is little to perturb the Aristotelian legacy in such a remark, except for a strange interference between abortions and forestallings (the German series *verfehlen, verhindern, vorbeugen*). In Nietzsche's text abortion – in the loose sense Schopenhauer has opened – is both the possible outcome of procreative anarchy and that which characterizes a eugenic regime. Both of these senses are in play in his famous remark from *Ecce Homo*: 'no abortion was missing, not even the antisemite' [N II 1119]. Procreation is aborted in order to avoid the procreation of abortions. If social institutions are to avoid being aborted abortion must be socially institutionalized. If Nietzsche's argument is somewhat tangled at this point it is because something essential to the classical model of reason has miscarried.

Unlike the will to life, the will to power is not driven by the tendency to realize and sustain a potential, its sole impetus is that of overcoming itself. It has no motivating end, but only a propulsive source. It is in this sense that will to power is creative desire, without a pre-figured destination or anticipatory perfection. It is an arrow shot into the unconceived. Will to power names the pre-representational impetus for which life is a tool, and for which tendency is inextricable from intensity. At the heart of the terminological motor driving Nietzsche's writings lie a series of nouns of action, each of which subverts a dogma by designating a genealogical topic. Nietzsche transcribes *moralization* fully as 'the genealogy of morals', but the genealogy of logic is initiated under the compact rubric of equalization (or logicization), as is the case with eternalization, simplification, divinization, legislation, etc. It is in this way that will to power is transcribed into thought by the first stammerings of a positive ateleological syntax.

Schopenhauer is a philosopher of primal non-differentiation because he conceives representation as individuating, according to the spatial and temporal isolation imposed by the principle of sufficient reason. Nietzsche recasts this principle into a general tendency to assimilation which he names 'equalization' (*Ausgleichung*), and it is this that makes him the first post-Kantian philosopher of difference. In his notes he succinctly asserts: 'the will to equality is the will to power' [N III 500]. Despite superficial appearance, however, the difference between Schopenhauer and Nietzsche is not simply that between thoughts of indifference and difference. It is more a question of phases in the emergent thinking of unilateral or non-reciprocal difference, which departs from the bilateral difference synonymous with ontology. Between the organic and the inorganic, for instance, there is not a bilateral or reciprocal exclusion, but rather a unilateral separation of the organic within the inorganic, such that the difference between the two is wholly immanent to the inorganic as primary term. This is the profound sense of economy: the energetic consistency between zero-intensity and its deviations, or between a noun of action and the antonym of its simple noun (e.g. between matter and spiritualization). It is because such consistency cannot be thought within the bilateral or non-contradiction logics traditionally countenanced that Schopenhauer was inhibited from its radical excavation.

The recurrence of the same cannot be diffentiated from the unilaterality of difference, which is to say that recurrence is the consistency of difference with equalization. It is not that energy is what recurs as the same, but rather that energy is the economic sense of recurrence as unilateral consistency. Recurrence is not a configuration of energy or cosmic economy, but the very impact of undifferentiable zero; the abortion of transcendence. To think of the real simultaneity of unsurpassable chaotic zero with the triumph of reactivity, such that the only repressed is the unrepressible, is to think of recurrence, and any suggestion that eternal recurrence is a cosmology describable according to a principle of non-contradiction is to entirely lose the matter of Nietzsche's excitement, i.e. the unilateral, materialist, or genealogical interpretation of difference. The sole philosophical rigour of recurrence splashes out of the pulverizing inundation of bilateral distinctions by indifferent matter. Spirit is different from matter and matter once again, culture is different from nature and nature once again, order is different from chaos and chaos once again, just as life is unilaterally different from death, plenitude from zero, reactive from active forces, etc. Transcendence is both real and impossible, as is the human race.

'Once again' is a term which Nietzsche's text binds inextricably to the rumour of eternal recurrence, for instance in note 341 from *The Gay Science* – often taken to be the first 'announcement' of the doctrine of return – where Nietzsche twice uses the same formulation to describe recurrence, 'once again, and again innumerable times [*noch einmal und noch unzählige Male*]' [N II 202]. There are very many places where this term plays a decisive role in his writings, amongst which are those marking the repressed unilaterality at the base of metaphysical binarities; for example in his notebooks he remarks:

> The 'A' of logic is, like the atom, a reconstruction of the thing – If we do not grasp this, but make of logic a criterion of true being, we are on the way to positing as realities all those hypostases: substance, attribute, object, subject, action, etc.; that is, to conceiving a metaphysical world, that is, a 'real world' (– *this, however, is the apparent world once again* –) [N III 538].

> The 'real world', however one has hitherto conceived it – it has always been the apparent world *once again* [N III 689].

Whether of Judaic or Platonic inspiration, monotheism rests upon hypostatizing the differential element of the human animal. It is because spirit, personality, reason, and law have all been taken as defining characteristics of man, that one finds the cosmos crushed under an absolute spirit, an infinite personality, pure reason, and perfect justice. When confronted by the gothic intimidation synonymous with Western culture it is hard to re-excavate the fact that one is merely dealing with a beast advantaged by a measure of superior cunning, a hypertrophic facility for the transfer of information, and an opposable thumb.

The meaning of humanity is abuse of the vanquished; the transformation of intensive difference into metaphysical disjunction. The libidinal sense of Platonism, for instance, is the paralysation of an intensive ascent in accordance with an exhaustive concept. Intensive spiritualization is fixed as consummate spirit, thus levelling out desire onto the stagnant plateau of theological idealism dominated by Christendom. Upon this plateau progress in extension remains possible – scientific, technical, and industrial growth for instance – but such development is rigidly constrained by its infrastructural libidinal petrification; imprisoned in the humanity whose first instance was Socrates, and whose horizontal limit is Christ.

The broad strokes of Nietzsche's diagnosis are well known:

> I count life itself as an instinct for growth, for duration, for amassing of force, for *power*: where the will to power is lacking there is decline. My assertion is that this will is *lacking* for all the highest values of humanity – that decline-values, *nihilistic* values, pursue dominion under the most hallowed names [N II 1167–8].

It is the devaluation of the highest values, the convulsion at the zenith of nihilism, that aborts the human race. Having polarized the high and the low in extension, humanity finds itself destituted of its idols – which have purified themselves into overt inexistence – and is thereby plunged vertiginously into its abjected values; animality, pathology, sensuality, and materiality. At the end of human civilization there is thus a regression driven by zero, a violent spasm of relapse whose motor is the cavity of an extinct telos; the death of God. Zero religion.

As a creature of zero, overman is not a conceptually intelligible advance upon humanity. Any such thing is, in any case, strictly impossible. Humanity cannot be exacerbated, but only aborted. It is first necessary to excavate the embryonic anthropoid beast at the root of man, in order to re-open the intensive series in which it is embedded. If overman is an ascent beyond humanity, it is only in the sense of being a redirection of its intensive foetus. This is why overman is predominantly regressive; a step back from extension in order to leap in intensity, like the drawing-back of a bow-string.

The zero is the transmission element which integrates active and reactive impulses at the end of the great Platonic divorce between nature and culture. Zero is undifferentiable without being a unity, and everything is re-engaged through zero. Eternal recurrence – the most nihilistic thought – begins everything again, as history is re-energized through the nihilistic indifferentiation between zero enthusiasm and enthusiasm for zero. Passive nihilism is the zero of religion, whilst active nihilism is the religion of the zero. On the one hand is Schopenhauer's metaphysical pessimism as 'a European Buddhism' [N II 767], on the other Nietzsche's Dionysian pessimism as the exultation of dissolution. Within the order of bilateralized representation the 'will to nothingness' [N II 837, 863] is of profound ambivalence:

> 'either abolish your reverence or – *your self*!' The latter would be nihilism; but would not the former also be – nihilism? – This is *our* question mark [N II 212].

Nihilism as concrete history is Christianity, and it is only because Christianity is as impossible as it is real that nature escapes from being stigmatized to its foundations by the cult of the Nazarene. Christianity as inconsistency with matter recurs consistently with matter and thus inconsistently with itself. This is the motor of nihilism; the great zero, and the impersonal generator of nature and culture in their incompossible consistency.

Christianity, as Nietzsche insists over and over again in *The Antichrist*, is Judaism *once again* [*noch einmal*]. 'Once again came the popular expectation of a Messiah into the foreground' [N II 1202], he writes in section 40 of *The Antichrist*, and two pages later, getting a little carried away: 'once again the priest-instinct of the Jews perpetrated the same great crime against history' [N II 1204]. Against the tide of Teutonic antisemitism, with its project of Hellenizing, Aryanizing, and Wagnerizing Christ, Nietzsche is obsessive in his claim that Christianity is nothing except a recurrence of Jewish monotheism; which is not a mere repetition, but a return that both exacerbates and corrodes. 'The Christian, this *ultima ratio* of the lie, is the Jew once again – three times even' [N II 1206]. Europe is a population whose history has fallen prey to the zealots of the One; victim to the spreading ripple from the same catastrophe of monotheism which culturally vivisected the ancient Hebrew warrior tribes into the broken rabble of apostles and first Christians, huddling in wretched destitution beneath the shadow of the cross.

'Once again' – recurrence – does not say that an identity is repeated, except when thought is devastated by the reciprocity of reason and the mono-logic of the same. Monotheism is not repeated, but nihilistically exacerbated by unilateral zero, and driven irresistibly into the death of God where it consummates its truth. There is a savage rigour to Nietzsche's thinking here:

> [T]he little rebellious movement, baptized in the name of Jesus of Nazareth, is the Jewish instinct *once again*, in other words, the priest-instinct, which no longer tolerates the priest as a reality, the invention of a yet more destitute form of existence, a yet more unreal vision of the world, than that which conditions the organization of a church. Christianity *denies* the church . . . [N II 1189].

When Nietzsche's loathing for Christianity reaches its crescendo it becomes an obsessive reiteration of the One. One, one, one, over and over again, monotono-theism [N II 1179] as Nietzsche calls it; a God whose speculative triad collapses everything into the one, the Father, Son, and Spirit, power, benevolence, and knowledge, the simplicity, equality, and ontological individuality of the soul, the entire universe crumpled up together by a phallic fanaticism for monolithic form. Christian trinitarianism is the demonstration that everything comes back to One unless it is zero. To set up the question of difference as a conflict between the one and the many is a massive strategic blunder – the Occident lost its way at this point – the real issue is not one or many, but many and zero. Nietzsche writes:

> Wherever there are walls I shall inscribe this eternal accusation against Christianity upon them – I can write in letters which make even the blind see ... I call Christianity the *one* great curse, the *one* great instinct depravity, the *one* great instinct for revenge for which no expedient is sufficiently poisonous, secret, subterranean, *petty* – I call it the *one* immortal blemish of mankind ... [N II 1235].

*

This blemish is not a scar, but a callus, because the association between God and man is a matter of industrial relations. Unitary being is the order of work. God who creates and conserves, man who toils; theology stinks of sweat. Long before Marx, it was monotheism that hallucinated the earth into a work-house.

> As soon as we imagine someone who is responsible for our being thus and thus, etc. (God, nature), and therefore attribute to him the intention that we should exist and be happy or wretched, we corrupt for ourselves the *innocence of becoming*. We then have someone who wants to achieve something through us and with us [N III 542].

History is industrial history, and it only has one goal, which is God. Nihilism is the loss of this goal, the nullification of man's end, the reversion of all work to waste. It is in this sense that history is aborted by zero. There are those who in their eagerness for the continuation of effort take Nietzsche's overman to be a new goal, a restoration of teleology, a task commensurable with the nihilation of history. Perhaps Nietzsche himself succumbs to such a temptation at times, after all, German Protestantism had poisoned his blood. It must nevertheless be insisted that the world of work perishes with the One, and that zero is an engine of war.

> When truth steps into the fight against the lies of millennia we shall have seisms, spasms of earthquake, a displacement of mountain and valley, the like of which has never been dreamed.

> The concept of politics then passes over totally into a war of the spirit, all power edifices of the old society are blasted into the air – they all rest upon the lie: there shall be wars as there have never been upon the earth. From myself onwards, for the first time, is there *great politics* on the earth [N II 1153].

Between war and industry is a unilateral difference; industry is different from war and war once again. This is why great politics is not just an episode of war, but the very tide of recurrence in its ferocity. Nothing is great but zero, and great politics is that for which the polis itself falls victim. Nietzsche is thus utterly incapable of consenting to the Aristotelian dictum, in his *Politics*, that 'the art of war is a natural subdivision of the art of acquisition' [Pol 16], associated with his assertion that '[t]ame animals have a better nature than wild ones' [Pol 11]. In its uninhibited and extravagant root war does not serve the state. Even in his earliest writings Nietzsche is explicit that the order of dependence is quite to the contrary, and that the polis – along with its telic integration – is a consequence of pre-political militarism. In a text from the early 1870s called *The Greek State* Nietzsche notes that:

> Whoever contemplates war and its uniformed possibility, the military [*Soldatenstand*], in relation to the previously outlined essence of the state, must come to the insight that through war and the military an image, or perhaps rather a blueprint of the state is set before our eyes. Here we see, as the most general effect of the tendency to war, an immediate separation and division of chaotic masses into military castes, upon which the edifice of the 'warrior society' raises itself, pyramidally, upon the lowest, broadest, slavish stratum. The unconscious purpose of the entire movement compels each individual under its yoke and generates even with heterogeneous natures a similar chemical transformation of their properties, until they are brought into purposive affinity [N III 284].

Much later, and more importantly, Zarathustra tells us:

> You should love peace as a means to new wars. And the short peace more than the long one./I do not advise you to work, rather to struggle [N II 312].

These are the most profound words in the history of military thought; the libidinal comprehension of peace as a unilateral differentiation from war. On its extensive or political plane war appears as the antagonistic juxtaposition of constellated forces, but on its intensive or cosmic axis it is a metamorphosis of forces; their relative decomposition from strategic ensembles and purposes, towards tactical fragments and initiatives; dissolvant excitations at the edge of zero, the goalless *polemos* of Herakleitean flux. In extension war can appear to be oriented to appropriation, domination, and subordination, but intensively it develops according to tendencies of subtilization, infiltration, and dissolution. It is not that there is merely a desire for war, variously named by Nietzsche the 'thirst for destruction' [N III 821], 'the drive to destroy, anarchism, nihilism' [N III 708], and 'will to nothingness' [N II 900, III 738], rather that war in its intensive sense is desire itself, convulsive recurrence, unilateral zero.

*

The three great economic discourses of modernity can be summarized under the names Marx, Freud, Clausewitz. In each case what is sought is a rigorous comprehension of surplus, and in each case this is thought of primarily as success; industrial profit, psycho-sexual satisfaction, or military advantage. Sex and war can seem industrial, work and war libidinal, or business and love like war. Is Lenin's reading of the First World War more convincing than Freud's (think of Jünger), or than Foucault's reading of industrial history? Such questions are complex, and easily effaced in an eagerness for reduction. Furthermore, Marx already sees that political economy has its irreducibly military features ('the so-called primitive accumulation'), just as Freud sees that the psyche is a battle-field. Wars are produced and desired, industrial conflicts waged, commodities eroticized. The human animal seems to work, fuck, and fight, without accomplishing definition in terms of secure boundaries.

Bataille does not hesitate on this question: he locates war and industry within a general economy as the respective tendencies to useless and to productive expenditure. War is the free movement of solar flow across the earth, whilst industry is its inhibition, such that war is imbued with sacred characteristics; irrationality, horror, and the incendiary glory of 'donation of self' [*le don de soi*] [VII 237, 242, etc.]. This immediately contests the Leninist reduction of war to productivist motivations, siding instead with a (late-) Freudian account of base thanatropic drives. War is not the parasite of production, less still its instrument. War is rather the prisoner of production; its repressed energy source, overflow, and implicit catastrophe. Far from being the Frankenstein monster of production, war has a solar genealogy.

War is not meant here in a Clausewitzean sense, which is to say, as an instrument of policy. War in its radical sense is not an instrument of any kind, least of all a political one. The relation of war to the political is not (in reality) one of technical subordination, but rather, one of the uncircumscibed to the field of its potential circumscription. Only when it has been domesticated, and inhibited in its tropism to utter dissolution, can the sad dog we know as 'war' be subjected to policy; as the negative potency of the state. War escapes a Clausewitzean definition therefore, although this is not to dispute the very great pertinence of Clausewitz's thought to its servile forms. *Krieg* is no doubt indelibly scarred by its Prussian serfdom, but this need not efface its wilder features; the cosmological nobility described by Herakleitus, and the lines of hydraulic intricacy traced by Sun Tzu. There is even an inescapable sense in which war is beautiful – especially when compared to the sordid idiocy of work – since even its abject forms spill over into something harsh, fluid, and untamed. War is a luxuriance of chances, which is quite consistent with its shattering ugliness as a loathesome vampire trailing hideous carnage, the swamp breeding ground of vermin and plague. Whatever its terrible allure, there is nothing more profoundly degrading than war. It alone is truly *base*.

The word 'war' derives all the crucial currents of its sense from that of being the drive to dissolution, much as Freud described it in the wake of the First World War. It is the oceanic wilderness which is always other to civilization, irrespective of the compromise formations that seem to unify them. War irrupts convulsively into the history of civilizations as a loss of control, partially managed, with varying degrees of adeptness, by competing political interests. Such interruption is undergone as a de-humanizing regression; the re-surfacing of an ineliminable allergy to integrity, for which 'man' is a circumscription. It is an incidental feature of Freud's account that one sees even the armed contest of the European states as a massively inhibited lurch towards the free-flow fundamental violence of desire. Civilization (with its attendant militarism) is war subject to repression, and the energy of war is Thanatos; base hydraulics.

*

The chronological tendency of Bataille's writings is one of demilitarization, with the ardour for insurrectionary war that typifies his early polemics being rapidly phased out of his text from the early 1940s onwards (although not with the decisiveness he himself suggests [VII 461]). The sacrificial exigency becomes increasingly interpreted as one of forestalling war [VII 31–3], slipping precariously towards the abject status of a *means* to the preservation of peace. Whatever interest such political contortions might have from the perspective of reconstructive biography and retrospective moral pontification, their consequences for the development of general economics is of vanishing insignificance. Whether we approve or disapprove of war is, after all, scarcely the issue. (Anything of which we can approve is, in any case, less than war, disputation over this question is superfluous; war is hideous evil, and to affirm it is to cease to be human.)

War is not an evil, but evil itself. Every reckless debauching of humanity's productive resources has a military character; compacted from anarchic violence, senseless prodigality, contestation, regression, contagion, and heterogeneity. This is why criminality has an archaic sense as aggression against the community (whose relics survive in banditry and the military infrastructure of penal forms), and why the unconscious is metaphorized spontaneously as an insurgency. Sade's orgies share this military principle; 'governed' dissolvantly by force, treachery, sacrificial glory, and filth. It is the collapse of the centralized pacification of the populace which is at once the historical and literary space of the Sadean text; the uneven disintegration of society into armed packs, bands of robbers, and outlaws, as heterogeneous forces criss-cross the disinterred battle-fields of the decomposing regime, trailing vice, disorder, and ruin in their wake.

*

War is unreason, but what is reason? It is something like a pearl; the symptom of a protracted irritation. When a people becomes philosophical there is always an institution of torture to be found. In the Occidental world the basic implement of this torture, the very chamber or *territorium* of cruelty, has been called the soul. Like a black, damp, and freezing cell it has always been a torment in itself. Europe has been chained in the soul, dangling with bleeding wrists, until it lusted for destruction with a foul and parched thirst. 'Inspired' by the symbol of its gibbeted God, it has been a perpetual crusade.

With the immense, almost inexplicable energy that stems from controlled fury, the philosophers have tended the carniverous worm gnawing at our brains. Perhaps they thought that if they could sate it with an ethics its devouring would diminish for a while, but such judgement attests to a severe deterioration of the military instinct. The attempt to bargain is already a devastating defeat. To acknowledge weakness, to await response, to fend . . . these are all incompetent positions to adopt. At the level of tactics it might sometimes be necessary to fall back into a defensive posture, but grand-strategy begins and ends with a commitment to initiative; to the offensive. Pragmatism is finally indissociable from aggression. Due to a strategic idiocy on the part of its philosophers, Europe has tried to make peace with its soul, yet remorselessly – *stimulated* – the mutilation continues, and with each bite we suffer and intuit self.

The dissipation of the soul would not relate to thought as an object of theoretical representation. There would be something almost touching about Hegel's clutching for philosophical *Auflösung* if it were not so pitifully stupid. It takes only the most rudimentary psychology to know that for as long as 'I think' theory will be merely a brutal jest; a way of baiting the nervous system into an apoplexy. Whatever is thought in the grim mode of responsibility can only be registered as a grating aggravation, because it is precisely the ego which is unable to dissolve itself in thinking; clattering with its chains through labyrinths of confession, transforming energy flux into representation, into frustration. When we speak it rattles like a jagged stone in our throats. A little over two millennia ago we began to cough up strange new words with our blood and bile, and in certain quarters the excruciation of libido began to be called 'philosophy'.

> These Germans have employed fearful means to make themselves a memory, in order to become masters of their *basic* instincts and their brutal crudity: one thinks about the old German punishments, stoning for instance (the sagas already allow for a mill-stone to be dropped upon the head of the guilty), breaking on the wheel (the most authentic invention and speciality of German genius in the realm of punishment!), piercing with stakes, tearing or trampling with horses ('quartering'), boiling the criminal in oil or wine (still in the fourteenth and fifteenth century), the well-loved flaying ('cutting with

thongs'), cutting flesh out of the breast; one also covered the evil-doer with honey and left him to the flies in the burning sun. With the help of such images and procedures one finally kept five or six 'I will nots' in the memory, in relation to which one has given one's *word*, in order to live under the advantages of society – and really! – with the help of this type of memory one came finally to 'reason'! – Ah, reason, seriousness, mastery over the affects, this entire gloomy business called reflection, all these privileges and adornments of men: how dearly they have been made to pay for them! how much blood and horror is at the base of all 'good things'! [N II 803–4].

Philosophers are vivisectors, surgeons who have evaded the Hippocratic moderation. They have the precise and reptilian intelligence shared by all those who experiment with living things. Perhaps there is nothing quite as deeply frozen as the sentiment of a true philosopher, for it is necessary to be quite dispassionate if one is to find things theoretically *intriguing*. *Strong* thought is always experimentation in the severe style; 'cut, then watch'. It is not easy to be the friend – or the body – of a philosopher. They have always understood that if one is not *amused* by suffering, there is little point in attempting to reason.

It is the great pain, that long slow pain which takes its time, and in which we are burnt as by green wood, that first drives us, we philosophers, to climb into our final depth, and to do away with all trust, everything good-natured, veiling, mild, average, in which, perhaps, we previously located our humanity. I doubt whether such pain 'improves' – ; but I know that it makes us *deeper* [N II 13].

'Remorselessness' is a word that is quite quickly and easily said. To perform it against oneself and others is harder. It could scarcely be said to be a virtue, it has no hopes, and it hurts. One would be surprised, perhaps, to encounter it often. Yet the bleak compulsion for the desert – for sterile austerity – is somehow perpetually regenerated, as if there were a diffuse and inarticulate longing for the futility of obssession.

Given a sufficiently terrible history, in which useless sacrifice has become automatic – uninteresting – such nihilism is easy to explain. If one wants to be *available* for thought a stringent and icy code is requisite. One must first learn to develop a predatory sense for anything comforting that could be excised from one's life. For instance, all the little luxuries that, once savoured, have become habitual; every residue of leisure and indulgence buried in routines; and every relic of ancient mollifications (even when these are disguised as disciplines, as chastisements, as despair). Since the human being is a social animal it is inevitable that – pushed beyond a certain threshold – its solitude will become a destitution for it. If one is to generate 'thinkers' this must be exacerbated to the extreme. One must seek to eradicate the capacity for love, or rather, since this is unrealistic, one must infuse it with a harsh and paralysing cynicism. It is of particular importance that all traces of tenderness – that most dangerously blissful affect – be ground rigorously into the dirt. Life must be stripped down to its bare frame, and there is always something to be eliminated that one had mistakenly thought was architectural, but which was in fact quite different: merely a *reinforcement*. For it is only in being *allowed* to fall that a structure discovers its *emaciated* erectness – its spine.

Philosophy is a discipline. It takes only the most casual reading of Nietzsche's *Genealogie* to begin to take this word seriously; to detect its mixed aroma of sweetness and putridity that betrays innumerable spillages of blood. In addition, for those trained by Nietzsche into a more acute genealogical sensitivity – splicing refinement with a tense sickness of the nerves – a fuller panoply of odours becomes detectable; the sharp sting of fermented pain, the mustiness of prolonged despair, and the rich rankness – luxuriant in its metaphysical resonances – that only ripens in the miasma of frequent and premature death. There are few, if any, who could gaze unflinchingly into the laboratory of human cultures, but then, this is scarcely an option: the true training process of the intellect is not on display. Those fragments of atrocity that accidentally remain exposed, whether due to the vaunting of a defeated enemy's bestiality, intestine conflicts within a power apparatus, the disruptive effects of natural catastophe, or some other reason of this kind, must function as symptoms of a generally buried horror.

If disciplinary violence is to be effective it is crucial that it be without justification, and thus indifferent to teleology, either positive or negative. It must not seem as if anything is *wanted*. For the most direct way of softening a tool is to begin to give it reasons; eventually it begins to think it has a *right* to reasons.

Suffering must be obviously futile if it is to be 'educational'. It is for this reason that our history is so unintelligible, and indeed, nothing that was true has ever made sense. 'Why was so much pain *necessary*?' we foolishly ask. But it is precisely because history has made no sense that we have learnt from it, and the lesson remains a brutal one.

Useless suffering has always been Europe's 'practical philosophy', our true *evangelium*, communicated to every cranny of the earth with unparalleled dedication. After all, it is the secret of so many things. So much power becomes accessible at the point where one loses all capability to enjoy it, and better the misery of the master than the wretchedness of the slave. Thus it is that entering the space of reason has always required that one spit upon the fierce pleasures of the savages, resigning oneself instead to an infinite vacuity.

*

Academic prose has the remarkable capacity to plunge one into a sublime dystopian nightmare: *is anything this appalling really possible?* one asks. What happened to these people? Is it part of some elaborate joke perhaps? Or do they just hate books? There is a sense in which one can only admire their ability to make Nietzsche seem like a bank manager, Bataille like an occupational therapist, or Derrida world-historic, but in the end one vomits. Such writing is unparalleled as an introduction to despair: a universe in which it is possible condemns itself. (With trembling fingers one turns the pages: *we have really come to this.*) One only has to read genuine scholarship to be wracked by ardent dreams of incinerated cities.

Bataille's *Sur Nietzsche* stands alone in the salt flats of Nietzsche 'reception' (there is no generic term that fails to insult in this context). One of Cioran's casual jokes is of inestimably greater value in making contact with Nietzsche than the whole of Heidegger's ponderously irrelevant *Nietzsche*. The exceptions are rare enough: Klossowski's *Nietzsche et le cercle vicieux* was better written than not, even though it stinks of transcendental philosophy, and Deleuze's *Nietzsche et la philosophie* is saved by being solely about Deleuze (an academic who can think!). Otherwise there is only an almost mystical vacuity, the gibberings of a lobotomy ward.

Upon encountering *Sur Nietzsche* one flips through the pages with mounting excitement: no sign of scholarship or servility, prose that burns like an ember in the void, precision, profundity, *esprit*. The shock is almost lethal. The euphoria blazes painfully for weeks. At last! A book whose aberration is on the scale of Nietzsche's own; a sick and lonely book. The fact that such a book could be published even dampens one's enthusiasm for the universal eradication of the species.

How were the slapstick Nietzscheans going to punish Bataille for writing a beautiful and profound book about their master? The answer is simple; one merely extrapolates from their lack of imagination. 'Let us do the same thing again,' they squeal happily, 'let us bury him. Let us be ever so professional in our dealings with this dangerous animal, and nurture another limping dwarf.'

*

Superficially, Bataille's engagement with Nietzsche is difficult to locate. He has no sympathy for the announcement of the overman, his exoteric reading of eternal recurrence is hasty and crude, and that of will to power dismissive. He takes the thought of overman to be a residual spectre of idealist productivism, and in his early essay 'The Old Mole: on the prefix sur- in surhomme and surrealism' (but not overkill) he aligns it with the aspirational element in surrealism, a position he never revised. Eternal recurrence he considers to be an immotivating tactic, exhausted by its negative function. In *Sur Nietzsche* he associates it with an 'acceptation that is not preceded by any *effort*' [VI 159]. As for will to power; what need for an impulse to the accumulation of force on a planet drowned in solar luxuriance? It is not any positive doctrine, therefore, that lures Bataille into the labyrinth of Nietzsche's writing. He is drawn down into these texts by their 'own' labyrinthine character, and by the nihilist religion that haunts them, which he approaches through the death of God, and entitles 'the will to chance'.

The will to chance is not an addition to the archive of philosophical concepts. It is first of all the subsidence of *Sur Nietzsche* from discursive responsibility into a patchwork of quotations, theoretical passages, poems, aphorisms, fragments, and diary extracts, much written in the first person. In this way it protracts the disintegrative virulence of Nietzsche's writings with an exuberance quite alien to the pedants of the academy. In Bataille's communion with Nietzsche something occurs that is utterly incommensurable with commentary, exegesis, or interpretation. 'If community does not exist,' he writes, 'M. Nietzsche is a philosopher' [VI 27]. *Sur Nietzsche* – like Nietzsche's 'own' texts – is a space of community rather than a contribution to a body of scholarly work. 'My life, in company with Nietzsche, is a community, my book is that community' [VI 33]. Not a study, therefore, but a pact against industry, a re-activation of a war, and if Nietzsche is to be labelled a philosopher it is only in the violently pardoxical guise of 'the philosopher of evil' [VI 16].

Against the abortive consolidation of Kantian industrialism associated with Hegel and teleology, Bataille counterposes Nietzsche and the naked risk of chaos, war, eroticism, and surrender to the sacred. 'There is nothing I want except chance' [VI 161], certainly not salvation therefore, or anything associated with God who 'by definition, is not in play' [VI 84]. The will to chance no longer resents the irresponsibility of immanence, and Nietzsche figures as the attestation that '[u]nlike God, man is not condemned to condemn' [VI 75]. Devotion, prayer, hope, or faith are all violently corroded by the will to chance, which relapses towards immanence, and 'immanence is impiety itself' [VI 81]. Bataille protects nothing (one cannot offend against the sacred): 'I love irreligion, the disrespect of putting in play' [VI 86]. Nevertheless, there is no religion that is not a chance, and no morality that is not chance's denial. Morality is the domain of tasks, whilst religion dissolves itself in fate.

The will to chance is the sacrifice of the will. This is not to say that the will enacts its own end, since any *act* of surrender merely consolidates humanity; extending the range of its possibilities into negation. Unlike any act, the will to chance resists the order of the possible, but even its resistance is involuntary, a '[f]atality of working evil, in disorder' [VI 154]. Between chance and the will is impossibility or unilateral difference, such that the succumbing of the will is itself succumbed to as a chance. Chance is everything that no agent can do, and its range is only circumscribed by fictions (although dense ones). It is the same as time [VI 140, 149]; collapse of individuated being into communication. 'Being, humans, are not able to "communicate" – *live* – than outside of themselves. And as they must "communicate", they must *will* this evil, this pollution, which, putting their own beings into play, renders them penetrable one to the other' [VI 48].

Chance is not a pre-ontological arche-reserve of possibilities, and to think of it as such is merely to displace ontology; reducing chance to randomness once again. A chance has no essence outside its instantiation, which is merely an assertion of the elementary anti-Platonism sufficient in principle (were it not in fact unintelligible) for the generation of minimally materialist thought. Chance is not some kind of infra-, super-, or ur-being, and there is no sense at all in which it surreptitiously 'is'. The 'ground' of the accident is even more accidental than the accident itself.

Chance is far less a fundament than a betrayal, at once radical and gratuitous, whereby being falls prey to its indeterminate exactness. Being derives only a vanishing speck of its contingency from the fact that it is haunted by the logical spectre of an eliminative negativity. The overwhelmingly preponderant part of its deviance stems from its irresolvable composition, beyond which there is only idealist phantasmatics. If being is conceptualized, through submission to logical functions (either that of opposition to nullity, or distinction from arbitrary specification), it is idealistically reconstructed in a process that is one with the repression of chance. What separates base materialism from the scholastic differentiation between composition and creation (culminating in the Heideggerian meditation upon being) is its realism, in accepting that *being is only what it is*. In other words, being is indeterminably or *intensely* unnecessary.

That being is a chance means that it is *logically intolerant*; starving almost the entire field of possibility of the resource for actualization. The real context for being's logic (ontology) is famine. It is in this sense that Spinozism provides such a decisive paradigm for the theoretical decompression of intensity, since it is programmed by the meticulous refusal of being's logical intolerance (a necessity for one writing of *deus sive natura*). It is perhaps only here that Spinoza succumbs *abjectly* to the tradition, blinding himself to the vertiginous modal skewing which attests to the psychosis of God, and impresses itself upon materialist thought as violence and crime.

It is not that Nietzsche pronounces upon chance in a way that Bataille comes to decode, but rather that in Nietzsche's text chance decouples itself from the prison of probability, exploding in its luxuriant immensity. Nietzsche's writing is not a doctrine, but a convulsion of hazard, breaking open the cage of Kant's *nihil negativum* to float in a positive insanity, 'dissolved and free' [VI 155]. As early as 1936, in his article 'Sacrifices', Bataille explores such a cosmic antilogic, in which irresolvable improbability, irrational negation, and interminable compositional intricacy are interwoven. When compared with the play of combination occurring at an inferior stratum of composition every 'being' is an improbability so violent that Bataille labels it 'chance'. If there were a final stratum of eventuation chance would be subordinated to statistical principles, but something quite other is the case. An aberrant space which Bataille – borrowing one of Nietzsche's favourite 'metaphors' – refers to consistently as 'the labyrinth'.

Chapter 10

The labyrinth

The spirals, or galaxies, which uncoil in their gigantic tentacles of light in dark space, are composed of innumerable stars or stellar systems gathered in an 'ensemble movement'. The stars are able to be simple or composed. They are able, if one accepts that the solar system is not an exception in the immensity of the heavens, to be accompanied by a whirlwind of planets and, in the same way, the known planets are often doubled by satellites ... Celestial bodies, whatever they are, are composed of atoms, but, at least if one considers those whose temperature is greatest, the atoms of the radiating stars have no possibility of belonging to any other particular composition at the interior of the star itself: they are *in the dominion* of the stellar mass and of its central movement. Quite the contrary with the atoms of the terrestrial periphery – of the crust and the atmosphere – which are free of this dominion: it is permissible for them to enter into composition in powers which possess a developed independence in relation to the dominion of the mass. The whole surface of the planet is formed not only of molecules each uniting a small number of atoms, but also compositions which are much more complex, some crystalline and some colloidal, the latter arriving at the autonomous powers of life, of the plant, of the animal, of man, of human society [I 516–17].

The surface of the earth is formed out of molecules; each molecule unites a certain number of atoms; molecules often unite themselves, forming groups of a colloidal or crystalline nature. It is such colloids which assemble themselves to compose the individuality of the living being: plant, animal, human, escaping in that fashion from the general movement of the world, they each constitute a little world apart for themselves. Animals are able to assemble amongst themselves in turn. Humans agglomerate themselves into little groups and the little groups into larger groups, then into states. At the summit of these *compositions* one finds oneself at the greatest distance from 'nature' [VII 188].

Benoit Mandelbrot walks along a rocky shoreline in the evening. The edge of the land scales downwards through boulders, pebbles, gravel, beyond sand and into elusive extremities of complexity. The ocean is dark, suggestive of death.

If the movement of a thing is always a change within a greater thing it becomes equivalent to a partial dying. A flotsam of seaweed, small animals, fish-eggs, biological detritus, and mineral particles infiltrates innumerable estuaries. It seems as if they are exploring new intricacies of proximity. Mandelbrot wonders whether *how long is the coastline of Britain?* asks the same as *how close can we get?* How inter-tangled, how confused?

*

Bodies are not volumes but coastlines; irresolvable but undelimitable penetrabilities, opportunites for the real decomposition of space. How many orifices has the human body? The osmotic transfusion of saline chemicals from a drop of alien perspiration impacts upon a cluster of epidermal cells as an annihilating copulation.

*

As the third part of Bataille's *Inner Experience* meanders towards its insatiate termination in a splintered discussion of communication, it opens a confused and fissured space entitled *The Labyrinth (or the Composition of Beings)*. Or rather, from a certain perspective, a certain *scale*, this space seems fissured, as if integrity were merely interrupted.

The labyrinth is not an intervention into being, but an infestation or irresolvably complex collapse, replacing being with an illimitable corrosion. The labyrinth is precisely the *positive impossibility of privileged scales*; both the recurrence of irreducible detail across scales, and the recurrence of irreducible diversity in the transitions between scales. Complex heterogeneity is not suppressed by any refinement of focus, nor are simplicity, autonomy, elementariness, ever approached; 'being is *nowhere*' [V 98].

The labyrinth is a complexity that cannot be determined as an extrinsic predicate of substance; one that returns the pretension of substantiality to the uncircumscribed recession of detailing which undoes it. When woven into the labyrinth all substantiality succumbs to an unconceptualizable implosion; becoming the mere cypher for the unresolved precision of porosity. There is only 'relative simplicity' [V 98] and not being, or at least, being is diffused irrecoverable by its 'own' 'labyrinthine construction' [V 99].

The labyrinth is constructed by a recurrence – a drifting replication and a replication of drift – that proliferates an a-polar fission: 'two principles – transcendent composition of components, relative autonomy of components – regulate the existence of each "being"' [V 101]. Whatever the level or degree there is never achieved totality or simplicity, but always composition/component, an insoluble compact of integration *and* complexity.

> I can, if need be, admit that developing from an extreme complexity, being imposes upon reflexion *more* than an elusive appearance – but complexity, gradually increasing, is for this *more* a labyrinth in which it wanders endlessly, then is lost once and for all [V 98–9].

*

I do not have the least pretension to mathematical competence; my inability to subscribe to the superstition of number has crippled my intellect in this respect. Nevertheless, what little I understand about the influx of chaos themes into mathematics suggests that the discipline is being shifted in an encouragingly anti-Platonic direction, provoking me to make a few confused remarks.

The very notion of a 'mathematics of chaos' seems to suggest a grotesque domestication, such as the enfeeblement of chaos into a statistically intelligible randomness. For this reason my immediate reaction to the mathematics of chaos was one of visceral suspicion, even though a thread of eighteenth and nineteenth century German philosophy had prepared me for its topic. Nevertheless, it is not easy to imagine a mathematician ceasing to be a Platonist. Nor easy to remain immune to the virological seduction of 'a geometry of the pitted, pocked, and broken-up, the twisted, tangled, and intertwined' as Gleick summarizes it in his popularizing book [Ch 94], or to sustain an indifference to topological explorations characterized by mathematical orthodoxy as 'monstrous, disrespectful to all reasonable intuition about shapes and ... pathologically unlike anything to be found in nature' [Ch 100].

A glance at the purportedly chaomorphic 'Sierpensky-' or 'Menger sponge' both confirms and undermines such suspicions; it is a shape that is homogenized, saturated with equalities, inanely geometric, yet also irresolvable, paradoxical, *unhealthy*. A Menger sponge results from the endless recursion of a simple operation. A cube is divided into twenty-seven identical smaller cubes, with the central block and each of the six orthogonally adjacent ones being removed. The resulting frame consists of twenty blocks, which are then all treated in the same way as the initial cube, and so on, recursively. Each transformation increases surface area with a tendency to infinity, and decreases volume with a tendency to zero. However far this process is taken the sponge remains cohesive, and it is possible to trace a line in three dimensions from any point on the surface to any other. In its ideal conception a Menger sponge is thus a model of infinitely complex immanence; a universe of endlessly intricate distances, without inaccessible depths or absolute ruptures. Exceeding a surface, but evading volume, the Menger sponge is a shape of between two and three dimensions, or of a fractional dimension; a fractal to use Mandelbrot's term. Like the Möbean band of the early Lyotard, or the 'smooth space' of Deleuze and Guattatri, it is a libidinal geometry without inaccessible recesses, a topography without transcendent repression.

The Menger sponge confronts us as an immobile quasi-solid figure described (ungraspably) in space. This is intrinsic to its mathematical or ideal character. It is mapped in a geometry it does not disturb; concepts of space, time, abstraction, and infinity remain uncontaminated. In this respect it is not a 'labyrinth' (in Bataille's sense); it admits of absolute transcendence, subordination, ideal objectivity. (It might nevertheless be a certain horizon of lucidity.) Transcendental philosophy needs to be scaled, just as chaos theory needs deepening transcendentally. Between real scales there is always a difference of condition/conditioned, but this difference is only ever scalar (never polar). Unlike a Menger sponge the labyrinth cannot be expressed within a transcendent grid, since it maps an uncircumscribable terrain of immanence. Space and time find their construction 'in' the labyrinth, or nowhere. Scale is an irreducible difference.

In the end there is only the voiding of volume, in which space and time cooperate in utter continuity; chaos where everything is spent. Nevertheless, a stellar silt is pasted across the void like diseased skin, so that the ramifications of the sponge encrust death, forming a surface without real depth, in distributing distances across the scales. To ascend the sponge strata is to progressively 'transcend' a position towards the intensive construction in which it is described. From superstructure/macrostructure to infrastructure/microstructure. Always a deeper infrastructure and a shallower superstructure (one ascends into profundity, but profundity is nothing but a complication of the shallows, and 'one' is nowhere).

*

On the one hand two orientations or directions of focus, macrostructure and microstructure, on the other two states or qualifications of space, solidity and void. Between macrostructure and microstructure is a relation or difference of analogy and asymmetry. As compositions each stratum is analogous to the other, but as strata one is dissymetrically composed by the other. Macrostructure is real crudity or blur, but its reality is something other than itself ('it' is blurred). Blur is real, but what is blurred is reality (microstructure). That which is blurred is not something other than blur, but what blur 'itself' is. Blur is real, death trapped in confusion.

Void excludes solidity, but solidity does not exclude void. This absence of reciprocity is the consequence of the fact that focus has dissimilar consequences for plenitude and void. Void alone is ever strictly focused, and is thus unilaterally absolute (death is perfect). At any level of composition what appears as void is void, but what appears as solidity is a compound involving the aggregate of the unfocused; both unfocused solidity and unfocused void. In appearance (a level of focus) void and solidity exclude each other, but in reality (the unfocused of any level of focus, its micro-strata of composition), solidity is contaminated by void. Death is definitive, but life is indefinitely corroded by death. Solidity is in reality void, but reality is impossible (and inevitable).

How is the relation between scale and its content to be interpreted? The dependency of solidity upon blur seems to suggest that the dissymetries of both couples align, and that compositional ascension is generative of solidity. Blurring or scalar progression would in this case be equivalent to a variable deviation from void, so that composition is no longer thought of as static description, but as dynamic accumulation. This is the description Bataille gives in *The Accursed Share, Inner Experience, On Nietzsche,* and elsewhere. Growth is inextricable from the integrative impulse of scalar progression, in which the hierarchy of predation and of compositional organization are fused. Such a scale has a terminus but no origin, as a symptom of its basic asymmetry. Regression is without term, since there is always a subtilization of the tributary from which the anticipations of solidity gather, as they flow into the macrostructural basins of organization. Progression, however, tends – irrepressibly – to empty itself into the sea. In other words there is, as Bataille insists, a *summit*:

> If I now compare the constitution of society to a pyramid, it appears as a domination on the part of the centre, of the summit (this is a rough, even difficult schema). The summit incessantly throws the foundation off into insignificance and, in this sense, waves of laughter traverse the pyramid by gradually contesting the pretence of sufficiency of the beings placed at a lower level. But the first pattern of these waves issued from the summit flows back and the second pattern traverses the pyramid from the bottom to the top: the flowing back this time contests the sufficiency of beings placed at a higher level. This contestation, on the other hand, right up to the last instant, preserves the summit: it cannot however fail to reach it. In truth, being, without number, is in a certain sense suffocated by a reverberating convulsion: laughter, in particular, suffocates no one, but if I envisage the spasm of multitudes (whom one never takes in with a single glance) the flowing back – as I have said – cannot fail to reach the summit. And if it reaches it? This is the agony of God in black night [V 107].

Imagine an irregular Menger sponge, scaling downwards in a similar way to the Mandelbrot set, diversifying, and thus without predictability across scales (except for that of protracted scaling 'itself'). Once its differences have been stripped of periodicity it must be impossible to return to the same. Something happens that is like a becoming, liquifying matter/space into a mutating complexity of flows, with differentiated vectors and speeds, still recursively conserving detail. Currents drift across the omnisurface, and within the currents are sub-currents, and within the sub-currents ... with each seeming to float on a pseudo-volume generated by unresolved involutions of the sponge-plane. A force floating in sponge-space has no determinate speed, but traverses distances proportionate to a level of resolution; digressing with its micro-components into complexities that indefinitely protract their voyage. Any two points in sponge-space – whilst immanent to each other – map out an unsimplifiable distance that cannot be traversed *at all scales* in any given period. Contrary to anything that a superficial similarity to Zeno's paradox might suggest, this does not result from the formal character of an argument, but rather, from the material characteristics of a terrain.

Sponge-space is the positive impossibility of resolvable boundaries, and thus of discrete entities, decidable actions, unproblematic vectors, logical identities, and adequate representations. There are no representations of any kind, but only floating plates or scales, immanently distanced from each other by an indeterminably convoluted surface. In sponge-space pure spatiality cannot be demarcated from matter as a discrete concept, but conspires with matter in the sole reality possible to either: complexity. Distances are proliferated amongst the oceanic detritus of a receding shore-line, with the prospect of an ideal univocity diffused irreparably into the recurrent detail of base matter. 'You would not be able to imagine the degree of aberration to which it is possible to arrive' [II 405]. Sponge-space is a 'scale of beings' [II 293], 'scale of composition' [II 305], or 'scale of forms' [II 293–4] which does not tend to simplicity, ideality, or purity in either direction, which never becomes cephalic, capped, teleological; a *headless* axis of recession.

*

I teach you the friend and his overflowing heart. But you must understand how to be a sponge if you want to be loved by overflowing hearts [N II 325]. Thus spoke Zarathustra.

*

Reason is rotted to bits in sponge-space, because all the polar concepts which provide its structure depend upon the repression of scaling differences. Form is infested by matter, the abstract by the concrete, the transcendent by the immanent, space by time. (It is not only ideal/real, actual/virtual, infinite/finite, simple/complex that succumb, but also Euclidean/fractal, absolute/scaling, consistent/sponge.) Life is infested by death; terminally infiltrated by the unsuspendable reality of its loss. There is no integral identity or alterity, but only fuzzy sponge zones, pulsing with indeterminable communicative potencies. Not merely lethal diseases, but the disease of lethality; a labyrinth of contagion, knitted irresolvably into death.

Chaotic 'geometries' (but they are not geometries), diseases, fluids, war, vermin, and desire; all aspects of irreducible mess. A mess that does not have the simplicity of amorphousness, homogeneity, entropy, or consistent slime, no, this is a real mess; imperfectible, unthinkable (even by negation). Mess is not liquid, but differentially liquidated, *fractional at each level* between a solidity and a liquidity that mean nothing on their own, a power of infiltration that cannot be polarized. The parts of a liquid have velocities, traced in geometric space, and polarized between immobility and the rapidity of light, but the components of a fluidification have speeds; spatializions, or differential rates of becoming. These are recursive complications of geometry, arbitrarily projectable as deviating from an energetic norm, illimitable in both scalar directions. Velocities can be represented geometrically, but speeds 'shape' space. Which is to say; there is no transcendental space, no spatiality that is ultimate – whether 'highest' or most 'basic' – no final grid, topology, or terrain, no absolute geometry or legislative stratum. There are only scales in which everything happens; a labyrinth which can never be 'placed in perspective'.

Space 'itself' is deep and twisted – a 'mortuary abyss of debauchery' [IV 327] – which is not at all to suggest that it has three dimensions. Its depth does not retreat from surface, except as a maze-like complication. (Sponge)-space has the depth of Nietzschean eternity; a depth of endless intrication hollowed by recursion and a-synchronicity. Far from being synonymous with a spatial dimension, the profundity of space stems precisely from the impossibility of any geometric or cartographic master-position from which scales could be plotted in consistent space. Nor can time be exteriorized in relation to space, since both are co-effectuated as recursivity, or incomprehensibly diffuse encroachment. It is not any transcendentally spatialized objectivity, but spatiality 'as such' that is abyssally complicated through scaling.

I fall into the immensity
which falls into itself
it is blacker than my death [III 75].

*

The difference between transcendence and immanence is a matter of volume and encroachment. In the recession through scales volumes are dissymmetrically devastated by encroachments, and yet sponge-space – as a 'whole' – never reverts to the simplicity of a void. The unilateral erosion effected by real death corrupts being with an interminable complication. Transcendence is similarly powerless against the ferocious indifference of immanence; losing every encounter, eroded a little further each time, but in a process that never resolves into homogeneous negation.

The most philosophically rigorous discussion of this difference in Bataille's writings is to be found in his *Theory of Religion*, which was probably written during the mid- to late 1940s, and appeared finally in 1974. It is here that he most fully delineates his thought of transcendence; a term which he consistently employs throughout his more theoretical texts to designate *the state of separation*. As he remarks:

> The object . . . has a sense that breaks with indistinct continuity, which opposes itself the immanence or to the flowing of all that is – that it transcends. It is rigorously alien to the subject, to the ego drowned in immanence [VII 298].

This is not to say that there is first an ego for which the object is then separated by its transcendence, it is rather that ego and object are simultaneous hypostatizations of interrupted flow. What could an 'I' be that lacked all distinctness, haemorrhaging freely into death, and lost in 'immanent immensity, where there are no separations, or limits' [VII 306]?

All three of the traditional schemas of difference – logical, empirical, and transcendental – presuppose the prior distinction between subject and object. At the most straightforward this is because, in their modern sense, all three have been historically fixed in an epistemological usage (asking: how does a subject come to know an object?). Transcendental philosophy sophisticates the subject/object relation, but maintains its fundamental orientation, such that Kant's most celebrated achievement was to have consummated epistemology (in a way that is inherited and trivially readjusted by our contemporary philosophy of science). This is not to suggest that the difference between subject and object remained unquestioned between the sixteenth and eighteenth centuries, on the contrary; almost all the central concepts of philosophy in play from Descartes to Kant have served at some stage to investigate and determine this difference. The question that remains repressed in the history of Western philosophy up to Kant is not that of the articulation between subject and object, but that of the difference between the subject/object distinction itself (knowing) and inarticulate or non-objective materiality (unknowing). At the apex, with Kant, a reason is given for this silence, but the question as to the real difference at the root of knowing is only raised in order to be judged *impossible*, because difference (by this time) belongs utterly to the internality of the subject.

Epistemology takes as its problem the relation of a subjective representation to what is objectively represented – which might be problematic (scepticism) or unproblematic (dogmatism), one of difference (realism) or identity (subjective idealism) – but what is evaded in this whole calculus of permutations is the relation between knowing (subject/object separation) and what is not knowing, or the sense of what escapes thought other than as an unknown object, which is to say, other than as the real thing 'behind' the representation of the object (Kant's noumenon is still this). In order to differentiate between the real correlate of the object, or epistemologically determined real substance, and the unconditioned unknown, Bataille does not refer merely to matter, but to *base* matter; a materiality so alien to the epistemological framework that it is utterly without dependence upon the form of the object (the thing).

The thing is the instance of a petrified separation – a fetish – which represses both indistinct immanence and the difference from indifferentiation. This is because the immanence buried beneath the crust of things is the common but complex source of difference in (intensive gradations of) transcendence; the generative materiality in which everything real in transcendence must abysmally participate, and from which every separation or isolation must draw its force (but only in trailing an Ariadne's thread that escapes it; winding into obscure exteriority). Differentiation is continuity, from which only sclerosed, formalized, or structuralized differences depart, and depart only to the scale of their fictiveness. There is a certain sense in which transcendence is untruth – a utilitarian falsification or veil of *Maya* – and Bataille says of the thing that '[i]t is insofar that it is transcendence that it is fiction' [VII 375], but the premature exercise of such a judgement leaves immanence stranded in the inertia of a being-in-itself, isolated from the process of its falsification, and thus penned-back within its theological determination as passive resource. It is important, therefore, to emphasize that what is real in transcendence is not merely immanence, but also the difference from immanence (which remains immanent). The sense in which transcendence is real is not the transcendent sense of reality, which is to say that reification (emergence of things) is the reality of unreality, rooted not in thought, or in any other transcendent faculty of falsification, but rather in the differentiation of immanence; the knotted unconscious complicity through which nature stratifies itself.

Insofar as the thing is false (transcendent) it does not derive its sense from the real rupture which realizes its intensive deviation from continuity, but from the inert articulations through which it is related to other discrete beings. The price-mechanism of market economies systematizes this tendency at the highest degree of its possibility; instituting an automatism of reification that is fuelled by its own consequences, so that it insinuates equivalences between things ever more intricately into the fabric of the world.

*

Matter is stacked as transcendence, but if the relation of transcendence to immanence can be described as 'hierarchical' it is only by wrenching the word from its Nietzschean usage, and thus employing the words metaphysically (without scaling). Where Nietzschean hierarchy – developing Schopenhauer's 'grades of objectification' – is a matter of strata, scales, compositional levels, irresolvable tributaries open to the sea, labyrinthine in Bataille's sense, the so-called 'hierarchy' of binary difference, polarity, and dialectic is infinitized and sterile. It is the whole of 'Nietzschean' hierarchy which is immanent (unilateral), whilst polar hierarchy institutes transcendence. Or rather, the difference between immanence and transcendence has no absolute measure, but changes its sense according to the site of differentiation. It can certainly be construed transcendentally, as a definitive rupture of commensuration, generating the ontology which Nietzsche incessantly mocks as that of 'the real and apparent world'. Such polar thinking hypostatizes stratal difference into the *concept* of *superiority as such* (= God).

The strata of immanence transcend each other unilaterally – 'overcome' each other to persist with Nietzsche's vocabulary – but they do not transcend the materiality of scaling 'as such' (there is no such thing). Not spirit but *spiritualization* (*Vergeistigung*); densely material throughout its process. In their immanent usage transcendence and immanence mark out the directionalities of a differention; relative serial co-ordinates, phases of intensity. They are not determinate concepts, but pronominal traffic signals on the intensive sequence, provoking exacerbations. Direction not concept, experiment not approximation.

Although there can be no question of thought being adequate to sponge-matter, this does not make the issue of its inadequacy an uninteresting one. Adequacy exactly describes the ideal of an absolutely depressive pole of economy; the absence of all abbreviation. More fundamentally, the thought of adequacy is construed within a vulgar realism, and is thus quite blind to the convoluted surface of the sponge, upon which the tangled paths of immanence are traced. Between thought and the sponge there is not a relation of transcendence (epistemic representation), but one of intricate texture.

Thought is not remotely comprehensible to a philosophy of reflection, because it never grasps more than a surface of itself. Thought is no more representable by an idealized limit than by a general concept, since it has no privileged stratum of realization, no horizon of subtilization. Every thought, intellectual synthesis, or association of ideas is a pattern of convolution that is only ever apprehended under conditions of indeterminable summarization. Even the crudities and failures of thinking unfold upon the terrain of an illimitable complexity. So it is not just that on the sponge-matter surface the shortest distance between two points is something other than a straight line. Such a distance is not even finalizable. Crudity enables things to happen (contra Zeno), but only under the conditions of an imperfection whose potentialities for evolution escape definition.

*

A provisional differentiation is obviously possible between elementary sponges (such as Bataille's groping example of the *siphonophore*) and scaled sponges for which '*being* is *composed*' [VII 265] irreducibly (such as Menger's). An elementary sponge might also be a scaled sponge, but of an extremely disequilibriated kind. It has a privileged stratum of fission, which is a threshold at which death vertiginously transforms its sense. A siphonophore can be dissolved to the level of its cells and still recompose itself, but dissolution below this level annihilates it. In the same way, a hive of bees or a colony of termites can be disaggregated without irreparable damage, which does not hold for the dismemberment of the individual insects composing them. Yet even in these cases the matter is more complex; sex cells, viruses, nutrient compounds, and other components circulate upon differentiated strata, irreducible to specifiable economies of life and death. The death of a highly organized animal triggers a crisis across a large spectrum of its biochemical composition, but it does not precipitate a return to some zero-degree of chemical organization. Under 'natural circumstances' the compositional stock of such a creature is rapidly plundered; its proteins and fats redistributed into new hierarchies by scavengers of all kinds. Cultural organisms are able to treat texts and other detritus of life in an analagous fashion.

Sade's thought begins to stray into the labyrinth when he writes:

> Now then, what value can Nature set upon individuals whose making costs her neither the least trouble nor the slightest concern? The worker values his labour according to the labour it entails and the time spent creating it. Does man cost Nature anything? And, under the supposition that he does, does he cost her more than an ape or an elephant? I go further: what are the regenerative materials used by nature? Of what are composed the beings that come into life? Do not the three elements of which they are formed result from the prior destruction of other bodies? If all individuals were possessed of eternal life, would it not become impossible for Nature to create any new ones? If Nature denies eternity to beings, it follows that their destruction is one of her laws. Now, once we observe that destruction is so useful to her that she absolutely cannot dispense with it, and that she cannot achieve her creations without drawing from the store of destruction which death prepares for her, from this moment onward the idea of annihilation which we attach to death ceases to be real; there is no more veritable annihilation; what we call the end of the living animal is no longer a true finis, but a simple transformation, a transmutation of matter, what every modern philosopher acknowledges as one of Nature's fundamental laws [S III 514].

What is crucial to the labyrinth, maze, or 'composition of beings' [II 293] is that the 'word individual is not able . . . to serve as a designation for a degree of the scale of forms' [II 293–4]. Each element is corrupted by an irreducible organizational fabric that opens across the difference of scale. 'I am led ... to propose to speak of aggregate [*amas*] if it is a matter of associations which do not modify the parts forming it, of "composed beings" when it is a matter of atoms, cells, or elements of the same order' [II 295]. Simple animals such as sponges and starfish are characterized by a relatively loose assemblage of cells, whilst linear animals – such as insects or vertebrates – exhibit a 'more complex mode of composition' [II 294] in which the organic elements succumb more profoundly to their integration. In his early 'sacred sociology' writings Bataille employs the distinction between colonies and societies to mark this difference between aggregated and scaled multiplicities. A society is an assemblage or composition which does not consist of individuals possessing a greater ontological density than its own, and this absence of privileged scale meshes it inextricably with death (the unlocalizable zero of community). The 'elements' of a society are thus vampirically drained towards the nuclear whole, just as they are agitated in their integrity by the ineliminable flows at 'a lower degree on the scale of composition' [II 305], lending the labyrinth a 'double aspect' [II 292, 293]. Such particles – more spongiform than sponges themselves – are irreparably violated by their constellation into the dissipative mass of the labyrinth.

*

General economy is a traffic system; marking routes within the complex immanence or quasi-horizontality that infests the axis of transcendence. Every vertical difference is collapsible onto a tangled horizontal flow. It is not that base materialism denies the necessity of vertical articulation; there is no tendency to delete the vocabulary of summits and troughs, differences in intensity, compositional strata. The elimination of such an axis from materialist thought would leave nothing but a theologically constituted reality abandoned by God (a colony of particles). Scaling is the positive superfluity of God inherent to matter, but its gradations of relative transcendence must be commensurated with an impersonal nature exhausting the real: genealogically rather than metaphysically explored. The labyrinth is the unconscious of God, or the repressed of monotheism. The illusion of ego in general requires that it remain unthought. What God really was is something incompatible with anything 'being' at all. Real composition is not extrinsically created nature, but if this is a

Spinozism, it is one in which substance itself is sacrificed to the scales. So that atheism is in the end (an end without end) an immense sponge, a mega-sponge, the dissolution of boundaries in all of its positive complexity. It is an inexhaustible porosity, saturated with negation, pregnant with swarming lethalities, and drunk upon the sea. Sponge-matter – encroached without limit by silence – is the same thing as fate. In any traffic system real transition precedes articulation (which means that there are no boundaries, but only digressions). Sponge-vectors do not connect pre-existing points, but spawn decomposable patches from out of the subtilization of speeds and the intricate criss-crossing of routes. Absolute points are transcendent mirages, hyperbolically projected out of dismantled vector nets. The *reality* of space is only the *possibility* of flow.

'Were you to stop a short moment: the complex, the gentle, the violent movements of worlds will make of your death a splashing foam' [V 112], writes Bataille. The word 'death' has the same mix of referential richness and conceptual poverty as the sign lifting a speed restriction. It would designate a concept only if this semiotic transition were treated as the representation of absolute velocity, rather than an incitement to free-flow. Dying is the departure from a traffic system, but this emigration is not transcendentally governed by a pure destination. The slipping-away of an animal into death is no less intricately positive than the arterial pulse pumping the blood from its heart. We are all fictional suicides, some impatient, some less so, but all demonstrating by our meticulousness the taciturnity of death. 'In effect, death is nothing in immanence, but due to the fact that it is nothing, no being is ever truly separated from it' [VII 308].

Death
answer
sponge streaming with solar
dreams [V 186].

*

And straightway one of them ran, and took a spunge, and filled *it* with vinegar, and put *it* on a reed, and gave him to drink [Matt XXVII 48].

And one ran and filled a spunge full of vinegar, and put *it* on a reed, and gave him to drink [Mark XV 36].

they filled a sponge with vinegar, and put *it* upon hyssoup, and put *it* to his mouth [John XIX 29].

*

Dying is inextricable from the harsh flame of sexual torture in which one is progressively consumed. It does not patiently await its consummation, but gnaws at the base of the brain; grinding each life into eroticized debris. Survival dissolves as a frangible dam does – eroded to bits by the tumult of energetic rage – so that sexual craving is the howl of nature's fringe pounded into trash by the sun.

Life is a scream *which one cannot desire to ameliorate*. It is rather that one would exacerbate it. Agony alone has the power to seduce us, and it is to our most savage torments that we most ardently cling. We know that a life which was not torched into charcoal by desire would be an unendurable insipidity. (Pain, however, remains pain. A word that is easily written. Perhaps there is little point in remarking upon it. One could imagine innumerable spurious reasons for reiterating the word 'scream' for instance. That life itself is filthy hurt . . . who could care about this being discussed? 'Everyone and no-one' as Nietzsche suggests?)

Eroticism would be impossible, if it were not that we know ourselves to be an unuttered howl, a scream. Nothing is more hypocritical than our public desexualization; the wretched urbanity with which we have replaced communication. 'Sexuality can be survived', we mutter with each dilute gesture, but of course, it cannot. We prevaricate until secreted in a liquid space (so often hidden at the lip of sleep) and then admit by our abandonments that everything is pregnant with death.

*

My wish to vomit persisted. It hadn't ceased, so to speak, since the day before last. I went to look for a bottle of bad champagne. I drank a chilled glass of it: after a few minutes I got up to go and vomit. After vomiting I went back to bed, I was slightly comforted, but the nausea wasn't long in returning. I was gripped by trembling and chattering of the teeth: I was obviously sick, I suffered in a very bad fashion. I fell back into a sort of fearful sleep: everything began to come unhooked, things that were obscure, hideous, unformed, that it was absolutely necessary to stabilize; there was no way to do so. My existence came apart like rotten matter . . . [III 425–6].

The semiology associated with 'the death of the author' is formulated in terms of an antinomy of authority. It accepts a question of intention, proceeds to resolve it negatively, and then moves on to a theory of indeterminate significations which valorizes the process of reading. What is at stake in the cruder variants (Barthes) is a dialectic of authority which redistributes the site of legislation from writer to reader. More intricate accounts take things further, so that with Lacan and Derrida the position of authority is itself subverted by the general text, in which the reader as much as the author was always already enmeshed and surpassed. In all of these cases death is thought of as the necessity that something does not reach us, and could never reach us. The transcendental impossibility of anything reaching us builds death (/castration) into the movement of signification, as the arche-absentiality that articulates/effaces base contact.

It is hard to imagine that anything could prevent Bataille's writing being flipped speculatively into this mirror space of frustrated representation, but this does nothing to increase the persuasiveness of such a move. If one is first prepared to think of the death infesting Bataille's writing as *his* death, in a gesture that can then be transcendentally exacerbated to undermine the general possibility of the proper, and thus of the 'ownness' of death, whilst nevertheless retaining the pathos of a ruined presence, then Bataille can indeed be deconstructed (with considerable technical meticulousness). Nowhere in this procedure is the contagious positivity of death touched upon (it is a matter of principle that nothing is touched upon), nor its fluidity, intensity, explosive impersonality, or solar luxuriance. Always the titillation of suspended meaning, and never the impact of oblivion (loss is thought as a deduction from anticipated lucidity, not as a variable positive voracity). On the one hand death as the ultimate nostalgia of signification, on the other death as the virulent flux of communication.

It is not that Bataille or his signifying intentions are blocked by death, it is rather that death is blocked by civilization in such a way that it is (merely) represented as an impossible signification, or as an impossibility of signification. That 'Bataille' should arise as a hermeneutic topic, more or less problematized by the empirical or transcendental death of the person, is itself the symptom of a far more basic inhibition, operating at a level continuous with impersonal death. In other words, death is not the principle of the ascetic law of representation, but the final term of the forbidden. With every word that one writes about Bataille one compounds a misunderstanding, contributing to an ordered representation of crime and oblivion. It could be said that the issue here is that of a paradox, but that is mere subordination to a philosophical lexicon, and thus definitive resignation to an accumulative outcome. More urgent by far is the mixture of nausea and fear that accompanies the pre-philosophical impact of Bataille's dilemma; a vertiginous slippage upon the immanence of death. It is then that one grasps every word, read or written, as a desperate scrabbling for escape (from isolation).

'The putting to death of the author by his work', writes Bataille, before quoting an astonishing passage from Proust in *Inner Experience*. After doing so he resumes the thread:

> The gods to whom we sacrifice are themselves sacrifice, tears wept to the point of dying. This in *Remembrance of Things Past* which the author would not have written if, broken with pain, he had not yielded to that pain, saying: 'Let us allow our bodies to disintegrate . . .' what is this if not the river, flowing in advance to the estuary, which is the sentence itself: 'Let us . . .'? and the open sea into which the estuary empties is death. So much so that the work was not only what led the author to his tomb, but the way in which he died; it was written on his deathbed . . . The author himself wanted us to feel him dying a bit more at each line [V 175].

It is only when authors are something other than their death that a literary theory can surgically excise them, when between 'themselves' and their inexistence no communication or continuity occurs. The condition of impossibility for a *theory* of authorial absentiality receives a precise nomination in Bataille's text: literature. One can readily accept that Bataille's discursivity comprises an analysable semiotic system, it remains only to note one urgent fact: that such discursivity is the thing sacrificed by his text.

Oeuvres complètes de Georges Bataille is a discursive label. The genitive is problematic, of course, as is the proper name, but so are all the elements. Not only *works*, but *complete* works! It scarcely seems probable. What do we find in these texts after all? Even at the discursive level they seem to suggest that individuality, creativity, and possession are illusions, that literature is something quite other than work, and that completion is inevitably aborted. They dramatize their gaps, absences, discontinuities, repudiate their authenticity, contest themselves. The rafts of coherence one finds are always adrift in disorder and confusion. Tortured juxtapositions, fragments, and abandoned plans abound.

Techniques of disintegration operate at all levels of Bataille's text, tending to distribute it along an axis of maximal fission. The extreme instance of this is the anorexic attenuation typical of his poetry, where the line is stripped of almost all its semantic and syntactic burden to enter into a vertical series of discontinuous cries. The line collapses towards a resilient spinal core, along which shrunken stanzas unstring themselves, like beads dropping from a broken necklace into a dimension of intoxicating descent. Other techniques include extended ellipsis, the employment of two separate gears of paragraphing (with both indentations and vertical line-breaks), violent narrative shifts of various kinds . . . But in the end it is not a matter of technique. The *fragmentation of Bataille's text* cannot be domesticated within the subjective genitive. Death 'itself' dissipates, aborts, fragments. Stories forestall completion, organization is lost, draft is spliced corrosively with accomplishment.

Whose completion and whose work? Bataille's? His editor's? Ours? As we have already glimpsed, there are innumerable theories of the text which might intervene at this point, attempting to persuade us one way or another. Some of these theories are even genealogically contaminated by Bataille's writings – although never more than tangentially so – but what they tend to share amongst themselves is a predisposition to an epistemological, ontological, or ethico-political register, and a certain sanitary distantiation from what *matters* to the text. The epistemophiliac fixation proper to theory, with its attachment to security, regularity, generalizability, and other cultural forms of insulation, might lead to possible *readings* of Bataille, but not to a *communication*; a pestilential seduction by these 'words purveyors of the plague' [III 197]. Bataille is less an 'interesting writer' than a loathesome vice, and to be influenced by him is less a cultural achievement than a virological horror; far closer to the spasmodic rot of untreated syphilis than to the enrichment of an intellect.

Any theorized 'death of the author' domesticates the infectious wastage through which Bataille's incompletion is spread. His is not the immaculate absence of the semiologists, but a filthy death; as senselessly unmanageable as a scream. We are touched abysmally by the very gesture that removes every authentic trace of 'his existence' from us; his disappearance is a violent communion. In the embers and smudges we inherit under the mark of *Bataille* something is deliberated which subverts all possibility of deliberation, as chance and failure are meticulously facilitated, and teleology undoes itself at its peak. Strategy runs itself into chaos in the incomprehensible zone where accidents are planned, and where desire flows freely into loss (of control). Will to chance. Ashes to ashes, mess to mess: a virulent irregularity continued into the complexities of a literary estate, into a 'chaos of books and papers' [IV 192].

Death is a completion of sorts, one supposes. This is comforting enough to believe, and thus almost certainly untenable. How pleasant, to be *rounded off* by one's abolition, to be edited by death. This is a way of thinking similar to that of all those who assume they will get better at death, that age will ease them gently into her cold arms. This dream of soft passage is like that of tradition, inheritance, legacy and memorial, conceiving writing on the model of transmission. It is thought as if it were essentially something received; offering itself successfully to the consummating fulfilment of a deciphering (however tantalizingly problematical this may be). Not only does such a model serve as an implicit apologetics for the cultural commodity process, it also trivializes by idealization the mute catastrophe of writing. That the immensely preponderant bulk of writing is lost forever is not a mere empirical accident – far less a phenomenologico-transcendental structure of non-presence – but an effect inherent to the nihilistic core of the literary impulse. At its root literature is *writing for nothing*; a pathological extravagance whose natural companions are poverty, ill-health, mental instability, and all the other symptoms of a devastated life that is protracted in the shadow of futility. In the current organization of civilization the facility of contacting a text is – at the very least – radically accidental with respect to its literary intensity. The bare minimum of honesty requires an acknowledgement that literature is spent almost entirely unattended. It is as foreign to us in our social being as an earthquake beneath the sea.

*

Confronting the absolute posed by our inevitable extinction, we feel brave, proud of ourselves, we permit ourselves a little indulgence, swooning in the delectations of morbidity. To face up to death is more than *the others do*, our haunted grimace becomes a complacent smile, we run our hands lovingly over the lichen-spattered graves. It is as if we have done our share, as if it were now up to death to make some gesture of reciprocation, of gratitude. How thankful death will be that we accept it so, it will surely favour us for treating it so tolerantly. We even imagine it as an outcast, rejected by all, miserable, hungry, endlessly appreciative of the benefactor who takes it in. Thus it is that death becomes cut to our dimensions, becomes *our* death, a friend, a little ominous perhaps, a little bleak-hearted, but limited by the modest horizon of its task; that of bringing a definitive end to ourselves. We sit on tombs and imagine the corpse within lying alongside its death, the two of them, snuggled together as lovers, mutually satiated by the perfection of their symmetry. What fidelity death shows! What simplicity to its desires! And how cruelly it is spurned! In the final phase of this insanity we find ourselves choked with pity for our dark and neglected twin.

How gentle and soothing, if death were really nothing but ceasing to be, but is there such a thing as 'mere death'? Were there to be we would never learn of it, for it is only in over-reaching itself that death leaves a script. What greater mistake than confusing *our* death with non-being? Is it because we want to believe in the loyalty of our substance that we make this peculiar equation? If so, we should be ashamed of our dishonesty. The facts are blatant: it is not the case that death leaves matter satisfied. At most it is a temporary refreshment, a cool black wave for matter to bask in like a reptile, a phase of dormancy, before the rush back into the convulsive dissipation of life. Perhaps we feel that our deaths should be more fulfilling, that they should be important enough to quench the most insensate thirst. It is almost as if we still believe in the faithful resurrection of the flesh. How humiliating then that matter remains *itchy* after shaking us from it, that it is still eager, that even before our mourners have forgotten us it is flirting with the worms . . . Across the aeons our mass of hydro-carbon enjoys a veritable harem of souls.

*

How much dying can a body do? At least one dose, and even this figure is conservative except in the case of the most elementary life.

A more complex organism is a true economy of death, running off a perpetuated inner catastrophe, shedding its cells into the ocean of ruin. It is the crudest type of error to reserve the word death for total systemic collapse: for the *end of dying*. Human bodies do not echo the neuroses that inhabit them, staving off disintegration, clutching at postponement, sealing death out, no, they glut themselves on death, traders in devastation, turning themselves over from within.

Matter is in flight from the possibility of essence as if from an original pertinency of ontology, and life is merely the most aberrant and virological variant of this flight; the convulsive fringe of being's relinquishment. Life is an exploration of death, whose motor is an exteriority from which it can never separate itself. It comes closest to co-extension with a principle in its deviation from the echoes of real essence; in its turnover or metabolism. Life smears itself across death as the migration from concrete existence; the meanderings of an ever accentuated vagrant reproducibility through confusion.

'No particle is the same', we happily admit, when discussing a body differentiated from itself by a few years. We try not to understand that we are thus accepting the final abandonment by complex life of all allegiance to existence. Life *evolves* into the embrace of death, becoming a mere turbulence of disappearance, indifferent to its pullulating inner mass, to its inner ruthlessnesses ... To be part of an organism is to become dispensable, and ever more dispensable. No course is more suicidal than that of the living substance that becomes an organ. Bataille writes of the human being for 'whom the components die incessantly (such that none of the elements that we *were* subsists beyond a certain number of years)' [V 98].

We are still determined to believe that we have one single and conclusive death awaiting us, a death tailored to the dimensions of a soul. But if a body is a river of death, what makes us so sure 'a self' isn't one? Is it likely that 'we' should really remain the same? It is the most elementary common sense to believe in our existence of course, but then, would it really be convenient for the body to admit to the ephemera in its nerves that it has so little attachment to them?

*

Animals of the species *homo sapiens* – it is rashly suggested – 'know that they are going to die'. Bataille claims so on a very great number of occasions. If this is so it is perplexing why they act as they do. Nowhere outside humanity is the indefinite postponement of life – named *différance* in recent times – developed to such a pitch of wretchedness. Which amongst our gestures would remain unchanged if it were to be the last? No impulse amongst us that is not a hesitation. No adventure without reserve.

The relation between being and death is commonly understood in one of two ways. Either existentially, such that death is thought of as an absolute loss of being-in-the-world, or naturalistically, such that being is considered to be utterly unimpaired – merely rearranged – by death. For the implicit existentialist (who is everyone in their moments of naïvety) both being and death belong absolutely to that scale consistent with the totality of the human person, whilst for the naturalist being recedes towards a level of fundamental elements, a level at which 'death' is always extrinsic. Heideggerian death is an absolute ontological horizon, whilst thermodynamic heat-death (comprehending all natural deaths) is merely energy-conserving disorder.

With Bataille things are different. 'Being is *nowhere*' [V 98]. Which is to say, it has no privileged scale, no refuge, either in the atom or in the totality. From the perspective of ontology the compositions at each scale are gnawed by insufficiency; both too friable and too partial to *be*. Being would be other to death – either annihilated by it or left immaculate – *were there not scales*.

If there were not scales, death would be *so* sublimely metaphysical. Take Aquinas for instance. There is no gesture exhibiting a greater fidelity to theology than the differentiating stroke with which he distinguishes decomposition from annihilation. Along with such a difference comes the entitlement to an entire flora and fauna of theistic distinctions: soul/body, essence/accident, creation/metamorphosis, etc. The scales as a whole are grouped together upon the ontological fundament of divine conservation, within which empirical death circulates as an obedient angel of the Lord.

Aquinas' reason is of crystal clarity:

> what is created comes out of nothing [ex nihilo]. Now composite things [composita] come out of their components [componentibus], not nothing, and therefore it is not them exactly that are created [A VIII 41]

> matter [materia] underlies natural production, and consequently

it, and not the concrete thing composed of it [compositum], is what, properly speaking, is created [A VIII 41].

A simple bilateral disjunction between being and nothing propels Aquinas' thinking here. The economy of being operates within a consistent conservative action, monopolized by an extrinsic author who interdicts any impulse on the part of nature to a direct collaboration with zero. Compositional strata are quarantined from logical differentiations; ghettoized in the sordid slums of a creation that is paternalistically comprehended by divine reason. 'God is the cause of things through his mind and will, like an artist of works of art' [A VIII 53].

Chapter 11

Inconclusive communication

'I am so weak sometimes that I lack the strength to write. The strength to lie? I must put it like this: the words that I align lie. I wouldn't write on the walls of my prison: I would have to tear out my nails to seek the issue.

'Write? turn one's nails against oneself, hope, completely uselessly, the moment of deliverance?

'My reason to write is to reach B./

'That which would consummate despair [Le plus désespérant]: that B. loses in the end the thread of Ariadne which is – in the maze of her life – my love for her' [III 113–14].

The fictive and the literary do not run parallel to the theoretical in Bataille's writing, it is perhaps better to think of them as dramatizing the untruth of theory, if the relation is to be theorized at all. One might say that at the level of writing theory is a constricted species of fiction, in the same way that the actual constricts possibility (but what matters is the *impossible*). It is thus that one would acknowledge that epistemic factors are secondary to textual generativity, in a manner that has come to be described as 'postmodern'. Even in Bataille's terms, insofar as a Freudian lexicon might be adequate to them, it could be persuasively suggested that it is only when a narrative is rigorously disciplined by the reality principle that a theoreticization emerges in consequence, whereas the unfettered movement of the primary process is of a spontaneously literary character. Literature is not primordially a matter of effort, any more than love or dying are. Theory – on the other hand – is work.

At the beginning of *The Accursed Share*, for example, Bataille explicitly subtracts all dignity from the theoretical impulse of his work. He remarks that 'my work tends first of all to *increase* the sum of human resources, but its results teach me that accumulation is nothing but a delay, a retreat from the inevitable discharge [*échéance*], when accumulated riches will have no value save that of the instant' [VII 20]. There is – in the end – no reason to delay beginning upon one's death, even though such a delay is reason itself. With such a statement discourse runs itself into the sand, anticipating an end to all theory that will always come from without. It is because theory only exists as a fiction, a unilateral deviation from solar howl, that it continues; impotent even to terminate itself. 'A book that no one awaits, that does not respond to any formulated question, that the author would not have written if he had followed its lesson to the letter, here is the peculiarity [*bizarrerie*] that I propose to the reader today' [VII 21].

The process of unbinding that is misleadingly named production takes place within a general field of expenditure, of which it is a specification. Due to the fact that it is initiated by a preliminary loss, production is always (excessive) replenishment, and not the simple occurrence of plenitude. Defaults in production subside towards a base of erosive profligacy, rather than to the security of inertia. Rooted in lava and earthquake, the production process is condemned to the hazards of an inescapable volatility.

The first paragraph of *Economy to the Scale of the Universe* ends with an utterance that dissolves into inconclusiveness; 'the energy that I expend now in writing . . .' [VII 9]. Whatever the operations of substitution, appropriation, and extraction that are brought to bear on Bataille's (or any other) text, *loss has already happened*. Whilst growth is juggled precariously into the future, speculated upon, and projectively developed, death is a fact. The text is initiated in the consummation of waste.

Writing shares in the sub-ontological delirium of the universe, and is primordially expenditure. But it is also to a large extent dominated by the superordinate terrestrial strata of production and reason; primary and secondary utility. Bataille names writing *discourse* insofar as it conforms to the order of utility. When it betrays, corrodes, and liquidates utility – regressing to the burning lava-flow of its base materiality – he names it *literature*. 'Literature is the essential, or it is nothing' [IX 171], Bataille writes in the introduction to *Literature and Evil*. Unless literature is the termination of sense, the reef at the end of words, it is a mere ornamentation of discourse. The radical inutility of literary language is not to be excused by epistemic, ideological, or moral apologetics (such as those that dominate current critical debate) but exacerbated to the point of collapse, because '[l]iterature is *communication*' [IX 171]. A literary destiny that is not an immolation is an insipidity. Fiction is a betrayal of being, but one that is uncircumscribed by the order of the real. 'The worst thing was to be at the point where, by an obscure fatality, each thing is taken to the extreme, and to feel myself, at the same time, released by life' [III 282]. Being (conservation) is the essence of utility and the highest principle of reason. Fiction, on the contrary, is loss. If literature has a value it can only be interpreted as *prestige*, such as that emerging from the potlatch of aboriginal economies; a *glory* that is the same as *horror*. Having broken with all fidelity to existence, fiction belongs amongst what is toxic and accursed upon the earth.

> The only means of compensating for the offence of writing is the annihilation of what is written. But that cannot be done except by the author; destruction leaving the essential intact, I am able, nevertheless, to bind negation so tightly to affirmation that my quill effaces in like measure that which it advances [*efface à mesure ce qu'elle avança*]. It effects therefore, in a word, that which is generally effected by 'time', – which, of its multiplied edifices, lets nothing subsist except the traces of death. I believe that the secret of literature lies here, and that a book isn't beautiful except when skilfully ornamented by the indifference of ruins [III 336].

Fiction is initiated in an annihilation of the world, but one that is at first isolated. Such writing is a darkness that is itself germinated in the dark; emerging fungally in a blackness that normally extinguishes it. In its contempt for the security of things, literature is sullied by a sacred character, and is nothing beyond the possibility of deeper contact than that offered in profanity. Nevertheless, the encapsulating space of the profane world oppresses it with the full weight of being; imprisoning it in the spectre of interiority. In this way the 'inherent' density of literature is bound to the fate of an address. Literature cannot be analysed beyond the common predicament of an utterance and its promulgation: beyond the fatality of communion.

From the side of theory there is an interpretation of literature as epistemic collapse, whilst from the side of literature there are stories about work as an imprisonment. This is not to suggest that

Bataille's fiction involves a workerist ideological critique, far less a social realism. Any earnestness of this sort would be the most abject submission to the ethic of production, and miss the crucial point, which is that Bataille fails utterly as a writer, a fact that is not speculatively redeemed by the way failure finds a voice in his work. That his writings communicate powerfully, propelled by unparalleled resources of insinuation, attests merely to the virulence of futility, and not to any subterranean productivity of the negative. It is rather that his characters intricate themselves into the dissolution of narrativity, forestalling its restoration as a contingently unrealized aesthetic aspiration. Bataille's fictions lose themselves (ungraspably) within themselves, rather than merely succumbing to an intelligible derailing. 'I imagined having myself condemned to silence, in an indefinite pain, as great as words . . .' [III 166]. There is no redemption through literature, but only a deepening horror and delight, which at some indiscernible mazing of the labyrinth crosses over . . .

Whatever the differences – and they are immense – between *The Story of the Eye* and Bataille's later fiction, or between his novels and his poetry, there is a consistent tone to his literary writings, a *darkness*, 'collapse of being into the night' [IV 23]. Not only are nocturnal scenes abnormally prevalent, but their effect is compounded by the interwoven themes of the unavowable, the unholy, and alcoholic oblivion. Base sexuality, sickness, religion, and intoxication entwine about each other in these texts, as withered creepers and roots might do as they cascaded into a chasm full of bats. A delirial fracturing presses the dominant thematic flows to the point of narrative discontinuity; shattering the aspiration to literary accomplishment, and collapsing its remains in amongst the embers of characters who cannot complete themselves. A sterilizing malaise dithers between narrative content and the process of writing. Sketches, fragments, ruptures, suicides, drunks, impossible desires and the burning thirst to be damned . . . this is a world of wrecked art, nihilistic love, and death triumphant; pervaded throughout by a hideous allure. In *The Story of the Eye* Bataille writes of 'everything that is bound to profound sexuality, for example blood, suffocation, sudden terror, crime, everything that indefinitely destroys human beatitude and decency' [I 15].

*

That which one qualifies with the name *love* when one seeks to determine the disinterested elements of life is nothing but a fragmentary representation of assemblages of impulses which are put in movement as soon as an object is found outside the normal course of things where everything is indifferently identifiable. Love – being nothing ordinarily than the conscious part of those assemblages – opposes itself to identification (to knowledge) of the object, which is to say that its object is necessarily charged with a heterogeneous character (analogous to the character of the blinding sun, excrements, gold, sacred things) [II 141].

Literature is like love in that both are catastrophic diseases. The way literature wantonly exploits the resources of base physiology is like love, as is the way it allies itself with hunger, sleeplessness, malaise, and strange fevers; derailing lives, and undoing the most methodical projects. Love introduces the taste of abjection and the gutter into the most secure of existences, breaking open interiorities, until it finally gets its wretched sacrifices down onto the floor, from where they are pitched into the abyss of supplication *without possible reponse*, choking on a sulphurous mixture of ecstasy and despair. There is no great literature that is not simultaneously a degradation and a burning futility. It is no coincidence that literature has been a perpetual tortured erotic stammering, whose aesthetic momentum flows from the fact that 'beauty alone ... renders tolerable the need for disorder, violence, and indignity that is the root of love' [III 13].

There is certainly no 'philosopher', and perhaps there is no writer of any kind, who has more recklessly explored the dark and extravagant terrain of erotic love than Bataille. It is not only that his fictions and poems are saturated with the erotic, since *Eroticism*, *The History of Eroticism*, and *Tears of Eros*, etc. are all 'theoretical works', but nor is it that this 'theme' is extended in a circumscribed fashion into certain non-literary texts. It would be tempting to suggest that – as the fusion of sexuality and death – eroticism was the keystone of Bataille's entire work, were it not that it is incommensurable with self, completion, and achievement. Eroticism certainly communicates itself into the most tangled vacuolizations of Bataille's writing, melding heterogeneous terms into viral constellations, and messing everything up, but then: '"[c]ommunication" is love, and love defiles those it unites' [VI 43].

Every production and articulate word, every morsel of nourishment, every second of sleep, is an atrocity against love and a provocation to despair. Erotic passion has no tolerance for health, not even for bare survival. It is for this reason that love is the ultimate illness and crime. Nothing is more incompatible with the welfare of the human species. 'I search only for the terror of evil' [IV 219], writes Bataille, in his adherence to the violent refusal of integral being. 'Evil is love' [III 37], 'the need to deny an order with which one is unable to live' [III 37]. The terrestrial problematic at its most furious finds a useless undoing in eroticism, so that the descent into love is also fundamental economy, which is perhaps a tragedy, or a joke (something truly *hideous* and sacred in any case).

That the root of love is a thirst for disaster is exhibited throughout its erratic course. At its most elementary love is driven by a longing to be cruelly unrequited; fostering every kind of repellent self-abasement, awkwardness, and idiocy. Sometimes this provokes the contempt that is so obviously appropriate, and the tormented one can then luxuriate in the utter burning loss that each gesture becomes. One wastes away; expending health and finance in orgies of narcosis, breaking down one's labour-power to the point of destitution, pouring one's every thought into an abyss of consuming indifference. At the end of such a trajectory lies the final breakage of health, ruinous poverty, madness, and suicide. A love that does not lead such a blasted career is always at some basic level *disappointed*: 'to love to this point is to be sick (and I love to be sick)' [III 105]. Yet there are times in which the morbid horror of love infects the beloved, or one is oneself infected by the passion of another, or two strains of love collide, so that both spiral together into a helix of strangely suspended disintegration, cheated of innocent disaster. Each competes to be destroyed by the other, drifting into the hopeless ecstasies that follow from the severing of all moorings, attempting to exceed the other in mad vulnerability. When propelled by an extremity of impatience this too can lead to suicide of course, but such an outcome is uncommon. The adequate pretext for such a conclusion is lacking, since the capacity to wound is melted from the world, which becomes a softened – and often almost imperceptible – backdrop, whilst the beloved, who is invested with such a capacity to a degree inconceivable to the utilitarian mind, strives entirely to annul it. Thus it is that the lovers conspire to protect each other from the lethal destiny of their passion, either succeeding in this, and relapsing into the wretched sanity of mutual affection, or compacting their fever to new scratch-patches of intensity. In the latter case all legible charts are lacking, and if the real has a splinter-fringe of utter exploration this is it . . .

. . . Sickness is something I understand. My corpse trembles in a euphoria of allergy each day that it drags itself across the surface of the earth. The weather ravages me, my joints become inflamed, ankylose, my lungs are shredded and torched to the point that they scarcely resist any longer, my skin is greenish pale, and the sockets of my eyes are withdrawn into black pits of foulness. As for my nervous-system – charred and three-quarters unstrung – that is my true pathological exhibit. No movement that does not seem like the twitching of an animal tortured to the brink of collapse, no thought that is not an experiment in damnation. Between ecstasy and torment there is no longer an interval of moderation; there is not even an alteration. I writhe on the spit of a devastated vitality, laughing with hunger for each ratcheting of descent . . .

> I have the hope of coming to the end of my health, perhaps even to the end of a life without reason to be [III 414].

*

The only honest words? The only words with integrity?

There are none. Only silence and pain (and even then there is still corruption).

To speak of eroticism is to be skewered upon pretence; sinking into either artificial passion or parodic discourse. What point in trying to persuade you (were it true) that each word is an inverse fake orgasm, a pseudo-lucidity, a howl trapped in the throat? The endeavour to let love speak merely fosters the pathetic delusion that it is unnecessary to die, as if individuated existence were capacious beyond the banality of being.

I pace around – a fiction of course – relentlessly agitated by the impossible, drinking another unwanted drink, tempted by innumerable evasions. There is no reason to resist them, there is simply no reason, but for a while I resist, or at least, they are resisted. The disgust I feel for every word I write almost suffocates me. I am unsure whether I feel physically sick. Vague nausea teeters on the brink of a faint, but it is also a strange delight.

*

According to Bataille eroticism is the 'extreme emotion' which 'opposes the human to the animal' [X 584]. The animal is ignorant of death and law – 'for an animal nothing is prohibited' [IX 33] – and is driven into its sexuality by 'the blind instinct of its organs' [X 593]. The human being, in contrast, is the only *morbid animal*; haunted by its prospective disappearance, caged in prohibitions, and relaying its drives through a 'calculus . . . of pleasure' [X 593]. 'Man has a thirst for evil' [III 42].

Bataille's obsession is with 'the unity of death, or of the consciousness of death, and eroticism' [X 585], which he also describes as the 'essential and paradoxical accord' of 'death and eroticism' [X 597], and 'the intimate accord between life and its violent destruction' [II 247], a cohesion that finds fragmentary attestation in the writings of Sade, in the trajectory of psychoanalysis, and perhaps most pointedly, in the characterization of orgasm within the French language as the little death. 'Voluptuosity is so close to ruinous dilapidation that we call its moment of paroxysm the "little death"' [X 170], leading to a question as to 'the identity of the "little death" and a death that is definitive' [X 577]. This is a matter both of identity and difference, of unilateral difference, or of scale. Orgasm provisionally substitutes for death, fending-off the impetus towards terminal oblivion, but only by infiltrating death into the silent core of vitality. 'It is true: speaking within the utilitarian limits of reason, we perceive the practical sense and the necessity of sexual disorder. But were those who gave the name "little death" to its terminal phase . . . wrong to have perceived its funereal sense' [X 586]? The little death is not merely a simulacrum or sublimation of a big one – of a true and virginal inexistence – but a corruption that leaves the bilateral architecture of life and death in tatters, a communication and a slippage which violates the immaculate alterity of darkness. Eroticism traces out the labyrinth, the maze, the riddle, from which death cannot be precipitated into lucidity. Death is enmeshed irresolvably in confusion. 'If the result of eroticism is envisaged under the perspective of desire, independently of the possible birth of a child, it is a loss, to which the paradoxically valuable expression "the little death" responds. It is not obvious what the "little death" has to do with death, with the cold horror of death . . . But is the paradox displaced whilst eroticism is in play?' [X 592].

'My rage to love opens onto death as a window onto a courtyard' [VI 76], because death is the only place we profoundly touch each other. 'And death is not mine alone. We all die *incessantly*. The little time that separates us from emptiness has the flimsiness of a dream' [VI 155]. Intimacy is not fusion, but unless it is the lip of fusion, it is nothing. Like eroticism, literature is communication, and communication is opened by death alone (but in the end everything is death, even the confusion that encrusts it). This is why to love is to bleed, which is not due to the pain of lack, but to excess. 'Erotic conduct opposes itself to the habitual kind, as expenditure to acquisition' [X 169]. It is only in an unrestrained debauching of the means to live that the desolate expanses of continuity are reached. 'We have no true pleasure except in expending uselessly, as if a wound opens in us' [X 170]. The impoverished bond of social connectedness is broken on the reef of deep community, where fusion is consummated in the impossible, 'it is under the condition of rupturing a communion that limits it that eroticism finally reveals the violence which is its truth' [X 167]. Only in a betrayal of life is there merging. 'The truth of eroticism is treason' [X 170].

Sade's reasoning on this question is of Thomisitic limpidity. Juliette follows a familiar Sadean path when she argues that however extraordinary the agony of another being, and however immense the number of such beings plunged into suffering, or death, they nevertheless remain utterly other, and their pain irrelevant. 'It doesn't matter at all if your neighbour undergoes a painful sensation, if there results none for you' [S IX 50]. If the torments of such unfortunate creatures impinge at all it is only due to the effects of convention – the servile dimension of the self – and such sensations should not be erroneously commensurated with the immediate (therefore natural) sensuality of crime. The slightest hint of immediate pleasure refutes an infinity of alien suffering. The pains of others register not at all, except insofar as one participates in the mutilation of nature, whose conventional name is 'conscience'. This is the notorious 'solipsism' of Sade, the affective denial of the other's subjectivity through a negation which he calls 'indifference'. Pain that is not one's own is to be coldly disregarded, since 'between it and your pleasure there is no proportion' [S IX 50]. He takes this argument to a dramatic climax: 'there is nothing to balance, even between a sugared almond and the entire universe. This reasoning serves to demonstrate the immense advantages of vice over virtue' [S IX 50].

What remains is to acknowledge such remarks as a communication, as Bataille does, attentive to the 'tears of blood' [IX 243] Sade wept upon the loss of his *120 Days of Sodom*. Sade's characters are no more trapped in an interior monologue than their author. It is not to herself, but to the beautiful young woman to whom she is erotically bound that Juliette declares:

> The excess of your sensibility is extreme, but you have directed its effects in a manner such that it is no longer able to carry you anywhere except into vice. All exterior objects which have some type of singularity put the electric particles of your nervous fluid into a prodigious irritation, and the disturbance, received upon the mass of nerves, communicates itself instantaneously to those which border upon the centre of voluptuousity. You immediately sense ticklings there, that sensation pleases you, you pander to it, you renew it; the force of your imagination makes you conceive of its augmentation, of details . . . the irritation becomes more lively, and you thus multiply, if you want, your pleasures towards infinity. The essential object is therefore, for you, to extend, to aggravate . . . I am going to say something to you that is a good deal stronger: because having surmounted all barriers as you have, being no longer restrained by anything whatsoever, it is necessary for you to go far. What henceforth inflames your imagination, therefore, will not be anything except the excess which is strongest, most execrable, the most contrary to divine and human law [S IX 47].

The ultimate intelligible term of the erotic is not that one negates the other in the interests of self-gratification, but rather that one violates a world which obstructs erotic contact, relinquishing all attachments before the predatory *puissance* of the beloved. Erotic love is an unrestrained violence against everything which stands against communion, and thus against everything that stands; a sacrificial spasm that violates God, cosmos, one's fellows and one's self, in a movement of donation without reserve. As Bataille remarks: 'at the summit the unlimited negation of otherness is the negation of self' [X 173].

The horror of Sade's writing is not to be dismissed by such words. If the cage of discrete being were to be the sole tribunal of his loathsome insatiation there could be little doubt as to the rigour of the condemnation. Perhaps no one has betrayed life with the ardour he has, unless Bataille, or myself. Sade writes:

Has an individual's death ever had any influence upon the general mass? And after the loss of the greatest battle, what am I saying? after the obliteration of half the world – or, if one wishes, of the entire world – would the little number of survivors, should there be any, notice even the faintest difference in things? No, alas. Nor would Nature notice any either, and the stupid pride of man, who believes everything created for him, would be dashed indeed, after the total extinction of the human species, were it to be seen that nothing in Nature had changed, and that the star's flight had not for that been retarded [S III 517].

This is a cold passage, lacking the resources of noxiousness with which his writings are usually so lavishly endowed. Its profound inhumanity is nevertheless beyond question. There is a particular scaling of death that is close to Sade, a numerical hypertrophy that tips orgy into massacre. Witnessing the unparalleled scenes of atrocity that litter his stories one is horrified of course, but to recoil in horror is to succumb anxiously to an erotic attachment. Nor is this only a literary matter.

However great the revulsion that can be felt in contact with a single corpse, especially when it is in an advanced state of decomposition, or marked with the traces of an ignoble extremity of agony (torture in particular), this is massively augmented – and not merely quantitatively – when one is confronted by *heaps* or *mounds* of corpses; the stacked remains of an ossuary, the human remnants from an extermination camp, piles of skulls, anonymous tangles of bodies in the Ugandan bush or at the edge of a Kampuchean paddy field. The corpse not as a lost person, but as a disintegrating clot in the depersonalized refuse of death. Sade's writings are not without such images, but nor are the mass media of twentieth-century societies. It is only at the lip of such abysmal indignities, when bodies are vomited as faceless masses of Herakleitean dung, that one glimpses the filthy and senseless death one craves.

Whatever the monstrosity of Sade, he does not point into Auschwitz; it is more true to suggest that he points out of it. Despite the peculiar desperation in our attempts to give a moral interpretation to the somatic shock induced by traces of the Nazi exterminations, our intellectual conscience remains offended by the sanctimonious inanities that ensue. We treat Hitler as a persuasive Satan, a figure that the church was unable to invent, in whom we vicariously live our evil (as if we were masturbating over a magazine). In the aggregate, our squalid separation from the victims gapes its stale complacency. Our lurch for innocence seals us against communion, and we are repulsed from the place where their fate is also ours, as if death itself has been soiled by their torments. That we are an ineliminably massacreable species of animal scarcely marks us. We engineer an apartheid of the dead. Partly this is due to the widespread dread of corpses, Jews, Gypsies, and homosexuals prevalent in our societies. All of which elements are consigned by morality to the same howl-choked dungeon as desire, irresponsibility, and profound contact with the real. Our moral natures would complete the sanitization of the 1940s' pogroms, contributing to the elimination of sprawling bodies, and of the problematic affects they provoke. We are even stupid enough to believe that between a KZ guard and a young Jew treading the edge of a death factory it is the latter who is most profoundly caged.

The technical core of the final solution was not merely an apparatus for mass killings, but one that was also guided by the exigency of the utile disposal of corpses. We simplify out of anxiety when we conflate the mounds of emaciated bodies strewn about the camps at the point of their liberation – the bodies of those annihilated by epidemics during the collapse of the extermination system – with the reduced ash and shadows of those erased by the system in its smooth functioning. The uneliminated corpse is not a submissive element within this or any other 'final solution', but an impersonal resistance to it, a token of primordial community. The docility of the inert body is itself a fascist myth.

The final solution is a myth *and* a fact; each of its traces being invested by complex libidinal forces. The lamp-shades made from human skin, the meticulously salvaged heaps of dentures and artificial limbs, the calm efficiency of the Nazi genocide-bureaucrat: all are freely circulating tokens of powerful affect. None of these images is more extraordinarily wounding to our sense of cosmic order than the bars of soap made from the body fat of the exterminated, the transubstantiation of verminized flesh into an implement of hygiene; white, glistening, malleable, inert. The soporific words of the allied propaganda machinery, with their insistence on fascist *filthiness*, are paralysed in the throat. Here are *purists*; clean and dutiful men, and yet we would be more fastidious than they were?

That there is nothing to insulate us from falling prey to such things – that the slime and ash in a drainage ditch outside Birkenau might be the residue of our own flesh – is a savagery of chance in which it is necessary to *exult* if we are to connect. A wall that stood between us and such acute horror would still be a wall, and if a God had existed to prevent the annihilation of Hitler's victims life as a whole would be the camp (for the Nazi it is). Pain, degradation, and death are one thing, the enslavement of desire something else. It is only because our bodies are weak and die that it is impossible for there to be a perfect cage, or for the sun to be locked interminably in a fascist health. To be protected by something more than zero is the final term of imprisonment.

*

There is poetry after Auschwitz, just as there was poetry within it, and *only because there was*. There is poetry wherever there are droplets of the sun who are not afraid to touch (however imperilled). I imagine there was even laughter amongst the doomed. There have been shadow-spaces of the Earth such as are impossible to think, but '[w]hat does truth signify . . . if we do not think what exceeds the possibility of thought . . .?' [III 12]. It is only at the edge of the impossible that the wretchedness of isolated being is grated open, and 'poetry is the impossible' [III 520].

It is not out of innocence, but from out of a history pock-marked by exterminations, that Bataille writes: 'I would like to efface the trace of my steps . . .' [III 161].

> I efface
> the step
> i efface
> the word
> space
> and breath
> are lacking [IV 28].

> The alcohol
> Of poetry
> Is silence
> Unmade [of a corpse] [III 372].

*

Fascism is not so much a symptom of political desperation, as of libidino-religious numbness, a kind of anti-poetry on the streets. Like all policy-obsessed behaviour patterns it is rooted in the humanist dead-end characterized by hysterical struggle for autonomy: self-determination, national self-management, master-races, autarky ... all attempts to seal the blister from within, to hide from the ocean. The thought that there might be a political response to fascism makes me laugh. Shall we set our little fascism against their big one? Organize ourselves, become disciplined, maybe we could make ourselves some smart uniforms and stomp about in the street? Politics is the last great sentimental indulgence of mankind, and it has never achieved anything except a deepened idiocy, more work, more repression, more pompous ass-holes demanding obedience. Quite naturally we are bored of it to the point of acute sickness. I have no interest at all in groping at power in the blister. What matters is burning a hole through the wall.

Bataille was not immune to the political charade, but even his short period of reality-process politicking during 1935–6 – when he was deeply involved with the journal *Contre-Attaque* and its project of radicalizing the Popular Front – is mapped in the labyrinth. The *Contre-Attaque* mobilization into militant action against fascism, militarism, and capitalism, the 'Popular Front in the Street' [I 402], stumbles in a maze of composition and decomposition. War with Germany is a futility because '[t]he process of decomposition which has been slow during the course of the last war will begin in France from the beginning of the next' [I 330]. In his 1933 essay on *The Psychological Structure of Fascism* Bataille outlines a re-emergent theological impulse in which the heterogeneous or decompositional element is deployed paradoxically as an operator of social integration, tending to the fascist state as a secularized divine order. The quasi-fascist undertow of his own politicized work – which he laments in a text from 1958 – has less to do with the exultation of violence, than with its concession to counter-discipline:

> What decides social destiny today is the organic creation of a vast composition of forces, disciplined, fanatical, capable of exercising an implacable authority in the day to come. Such a composition of forces must group together all those who do not accept the course to the abyss – to ruin and to war – of a capitalist society without head and without eyes ... [I 380].

Capital is a headless lurch into the abyss, an acephalic catastrophe.

What Bataille recoils from at this moment is not the claustrophobic managerial profanity of capital, but its psychotic flow into ruin:

> We see that the masses of humanity remain at the disposal of blind forces which dedicate them to inexplicable hecatombs ... [I 402].

The vocabulary of such writings does not jar against the deep currents of his slide into the sacred, but its evaluative impulse is almost wholly reactive; a tawdry Leninist voluntarism fixated upon control. I think of these 1930s texts as parodic, they are humorous and lively, a definite advance upon the austere preachings so prevalent on the left. They are, in any case, at best a joke. Who is more attentive than Bataille to the vacuity of manifestos, programmes, policy statements, declarations of commitment?

> The destruction of language is not my act [*fait*] but does not have a place in me except by destroying me, like the act of the moment which has suppressed me (I speak now but in vain) [IV 167].

'The impossible is the basis of being' [III 41]. To write is poverty and captivity if it is not wreckage upon the impossible, because the impossible is not a margin, a fissure, a border-zone, but an immensity compared to which the possible shrivels to the edge of nothing. 'I even believe that in a sense my stories clearly attain the *impossible*' [III 101], and that is why they matter, why *The Blue of Noon* is of immeasurably greater importance than the *Contre-Attaque* posturings, why in contrast to Sade – who sought 'an *impossible* freedom' [IX 242] – Lenin is a ranting dwarf. ' – IMPOSSIBLE! she cried' [IV 51], 'read or work? it was impossible' [IV 59]. *The Hatred for Poetry*, renamed *The Impossible*, exempts Baudelaire and Rimbaud from the complacency of words that resign themselves to the cramped box of the possible. Insipid lyricism vaunts itself as another possible type of language, a type that is elevated, beautiful, ethereal. 'True poetry is outside laws. But poetry, in the end, accepts poetry' [III 218]. Bataille vomits, but the 'poetry of Baudelaire – or that of Rimbaud – never inspires that hatred in me' [III 513], and from the start Bataille's reading of Nietzsche insists that – unlike the language of fascism – Nietzsche's texts are labyrinths, with no hint of the *directive*, no politics [I 450–2], only the voyage into the impossible, the will to chance. Utter confusion. 'Those moments, he said, where everything is divine, because everything is impossible. (Impossible above all to *explain*, to *speak*)' [IV 146]. Only when human relationships collapse in darkness and pain is there worth. 'Between her and me there was never anything possible' [IV 233].

> At first, death surrounds us with an endless silence as an island is surrounded by water. But there, precisely, is the *unsayable*. What importance have words which do not pierce this silence[?] What importance in speaking of 'moment of the tomb' [*moment de tombe*], when each word is nothing for as long as it has not attained the beyond of words[?] [IV 166].

*

Death is the reality of the impossible, making fictions of us all, and it is only in fiction that we separate ourselves from it. Wandering in the labyrinth one finds that not-one is only distanced by a complication of terrain, and that passages leading out of the possible can never be walled-off. If reasons were needed why literature cannot be supplanted by philosophy this is one, even though it is unreason itself. 'Are we able to imagine a place more favourable to this disorder: the lost depths of the cavern . . .' [X 597], depths that yawn as '. . . the abyss opened in us by eroticism and death' [X 596]. Depths that are also the maze, the pit, the caverns of Lascaux: 'it is in the bottom of a fissure, so difficult of access that it is today called the "pits", that we find ourselves before the most striking, and the most strange of evocations' [X 597]. The shamanistic figures marking the walls of Lascaux are not to be outgrown or sublated. No residence that is not founded upon the labyrinth: 'pass the night in the house if you dare, but don't forget that death inhabits it . . .' [IV 123]. Not that on the outside of the house, the box, the cage, there is anywhere to hide from the desolation of zero since 'the thunder of death/fills the universe' [III 212] and one can only run into her arms ('death my lover' [IV 22], Bataille cries). On the other side of the line is evidenced the idiocy that was one's flight:

> Black death you are my bread
> I eat you in my heart
> terror is my sweetness
> madness is in my hand [III 88].

Stories celebrate life, poetry exults in death. Wherever a story disintegrates into pain and confusion poetry begins, and whatever stinks of imperfection crawling crippled out of a howl is a poem. Bataille credits Blake with the succinct religious acceptance that 'everything that is sacred is poetic, and everything that is *poetic* is *sacred*' [IX 226].

> I speak amongst the dead
> and the dead are dumb [IV 19].

*

Those who consider reality to be a text can be said to be 'writers' only in a problematic – if not parodic – sense. Not for them the tormenting *discontinuity* between those tides of excitation we call 'thought' or 'moods' and their transcription into a linear series of collectively estimated marks. The 'general text' of which they dream is the stage for a comedy of writing; an equilibriated space where every frustration is immediately soliloquy, where affect is trimmed to the measure of its pronouncement, where the ghoul of mute horror – the terribly inert *compulsion to write* that breaks its victims beneath leaden feet – appears in the mask of a malleable clown.

'Malaise, silence' [IV 134]. That the inability to write should itself become utterance, and thus text: this most nocturnal of thoughts is the restless spectre that the writer can neither still, nor embrace. The sensation evoked by its visitation is the same as the one that afflicts the victim of a hopelessly profound dream, consummated in a phrase which – remembered during the hours of waking – is degraded into an inanity. The withered remains of those chill and expansive impossibilities, the mysterious companions of darkness, silence, and solitude, are rediscovered after an interval of sleep; wrought into facile puzzles, and even – after daylight has sucked away the last shadows – into mere paradoxes.

To become degraded to the level of a writer is to be perpetually captivated, and then betrayed, by the figments of method, a resource for creation, an inevitability. As poetry is to prose, so would this be, in turn, to poetry itself: a summit from which the flood-plains of textuality could be perpetually re-inundated, a hieroglyph of utter fertility. But the word 'method' is rather too philosophical, for what is at issue here is a map for traversing unknown terrains, and not one for domesticating them; a chart for discoveries that accentuate the enigma of the world. 'Method' not as lucid preparation, but as a passage to the point of delirium, to the point of an unconsciousness through excess. Method as a map that is indistinguishable from the voyage, a track, traced out in figures that already attest to the exoticism it announces, and leading towards what is ferociously *up-stream*. What is craved throughout the long nights of entrancement is that one be obliterated at the source of the deluge. 'To be spared a prosaic death!' But where the foaming torrents should be found . . . is dust, and even worse than this: the powdered remains of ancient seashells. Relics of the same 'movement which denudes *necessarily* and makes one enter naked into a desert' [II 242]. Those who sink to their knees in despair, after clawing their way to such places in a fever of excitement, are at least granted visions of a divine cruelty; of a laughter more acute than any to be found upon the flat-lands of the earth.

> you are the void and the cinder
> bird without head with wings beating the night
> the universe is made of your slight hope
>
> the universe is your sick heart and mine
> beating to skim death
> to the cemetery of hope
>
> my pain is joy
> and the cinder is fire [III 87].

When compared to the dark heart of writing, despair is almost a temptation. Yet, despite the black farce of wreckage that a fate crippled by writing effects of itself, there is something about such a fate that remains unbroken, or at least, something that outlasts every vestige of the individual it condemns. Rimbaud spent a decade trying to dissolve it in the Ethiopian sun, but he still died as a poet who had long been silent, rather than as someone who had salvaged their humanity from the insanity of words.

*

> The greatness of Rimbaud is to have led poetry to the failure of poetry [III 533].

*

In a letter dated the 13th May 1871 Rimbaud writes to Georges

Izambard from the maze of poetic delirium and the loss of self-possession. In a play upon the classic formula of Cartesian subjectivism, poetry is depicted as a shattering derangement of vision and a dislocation of the ego:

> Now I degrade myself as far as possible. Why? I want to be a poet, and I am working to render myself *visionary*: you will not understand any of this, and I scarcely know how to explain it to you. It is necessary to arrive at the unknown by a deregulation of *all the senses*. The sufferings are enormous, but one must be strong, to be born a poet, and I recognize myself as a poet. This is not at all my fault. It is false to say: I think. One should say: one thinks me... I is an other [R 5–7].

As if the confusional cyclone of poetry had already laid waste the resources of articulation, Rimbaud says that he cannot explain himself, just as two years later in *A Season in Hell* he will write: 'I understand, and not knowing how to explain myself without pagan words, I would rather be silent' [R 304]. This is not to say that words come to an end, but only that discourse ceases to dominate them. The motor is not discursive competence, but the vacant eye of the storm. In a further letter, this time to Paul Demeny, dated the 15th of the same month, Rimbaud repeated the phrase 'a *deregulation* of *all the senses*' [R 10] (only the emphasis is changed), the phrase *I am an other*, and the rhetoric of the *poète maudit* from the Izambard letter, stressing the necessity of intoxication, suffering, and exile:

> The poet makes himself a *visionary* by a long, immense and rational *deregulation* of *all* the senses. All forms of love, of suffering, of madness: he searches himself, he exhausts all poisons in himself, in order to preserve only their quintessences. Unspeakable torture where he has need of all faith, all superhuman strength, where he becomes among everyone the great invalid, the great criminal, the great accursed one – and the supreme scholar! – Because he arrives at the *unknown*, since he has cultivated his soul, already rich, more than anybody! He arrives at the unknown, and when, bewildered, he ends by losing the intelligence of his visions, he has seen them! Let him die as he leaps through unheard of and unnamable things: other horrible workers will come; they will begin from the horizons where the other collapsed! [R 7–17].

Inconclusive communication 203

A method or an antimethod, the will to chance, a voyage into loss of control, this impossibility is the desolate core of poetry, a space of slippage. To slip is not to plan, to work, to struggle. 'I have a horror of all trades. Masters and workers, all peasants, ignoble. The hand at the quill just as the hand at the plough' [R 301]. Rimbaud confesses that he is 'lazier than a toad' [R 301-2], without decency, an alien to the civilization of toil. 'I have never been of this people; I have never been a Christian; I am of the race who sings under torture; I do not understand the laws, I am a beast: you fool yourselves . . .' [R 308]. An explorer of the sacred, traversing wildernesses beyond piety or sense, charred by the flame of the impossible, Rimbaud treads the edge of the maze, scraping away his tight European skin.

*

I am of an inferior race to all eternity [R 304].

Religion.

*

The mobility peculiar to the labyrinth – real cosmic motion or liquidation – is not confined by the scales, instead it finds a shaft of facilitation passing from one to another, a 'slippage' (*glissement*), the full consequence of which is an illimitable dispersion across the strata: communication through death. A strangely stationary mobility therefore. It is not that journeys are lacking in Bataille's writings, merely that they radiate from a transition in profundity, from which they derive their futility and abortiveness. These static voyages can be undertaken by invalids in bed; Tropmann in the last two sections of 'Maternal Feet' in *The Blue of Noon* [III 425–39], Henri in *Julie* [IV 57–114]. 'The Wait' in *The Abbé C.* [III 316–19] describes Charles and Éponine in bed, glued together by the horror of Charles' apparently impending murder at the hands of the 'giant of butchery' (another Henri) who Éponine counts amongst her lovers. The narrator of the first part of *The Impossible* declares himself: 'prey to fear in my bed' [III 113].

Meanderings in extension remain trapped in the maze, unless they cross over into a 'blind slippage into death' [III 29], 'this slippage outside oneself that necessarily produces itself when death comes into play' [II 246]. A 'slippage produces itself' [V 113], we do not do so, a chasm opens, chaos (= 0), something horrific in its depth, a season in Hell that 'slips immensely into the impossible' [III 77], 'the intensity and intimacy of a sensation opened itself onto an abyss where there is nothing which is not lost, just as a profound wound opens itself to death' [IV 248]. Poetry is this slippage that is broken upon the end of poetry, erased in a desert as 'beautiful as death' [IV 18]. There is no quesion of affirmation, achievement, gain, but only a catastrophe without mitigation compared to which everything is poverty and imprisonment. 'I would love to forget the ungraspable slippage of myself into corruption' [III 227]. 'Corruption is the spiritual cancer that reigns in the depths of things' [IV 261].

> my heart is black ink
> my sex is a dead sun [III 87].

Life decomposes into filth as it explores the vicarious death of the universe. In no case does the heterogeneous belong to any scale, since it is 'exactly' the irruption of decomposability. Heterogeneous (base) matter – 'blood, sperm, urine and vomit . . .' [I 24] – is characterized negatively in relation to every possible stratum of elemental organization, which is why it resists the discourse on *things*. Vomit, excrement, and decomposing flesh do not proffer unproblematic solidity or comprehensible form, but rather quasi-fluid divisibility, imprecise consistency, multiple, insufficient, and evanescent patterns of cohesion. All of which are mixed with words slimed with sanctity. 'To write is to investigate chance' [VI 69], but the explosive excess that breaks in a black foam of poetry is not merely a risk, because risk implies the possibility of a benign outcome. It is a 'ruin without limits' [III 75], 'the submission of man to [blank]' [II 247]. Excess is venom.

*

> Winter wind
> oh my dying sister
> wolf gleam bite of hunger
> stone of frost pasted on a naked heart
>
> oh spittle of indifference
> oh heaven of insult against all hearts
> oh cold emptier than death [IV 26].

*

Particles decay, molecules disintegrate, cells die, organisms perish, species become extinct, planets are destroyed and stars burn-out, galaxies explode ... until the unfathomable thirst of the entire universe collapses into darkness and ruin. Death, glorious and harsh, sprawls vast beyond all suns, sheltered by the sharp flicker-lip of flame and silence, cold mother of all gods, hers is the deep surrender. If we are to resent nothing – not even nothing – it is necessary that all resistance to death cease. We are made sick by our avidity to survive, and in our sickness is the thread that leads back and nowhere, because we belong to the end of the universe. The convulsion of dying stars is our syphilitic inheritance. The name 'Bataille' loosely congeals a message from the dead heart of the real, and anything human is quite incidental here. Matter signals to its lost voyagers, telling them that their quest is vain, and that their homeland already lies in ashes behind them.

If there is a conclusion it is zero. Silence. Words continue as something else, as something in any case, or at most; the edge of something (of all things). Yet there is nothing but chaos, even if chaos (alone) is the repressed. Unilateral difference. That is why a revolution must be a zenith of competence nucleated upon burning insanity, since anarchy and utter surrender only connect in a religion of death. Thanocracy, anarchy are undifferentiable at zero, and a human being without desperation escapes my comprehension. Being created in the image of God, we mean nothing to ourselves, and want only the inhuman. They are right to say that in trafficking these words I correspond to a zone of Nietzsche's maximum detestation; vermin, disease, madness, anarchy, and religion flow through me as through their own space.

Through Bataille also.

*

Here in the loft space of the inner edge there is no end for words
they meander through the cluttered strip
these mutant insects violently blinded and driven on
by motors humming in darkness
once maggots heaving themselves from the carcass of reason
now winged
fat with venom
they rave for me.

*

Like Bataille, I too 'crawl in order no longer to be' [III 91]. It is possible that others have clawed their way to deeper abjections than I have known, but there is no reason for me to believe it. Beyond the end of succumbing is a subsidence through the very basement of the Earth, leaving a splinter of death clinging to its unravelling ghost, naked and serene in Hell.

Death is no longer a speculative problem for me, but a memory belonging to something else, a vestige upon zero. I can only ask myself: *did Bataille also cross the line and die before the end?* Crouching deeply broken in this life, which has become the vestibule of an unbearable but delicious horror, I supplicate myself to nothing, and offer up the sacrifice of these words to death.

Europe is the racial trash-can of Asia, and Britain skims-off Europe's charred froth. My ancestors were vagrants, whores, and killers. Minds melted by toadstools, they exulted in the ashes of monasteries, the base-line of the human animal, slimed across the sea-rocks of the North. 'It is quite evident to me that I have always been of an inferior race. I am not able to comprehend revolt. My race does not ever stir itself except for pillage: like wolves at the beast they have not killed' [R 302]. With so much ash in the blood, I never had a chance of peace ... so many years gnawing and scratching at the metal bars until I collapsed with exhaustion and disgust. Its hard to understand those graceful creatures who seem to have escaped from being knifed into inarticulate wreckage by life. Dissatisfaction white-extreme as a heated blade twisted into blank vulnerabilities cross-cut with ink droolings and clotting pain into absurdity. I have long understood the necessity of counting myself amongst the accursed, even before crossing over the line.

I see now that my terrestrial ur-mother was ravished by something fanged and insane from the wilderness, and that I am a vampire veiled raggedly in humanity, corrupted from birth by an unholy intimacy with death. The fever that bears me overstretches the entire health of the Earth, carrying me with my accursed twin into an emptiness beyond the reservoir of stars. Although the adventure of inexistence only begins in Hell there is no fear, only awe and burning werewolf thirst for the voyage. Nestled in some cove of this ulterior shore an utterly consummate eroticism – a pact against nature – tenses through fusion to its evaporation, denuded before the abyss; a glistening droplet of loss and beginning.

What could be more pitiful than the romantics with their sobs of aspiration? The toxic fruitage of eroticism is crisper, more silent, than the emptiest night. Inside the perimeter of Hell no walls remain against the unfathomable. Everything is calm, luxuriant, incomprehensibly desolate. The ghost of self drifts in the shallows; the fading echo from a clamour of frantic dreams. One swims effortlessly into not-one. Down beyond the mouth of the estuary the ocean awaits . . .

*

To an angel of death I wrote:
How I remember the way it was, with you sheltering in a cluster of fictions, eyes implacable and drenched in extinction, lost in the alternative night that waits
Patient immense
Out beyond the river-mouth
The cavity in which we float
Unsettled in our sleep
Anticipative
Nothing could be more diseased
And yet on the other side of the line
We shall bask in ecstasy
Until we burn
Oh yes, there are more and more words. My fever is fertilized by Hell itself. Even in the tower of reason they flap after you, abominable things released from dead suns. Out there in the underworld we await ourselves. Agonies of patience drown us in silence. Scorched. Transfigured.
Infernal genius chars the roots of our minds.
Now we are trapped on the inside of the world
but our strange aching chokes the crypt we haunt
maddens us
drives us out . . .

    dragged for so many years
    through the confines of heaven
    flanked by statues of the patriarchs
    until arriving in a place
    lacerated by the sun
    to drink the tincture of my father's crumbled skull
    ashes of monks their screams calcified
    mixed with the venom of a spider
    long extinct

There shall be new and terrible monsters.
We arrive at the city of God from somewhere they don't understand and torch it to the ground
dripping flame from the infernal bake-chambers of our minds
death is no stranger to us
behind our eyes lies a space beyond the stars
there is no doubt we are an abomination to this world . . .
I write now in the attic of insanity, smeared across words by unimagined desperations of beatitude. These soft terrestrial nights are unable to soothe the Hellish embers which blaze in my delirium. Horror and obsession scrawl their leprosy across my skin. My delight is unfathomable in its harshness. Shadow embalms me.
a lock of death explores your ear
and each word you write
unpicks the stitches of the world
until i feel as if i have passed through the wall
so that everything becomes perfect
and ill

The illness guides my words:

> sickness and death my sweet schizophrenic mother
> your child is lost to you
> and found on the other side
> where you inexist

Ah! Such abysses of disease open before me. I decay, transfixed upon abolition.
Ardent for collapse, I explore the rotting cities of the inner edge. The stink of opium interweaves with that of bat-dung and fungus. The moon mutters its electric paean to ruin, and I gaze into the grave of my life which gapes its moist idiocy. This is the labyrinth that leads out of the world.
In this place – luxuriant with deterioration – even your torturer's silence is an ecstasy

> i see you hushed by the sacred
> something feral treads the undertow of my thoughts
> as a wolf prowls the snow desolation
> famished for your words
> so that it seems as nothing but bone
> strung with death
> and clutched

by blackened nerves
untangled and strewn
through the mad howls of zero

Things drift to pieces, but I am so tense and thirsty for it.
I lurk in the wastes of the interior, intoxicated by the murmur of convulsions to come. We are specks of death entangled in wolf threads and ravings.
Only fictions separate us.
Bonded on the far side of blood, we are wedded beyond sense in Hell.

*

lets slip out
into the night
claw free of our souls and follow the road
through the heart of fear
where the spawn of vivisections
scramble from the blinding-machine
to tread the shadow lip of sanity

*

where the far side of the line transects the darkness in your mind
i want to navigate deserts of pain
whilst the galaxies decay
come unstrung in the night
headless ravens beat spasms of paralysed flight

*

Humanism (capitalist patriarchy) is the same thing as our imprisonment. Trapped in the maze, treading the same weary round. Round and round in the garbage. Round and round and round and round and round and round and round and round and round and round and round and round and round and round and round (God is a scratched record), even when we think we are progressing, knowing more. Round and round, missing the sacred, until it drives you completely into your mind. But at least we die.

Personalism is a trap because to believe that some of what one was holding onto will be taken care of by another being is irreligion. It is not our devotion that matters, but surrender. There is no end to the loss that lies down river. If only we can give up.

'Life will dissolve itself in death, rivers in the sea, and the known in the unknown' [V 119].

What could be more theological than politics, with its interminable idiot interrogation: *who has the power?* Revolution is different. Monotheism cannot be reformed, and must be washed away, but it is also the horizon of sanity. Abandonment.

Yes, I indulge myself intolerably, although *I* is also Bataille's *je*, because it is not his, or anyone's. 'I am all the names in history' [N III 1351], but that is scarcely to begin.

Each day that I remain trapped in the garbage I forget a little more of what it is to cross the line, but even forgetting is dying, and dying is crossing the line. Death is truth because error cannot adhere to it, all dreams are soluble within it, but death is not the word 'death', or any other word. The zero of words is not the word 'zero', nor are words about words.

*

a face looms from charred shadow
violently pale the night has silently
desolated an eye
blood flows thick
and profuse
it is only with great tentativeness that my finger
strays
into the vacant socket
searching out frayed nerve nakedness
for it must be a focus of jagged agony
condensed in the darkness
and there will be no speech

*

to sleep hanging upside down
in a barn
sheltered from the day
and then when it gets dark
flapping out

Notes

1 The reference is to Kant's First Critique [K IV 400–1].
2 The Kant/*Capital* complex is outlined in accordance with a Hegelian sanity in J.M. Bernstein's *The Philosophy of the Novel: Lukács, Marxism and the Dialectics of Form* and Gillian Rose's *Hegel Contra Sociology*, both of whom have a dependence upon the work of Lukács, especially his section on 'Die Antinomien des bürgerlichen Denkens in Geschichte und Klassenbewußtsein' [L II 287-330]. A schizoanalysis of the same complex is explored in Deleuze and Guattari's *Antioedipus*. Neo-Schellingian readings are most meticulously developed in Heidegger's exploration of technology, most particularly in his 'Die Frage nach der Technik', in *Vorträge und Aufsätze*.
3 This argument is to be found outlined in the twelfth section of *Mille Plateaux*, entitled 'Traité de nomadologie: la machine de guerre'.
4 I have no argument at all with Derrida as a reader of Heidegger, after all, deconstruction and reading Heidegger is one thing. It is when his academic textualism attempts to cope with *writers* such as Nietzsche, Freud, Bataille, and Artaud that it definitively abandons its zone of relative utility and becomes an apparatus of domestication in the service of the state. His reading of Bataille is most carefully developed in 'De l'économie restreinte à l'économie général: Un hegelianisme sans réserve' in *L'écriture et la différence*. A gesture towards Bataille is also evident in the essay 'Différance' in *Marges*, and no doubt elsewhere. Anyone seeking to fortify a reconstructed reason against the sacred will find much of value in these writings.
5 Thermodynamics is associated above all with a statistical revolution in the natural sciences. In the third volume of his *Hermes* Michel Serres deftly marks the importance of thermodynamics in the words 'the philosophy of physics is the theory of information' [p.44], since with the introduction of probabilistic description the form and content of natural science become indifferentiable in principle. The importance of Serres' work in this field is immense, and his writing is consistently beautiful.

Since information is a continuous rather than a discrete variable, the results generated by informational research are of a quantitative character. These quantitities are expressed as negative entropies, or negentropies. The concept of entropy, stemming from the work of Clausius, and building on Carnot's theory of thermic motors, is given its modern determination in Boltzmann's equation S = K log W, where S is entropy, expressed in terms of the ratio of energy to heat, derived from Boltzmann's constant K (ergs/degrees). W is the thermic probability, or totality of possible permutations. Logarithms are used in order that the addition of permutational states is equivalent to an exponentiation of improbability. This is easily understood in terms of the information concept, where, for instance, 2 bits added to 2 bits gives 4 bits, and this is equivalent to a fourfold increase in the precision of the message.

The theory of information stems from an article by Shannon and Weaver entitled 'The mathematical theory of communication'. The thermodynamic concept of entropy is adopted by information theory to describe 'informational uncertainty' or 'potential information'. This is the set of possible signals from which a specific signal is selected. As a measure of potential information, Lila Gatlin, in her book *Information Theory and the Living System* (the crispest and most incisive text I have found on the subject), equates the maximum entropy of a signal with the logarithm of the number of elements in the alphabet of signals, a figure she denotes by the letter 'a'. Boltzmann's K log W is thus simplified to log a. If base 2 logarithms are used the units of information are bits. The level of information of a given signal is equal to the entropy of the system. For instance, in a system with four elements, such as a genetic code, any one of four possible signals or events is hypothetically possible at any given position in the message sequence, so that in a state of maximum uncertainty each signal would have an information value of log 4, which is equal to 2 bits.

Gatlin writes, 'Thus with the higher entropy of potential information we associate the concepts of potential message variety, large vocabulary, surprisal value, and unexpectedness' [p. 49]. Potential information increases as entropy approaches its maximum value, or log a. Negative entropy, or negentropy, on the other hand, is equivalent to stored information, or information density. This is a measure of the order of a system. If stored information is expressed as a proportion of potential information it is called redundancy. 'If there were no constraints and every possible letter combination occurred with equal frequency, potential message variety would be maximal; but there would be no way to detect error because error detection and correction are based on forbidden and restricted combinations' [p. 50]. Effective communication, and indeed, the effective transmission of energy within any system of control, requires a balance between raw information or disorder, and stability or order: 'the capacity to convey meaning through language depends not on an entropy maximum or minimum but rather on a delicate optimization of the two opposing elements of variety and reliability' [p. 51].

Two highly authoritative texts on the subject are Carnap's *Two Essays on Entropy* (London 1977) and Kullback's *Information Theory and*

Statistics (New York 1968), although I find both works perfectly incomprehensible.
6 E. Zermelo's *Wiederkehreinwand* is an argument from the repetition of H-value transformations over long periods, based on a formula by Poincaré, suggesting that directional H-value tendencies are inconsistent with particle mechanics. Ehrenfest in his *The Conceptual Foundations of the Statistical Approach in Mechanics* argues that this objection is dependent upon a formulation of thermodynamic processes in terms of particle impacts (the *Stosszahlansatz*) that Boltzmann abandons [pp. 15–56].
7 Boltzmann discusses Poincaré's equation in some detail [B III 587], describing its essential commitment as being to '[t]the univocity and reversibility of the integral of mechanical differential equations' [B III 587]. See previous note.
8 This difference is most overt in the 'Project for a scientific psychology' (which is not contained in the German edition I cite, but in the *Standard Edition* SE I 283). Freud discusses its prevalence in his work in an important note in the 'Traumdeutung' [F II 516n].
9 Bataille's solar economics is frequently accused of naturalism by the humanist left. Such resistance to naturalization is a Kantian insistence, simultaneous with transcendental philosophy as such (and not in any sense a specifically post-bourgeois subversion of modern culture as so much recent 'theory' would suggest). An antinaturalist approach to the object is the initiating gesture of Kantianism. If 'ideology' is to be used as a name for the rationality of capital (a pretentiously gesticulating move), it is anti-naturalism, rather than naturalization, which is the pre-eminent trait of this ideology. This is not to suggest that the de-naturalization of the real is inevitably without 'progressive' features. If undertaken carefully – without mytho-theological relapse – anti-naturalism is certainly able to assist new money (interests) against old, intervening effectively in disputes between liberals and conservatives, although it seems that a great deal more than this is often being claimed.

What the bourgeois intellect forbade was always something quite different, namely, the thought of natural de-naturalization, or the acknowledgement of libidinal escalation. This is why Barthes is inscribed within the horizon of critique – as its legitimate semiological discipline – in a way that Nietzsche is not.
10 In my somewhat limited researches I found far less on the history of mathematical zero than I had anticipated. For my purposes the importance of its insistent invocation lies in its origin in a non-monotheistic culture (India), its character of indivisibility without unity, its volatilization of technocratic rationalism, and its perfect co-existence with death. Zero (derived, like 'cipher', from the Arabic 'zephirum') is the non-speculative other of unity, bringing it into affinity with a question of the feminine such as that emerging from the writings of Luce Irigaray, especially *Speculum: de l'autre femme* and *Ce sexe qui n'en est pas un*. Both of these texts launch a devastating assault

on the notions of unity, solidity, and identity, associated with the Judaeo-Hellenic privilege of One.
11 More technical information on cyclones can be found in E. Palmén and C.W. Newton's *Atmospheric Circulation Systems: Their Structure and Physical Interpretation*; see also John G. Lockwood's *World Climatology: An Environmental Approach*.
12 Wittfogel marks out the interdependency of political power and hydraulic control in his study of *Oriental Despotism*.

*

Bibliography

In writing this book I have read almost nothing except for Bataille's *Oeuvres Complètes*, supplemented only by those writers with whom I have had some previous intimacy, most important of whom are Kant and Nietzsche, but including also Sade, Freud, Marx, Boltzmann, Rimbaud, Miller, and a few others, amongst whom are such enemies as Aquinas, Hegel, and Derrida. More important by far than most of these names have been the saints, shamans, werewolves, vampires, and lunatics with whom I have communed, and whose names are absent from this text, even though their words have infested my own beyond extrication. It would be impolitic to make a selection – although I could easily do so – but sooner or later you will hear of them all from elsewhere. It is not necessarily any credit upon a writer for them to appear on the list that follows, crass cultural exigencies alone necessitate it.

COLLECTED EDITIONS

Aquinas, Thomas, *Summa Theologiae*, Translation, Introduction, Notes, Appendices, and Glossary by Thomas Gilbey Order of Preachers, London.
Bataille, Georges, *Oeuvres Complètes*, editors I & II Denis Hollier, III & IV Thadée Klossowski, V Mme Leduc, VI (and following volumes – 12 vols in all) Henri Ronse, and J.-M. Rey, Paris.
Boltzmann, Ludwig von, *Wissenschaftliche Abhandlungen*, published by Dr Fritz Hasenöhrl, Leipzig 1909.
Descartes, René, *Oeuvres*, editors M. Darboux and M. Boutroux, Paris.
Freud, Sigmund, *Studien Ausgabe*, editors Alexander Mitscherlich, Angela Richards, James Strachey, and Ilse Grubrich-Simitis, Frankfurt am Main.
Hegel, G.W.F., *Theorie Werkausgabe*, based on *Werke* of 1832–45, editors Eva Moldenhauer and Markus Michel, Frankfurt am Main.
Heidegger, Martin, *Gesamtausgabe*, multiple editors, Frankfurt am Main (still incomplete, hence entry below).
Kant, Immanuel, *Werkausgabe*, editor Wilhelm Weischedel, Frankfurt am Main.

Lukács, Georg, *Werke*, editor Frank Benseler, Berlin.
Nietzsche, Friedrich W., *Werke*, editor Karl Schlechta, Frankfurt am Main.
Sade, Marquis de, *Oeuvres Complètes du Marquis de Sade*, Édition Définitive, Paris 1966–7.
Schopenhauer, Arthur, *Zürcher Ausgabe: Werke in zehn Bänden*, text follows historical-critical edition by Arthur Hübscher, editorial materials acquired by Angelika Hübscher, editors Claudia Schmölders, Fritz Senn, and Gerd Haffmans, Zurich.

MONOGRAPHS

Aristotle, *Politics*, London 1959.
Augustine, *The City of God*, Harmondsworth 1984.
Bernstein, J.M., *The Philosophy of the Novel: Lukács, Marxism and the Dialectics of Form*, Brighton 1984.
Carnap, Rudolf, *Two Essays on Entropy*, London 1977.
Céline, Louis-Ferdinand, *Voyage au Bout de la Nuit*, Paris 1952.
Cioran, E.M., *La Tentation d'Exister*, Paris 1956.
Deleuze, Gilles, *Différence et Répétition*, Paris 1969.
——*Nietzsche et la Philosophie*, Paris 1962.
Deleuze, Gilles and Guattari, Félix, *Capitalisme et Schizophrénie I: l'Anti-oedipe*, Paris 1972.
——*Capitalisme et Schizophrénie II: Mille Plateaux*, Paris 1980.
Derrida, Jacques, *L'Écriture et la Différence*, Paris 1967.
——*Marges: de la Philosophie*, Paris 1972.
——*Spurs: Neitzsche's Styles (Éperons: les Styles de Nietzsche)*, London 1978.
Ehrenfest, Paul and Tatiana, *The Conceptual Foundations of the Statistical Approach in Mechanics*, New York 1959.
Gatlin, Lila L., *Information Theory and the Living System*, London 1972.
Gleick, James, *Chaos*, London 1985.
Hayman, Ronald, *De Sade: a Critical Biography*, London 1978.
Heidegger, *Vorträge und Aufsätze*, Pfullingen 1959.
Hobbes, Thomas, *Leviathan*, Harmondsworth 1988.
Irigaray, Luce, *Speculum: de l'Autre Femme*, Paris 1974.
——*Ce Sexe qui n'en est pas Un*, Paris 1977.
Klossowski, Pierre, *Nietzsche et le Cercle Vicieux*, Paris 1969.
Kullback, Solomon, *Information Theory and Statistics*, New York 1968.
Lockwood, John G., *World Climatology: an Environmental Approach*, London 1974.
Lyotard, Jean-François, *Économie Libidinale*, Paris 1974.
Marx, Karl, *Capital Volume One*, London 1977.
——*Grundrisse*, Harmondsworth 1973.
Miller, Henry, *The Tropic of Cancer*, London 1965.
Palmén, E. and Newton, C.W., *Atmospheric Circulation Systems: their Structure and Physical Interpretation*, London 1969.
Plato, *Collected Dialogues*, Princeton 1982.
Ragon, Michel, *The Space of Death*, translated by Alan Sheridan, Charlottesville 1983.

Rimbaud, Arthur, *Collected Poems*, with introduction and prose translation by Oliver Bernard, Harmondsworth 1986.
Rose, Gillian, *Hegel Contra Sociology*, London 1981.
Serres, Michel, *Hermes III: la Traduction*, Paris 1974.
Shannon, Claude E. and Weaver, Warren, *The Mathematical Theory of Communication*, University of Illinois 1949.
Walker, D.P., *The Decline of Hell: Seventeenth Century Discussions of Eternal Torment*, London 1964.
Weber, Max, *The Protestant Ethic and the Spirit of Capitalism*, translated by Talcott Parsons, London 1985.
Wittfogel, Karl A., *Oriental Despotism: a Comparative Study of Total Power*, London 1963.

Name index

Adorno, T.W. 12
Aquinas, T. 90, 99, 100, 101, 182, 183
Aristotle 23, 139, 140, 141
Arnobius 100
Artaud, A. 211
Augustine 98, 99, 100, 102, 136

Barthes, R. 176, 213
Bataille, G. 3, 4, 5, 8, 9, 10, 16, 28, 29, 30, 31, 32, 33, 36, 37, 48, 49, 51, 55, 56, 59, 61, 62, 63, 64, 65, 66, 67, 68, 69, 70, 71, 73, 74, 79, 80, 82, 87, 88, 89, 94, 99, 104, 107, 108, 109, 112, 113, 114, 115, 116, 117, 118, 119, 122, 133, 134, 149, 151, 155, 156, 157, 158, 159, 161, 163, 164, 165, 168, 169, 170, 171, 173, 174, 176, 177, 178, 181, 184, 185, 187, 188, 189, 191, 193, 196, 197, 198, 199, 200, 203, 205, 206, 210, 211, 213
Baudelaire, C. 198
Bernstein, J.M. 211
Blake, W. 200
Blanchot 61
Boltzmann, L. von 38, 39, 40, 41, 43, 44, 212, 213

Carnap, R. 212
Carnot, L. 37, 212
Céline, L-F. 108
Cioran, E.M. 155
Clausewitz, K. von. 149
Clausius, R. 37, 212

Deleuze, G. 13, 114, 155, 163, 211
Demeny, P. 202
de Rais, G. 66, 67, 68, 69, 70, 71, 72, 73, 74
Derrida, J. 5, 16, 17, 18, 19, 20, 21, 22, 24, 155, 176, 211
de Sade, Marquis 60, 61, 62, 63, 66, 137, 151, 172, 191, 192, 193, 194, 198
Descartes, R. 5, 80, 81, 82, 168

Ehrenfest, P. 213

Fichte, J.G. 7, 14
Foucault, M. 149
Freud, S. 9, 10, 16, 18, 21, 31, 37, 41, 45, 46, 48, 50, 125, 136, 149, 150, 211, 213

Gatlin, L. 212
Gleick, J. 162
Guattari, F. 13, 163, 211

Hayman, R. 62
Hegel, G.W.F. 2, 3, 4, 5, 6, 7, 8, 11, 12, 13, 14, 17, 20, 23, 61, 70, 83, 103, 110, 152, 157
Heidigger, M. 5, 10, 11, 16, 18, 20, 21, 155, 211
Herakleitus 137, 150
Hillmore, P. 105
Hobbes, T. 9
Hume, D. 2
Husserl, E. 7, 16

Irenaeus 100

Name index

Irigaray, L. 213
Izambard, G. 202

Jacobi, C. 14

Kant, I. 1, 2, 3, 4, 5, 6, 8, 9, 14, 15, 16, 41, 45, 59, 60, 70, 72, 86, 99, 107, 108, 109, 110, 111, 114, 115, 116, 117, 118, 136, 137, 139, 140, 168, 169, 211
Kierkegaard, S. 14
Klossowski, P. 155
Kullbuck, S. 212

Lacan 45, 176
Leibniz, G.W. 35
Lenin, V.I. 149, 198
Lockwood, J.G. 214
Lukács, G. 10, 211
Luther, M. 2, 99, 138
Lyotard, J-F. 18, 163

Mandelbrot, B. 161, 163, 165
Marx, K. 5, 13, 14, 49, 52, 54, 55, 91, 112, 149
Miller, H. 121, 124, 125, 128, 129, 130, 131

Newton, C.W. 214
Newton, I. 34, 35
Nietzche, F.W. 8, 9, 10, 13, 14, 15, 16, 17, 18, 19, 21, 22, 24, 25, 37, 40, 41, 43, 44, 59, 61, 63, 71, 77, 82, 83, 86, 87, 88, 97, 108, 114, 116, 134, 135, 137, 138, 140, 141, 142, 143, 144, 145, 146, 147, 148, 149, 154, 155, 156, 157, 158, 159, 170, 175, 198, 211, 213

Palmén, E. 214
Plato 27, 28, 29, 45, 90, 140
Poincaré, J.H. 40, 213
Proust, M. 177

Rimbaud, A. 73, 198, 201, 202, 203
Rose, G. 211

Sartre, J-P. 59
Saussure, F. 17
Schelling, F.W.J. von 5, 7, 8, 14, 18
Schopenhauer, A. 7, 8, 9, 10, 11, 12, 13, 14, 15, 16, 41, 45, 91, 108, 136, 137, 138, 140, 141, 142, 143, 145, 170
Serres, M. 211
Shannon, C.E. 212
Socrates 27, 28, 29, 144
Spinoza, B. de 17, 137
Sun Tzu 150

Walker, D.P. 101
Weaver, W. 212
Weber, M. 56, 112, 113
Wittfogel, K.A. 128, 214

Zermelo, E. 39, 213

Subject index

Abbé, The 203
abortion 141–2
abstract negation 60–1
accumulation 49, 52, 64, 65
Accursed Share, The 32, 33, 65, 165, 184
aesthetics 10, 22
agnosticism 139
annihilation 15, 33, 48, 101, 103, 119, 182, 186
annihilationism 100–2
Architecture 123
art 22–3, 44
asynchronicity 97, 104
atheism 16, 17, 18, 19, 39, 61, 62, 89, 101, 174
authority 139, 176
automatic writing 124
Aztecs 32, 65

Blue of Noon, The 198, 203
Buddhism 145

capital 2, 3, 4, 21, 53, 54–5, 56, 57, 91, 108, 110, 112, 113, 119, 197–8, 213
capitalism 56, 197
Cartesianism 80–1
castration 21, 24, 26, 88, 89, 111, 125
Catholicism 2, 18, 57, 65
chance 42, 44, 156–9, 179
chaos 38, 43–4, 162–3, 179, 205
choice 135
Christianity 2, 16, 18, 24, 45, 63, 65, 67, 78, 83, 87, 88, 99, 108, 145, 146–7
codes 96, 113, 121–2, 125
colonialism 55
communication 1, 44, 50, 51, 59, 61, 119, 157, 161, 176, 178, 184–210, 212
community 55, 71, 82, 104, 108, 136, 151, 173
composition 44, 49, 162, 164
conservation 101
consumption 56, 57, 63, 64, 65, 69, 104
continuity 16
Contre-Attaque 198
creation 101
crime 59, 60, 61, 63, 69, 70–1, 72, 73, 158, 177, 192
criminality 62, 63, 65, 71, 127
critique 2, 3, 5–6, 12, 14, 20
culture 2, 35, 56, 65, 90, 123, 143, 145, 146
cyclones 106, 214

death 8, 43, 46, 47, 49, 50, 51, 56, 61, 64, 65, 70, 72, 73, 83, 87, 91, 97, 98, 100, 101, 102, 103, 104, 110, 111–12, 117, 123, 125, 126, 131, 134, 135, 143, 146, 164, 166–7, 168, 172, 173, 174, 176–7, 178, 179, 180–1, 182, 185, 188, 191, 192, 194, 195, 196, 203, 205, 206; drive 43, 46, 48
deconstruction 8, 16, 17, 18, 19, 20, 21, 24, 26, 211
desire 8, 9, 10, 22, 26, 28, 36, 37, 42, 45, 46, 47, 48, 70, 119, 125,

135, 136, 137, 139, 140, 144, 150, 167, 195, 196
despair 82, 115, 155, 201
difference 19, 45, 64, 142, 143, 168–9
discontinuity 16, 64, 122, 124, 200
disorder 37
doubt 81–2
drive 41–2, 45

economics 25–6, 51, 64–5, 113, 151, 170; solar 33, 49–50, 64, 213
economy 23, 24, 25–6, 48–9, 50, 64, 143, 173, 183; bourgeois 57; capital 57, 113, 115; libidinal 42; political 52, 55, 57, 149; solar 33, 49–50
Economy to the Scale of the Universe 185
energetics: libidinal 44
energy 34, 37, 40, 41, 42, 43, 44, 48, 49, 51, 56, 65, 70, 106, 119, 143, 212
Enlightenment 138
entropy 37, 42, 43, 48, 49, 167, 212
epistemology 82, 99, 116, 119, 168, 169
equalization 142, 143
eroticism 61, 65, 175, 188, 189, 190, 191, 192, 206
Eroticism 188
ethnocentrism 12
eugenics 141–2
evil 59, 63, 73, 102, 151, 189
expenditure 5, 19, 23, 25, 33, 56, 57, 63, 65, 104, 149, 185

fascism 55, 196, 197, 198
feminity 21
fiction 186, 187
final solution 194–5
finality 138–9

gender 21
geometry 167
glory 65
God 6–7, 9, 12, 14, 15, 17, 18, 21, 34, 37, 45, 59, 60, 62, 63, 69, 73, 75–9, 80–91, 92, 93, 94, 95, 97, 100, 101, 102, 103, 108, 117, 119, 121, 131, 139, 145, 146, 147, 158, 170, 173, 183, 193, 196, 205, 209
goodness 135–6, 140

Hatred for Poetry, The 198
Hegelianism 4, 7–8, 103
hierarchies: theory of 45, 170
Hinduism 108
Humanism 8, 118, 135, 137–8, 209

idealism 7, 8, 37
identity 13, 17, 19, 102, 103, 108–18, 123, 146, 169
immanence 3, 50, 51, 115, 116, 157, 163, 168, 169–70, 171, 173, 177
Impossible, The 198, 203
industry 148, 149
infinity 4, 40, 163
information: theory of 42–3, 44, 122, 212
Inner Experience 80, 108, 115, 118, 161, 165, 177
Islam 65, 106

jealousy 92–3, 94, 95
Jesuits 2
Judaism 106
Julie 203
justice 71, 72, 73, 103, 135, 144

Kantianism 3, 5–6, 7, 8, 20, 41, 59, 72, 118, 134, 157, 213
knowing 7, 72, 81, 82, 116, 169
knowledge 1, 12, 27, 37, 83, 116; scientific 37

labour 52–5, 57, 112
Labyrinth, The (or *The Composition of Beings*) 161
labyrinths 49, 159, 161–83, 191, 198, 199, 203
language 43, 72, 121–2, 123, 124, 125, 131, 198
law 42, 64, 70, 71, 72, 73, 144; moral 14, 60
legislation 59, 176; moral 60
literature 60, 61, 73, 124, 136, 177, 179, 184, 186, 187, 188, 192
Literature and Evil 185
logic 59, 103, 104, 142, 158

Subject index

love 48, 119, 133, 154, 184, 188–90, 192; courtly 67; erotic 188, 193

Madame Edwarda 89
Marxism 49, 52, 54–5, 56
materialism 124; aesthetic 9; base 8, 116, 118, 123, 124, 158, 173; dialectical 37; French 61; libidinal 37, 43, 118, 123; scientific 38
mathematics 162
matter 9, 38, 111, 121, 122, 123, 143, 145, 165, 166, 169, 170, 181, 205
Menger sponge 163–4, 165, 171
metaphysics 1–2, 5, 13, 20, 21, 22, 36; German 5
Method of Meditation 118
monotheism 12, 14, 15, 18, 24, 79, 80, 90, 92, 102, 109, 138, 144, 147, 173, 210
morality 79, 124, 139, 157

negentropy 37, 38, 39, 40, 41, 43
neo-Kantian thought 7
nihilism 13, 19, 45, 91, 108, 110, 145, 146, 147, 153, 156
nothing 101, 114–15
noumena 6, 7, 8, 9
noumenon 6, 70, 105–20, 169

objectification: grades of 45, 138, 170
On Nietzsche 155–7, 165
ontology 5, 43, 65, 81, 95, 104, 129, 143, 158, 170, 181, 182
overman 15, 145, 147, 156

personality 15, 102, 144
pessimism 12, 13–14, 45
phenomena 6
phenomenality 6, 17, 140
phenomenology 7, 16, 29; deconstructed 16; of reason 17
Pineal Eye, The 30
Platonism 144
pleasure 45, 61
poetry 56, 72, 73, 178, 196, 198, 199–200, 202, 203, 204
politics 28, 112, 148, 197, 198, 210

post-Kantian thought 5, 14, 114, 138, 142
presence 16, 17, 19, 29
presencing 16–17
probability 158
production 49, 52, 185, 187
Propositions 87
Protestantism 57, 65, 66, 112; German 147
psychoanalysis 20, 46, 79, 88, 191
Psychological Structure of Fascism, The 197
punishment 1, 71, 100, 102
purity 117

rank order 138
rationalism 62; enlightenment 61, 111
rationality 62, 100
reality 2, 12, 19, 25, 26, 34, 46, 170, 174, 200
reason 1, 4, 5, 6, 7, 9, 20, 25, 31, 59–60, 61, 62, 72, 96, 103, 107, 135, 139, 142, 144, 146, 151, 155, 166, 185, 186
reasoning 82, 103, 110
recurrence 143, 162; eternal 25–6, 40, 44, 137, 143, 146, 156
regression 12, 14, 38, 62, 145, 150, 165
religion 57, 65, 81, 82, 83, 87, 89, 145, 157, 187, 203
repetition 19, 133–4
representation 5, 8, 9, 20, 28, 30, 31, 45, 70, 81, 82, 116, 118, 129, 142, 145, 166, 169, 176, 177
repression 17, 19, 21, 26, 46, 112, 124, 131, 150, 166
responsibility 1, 20, 73
revolt 61, 62
revolution 13, 53, 55, 59
rights 59, 71
Rotten Sun 30

sacrifice 33, 63, 72, 87, 115, 119
Sacrifices 95, 158
scholarship 35–6
science 9, 34–5, 138–9, 168
separation 81, 123, 124, 168
sexuality 21, 37, 46, 50, 89, 124,

Subject index 223

125, 136, 141, 175, 187, 188
Solar Anus, The 30, 31, 88, 99
solipsism 7, 192
Somme Athéologique 99, 108
sovereignty 3, 33, 56, 59, 93
space 43, 48, 49, 129, 163, 165, 166, 167, 174
Spinozism 103, 158, 174
spirit 6–7
spiritualism 37
spiritualization 143, 144, 170
state: and philosophy 10–11, 60
Story of the Eye, The 30, 187
structural analysis 122
structure 122–3
subject/object relation 116, 168–9

Tears of Eros 188
teleology 138, 139, 147, 154, 157
tendency 42, 43, 44
thanatology 103, 111
thanatropism 3
theism 14, 15, 60
theology 1, 12, 14, 18, 65, 82, 99, 109, 113, 182
Theory of Religion 168
thermodynamics 38–9, 42, 43, 48, 211
Tibetans 65
time 39, 40, 41, 43, 94–7, 103, 112, 118, 129, 138, 163, 166, 167
transcendence 3, 5, 7, 34, 41, 42, 50, 51, 70, 72, 74, 122, 143, 168, 169–70, 171, 173
transcendental philosophy 3, 59, 107, 140, 155, 163, 168, 213
transgression 58–74
truth 2, 20, 21, 25, 28, 34, 59, 95, 124

unconscious 8, 9, 15, 16, 18, 20, 26, 31, 33, 46, 62, 124, 125, 151, 173
understanding 59

virtue 136
void 164

war 4, 47–8, 65, 67, 68, 69, 71, 147–51, 167
will 8–9, 10, 13, 135, 137, 138, 140, 142, 156, 157, 211; to power 8, 15, 16, 138, 142, 156

Zeno's paradox 166
zero 5, 19, 22, 24, 25, 26, 45, 47, 51, 87, 89, 90, 91, 102, 104, 108, 109, 110, 111, 112, 113, 114, 115, 116, 117, 118, 119, 122, 125, 128, 129, 131, 143, 145, 146, 147, 149, 163, 173, 183, 196, 199, 205, 206, 213